Let us Worship the Lord

A plentiful resource for worship leaders

John Cox

kevin
mayhew

kevin
mayhew

First published in Great Britain in 2017 by Kevin Mayhew Ltd
Buxhall, Stowmarket, Suffolk IP14 3BW
Tel: +44 (0) 1449 737978 Fax: +44 (0) 1449 737834
E-mail: info@kevinmayhew.com

www.kevinmayhew.com

9 8 7 6 5 4 3 2 1 0

ISBN 978 1 84867 890 3
Catalogue No. 1501542

Cover design by Rob Mortonson
© Image used under licence from Shutterstock Inc.
Typeset by Angela Selfe

Printed and bound in Great Britain

CONTENTS

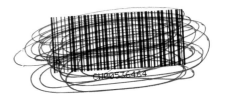

Prayers

Thoughts and reflections

In their own words – biblical characters

Old Testament

New Testament

Services for Holy Week and Easter

About the author

Having spent rather a long time at various universities including Cambridge, Oxford and the University College of Rhodesia and Nyasaland, John was ordained to a curacy in the diocese of Liverpool in 1968. He spent a second curacy in an inner-city ex-slum parish in Birmingham and became rector in the same parish. After a five-year period at Church House, Westminster where he was Senior Selection Secretary, helping to select ordinands, he was made Canon Treasurer at Southwark Cathedral and Diocesan Director of Ordinands and Postordination training.

Following four years as Vicar of Roehampton he moved to become Archdeacon of Sudbury in the Diocese of St Edmundsbury and Ipswich in 1995. When he retired in 2006 he was asked to be the part-time Diocesan Director of Education, a job he did for nearly four and a half years before retiring for a second time. It has been during these retirement years that John has been writing for Kevin Mayhew, in between being chair of governors at a primary academy, playing golf and enjoying river cruises. For details of all John Cox's books, please visit our website: www.kevinmayhew.com

Foreword

Ten years ago, Kevin Mayhew invited me to meet him to discuss what I might write for him. We decided on a book that looked at some basic aspects of faith relating them to daily life and experience. It was published as 'A risk worth taking'. I was sure that this was the one book I had it in me to write. Kevin convinced me otherwise and during these last ten years I have written some nineteen books, contributed to a number of others and edited a few more.

The books have varied in the subjects they have tackled, from the distinctiveness of church schools to stress related depression, from being a better PCC to parish courses for Advent, from reflections for Lent to why people don't go to church.

In this book I have gathered together a selection of material that I trust will be useful to those who are responsible for leading worship and who look for ideas on what might be said in the context of a service. The majority of the material, but not all, relates to the major festivals of the Christian year. There are introductions to those festivals, prayers, thoughts and reflections as well as some full services and 'monologues' from biblical characters. They are offered in the hope that they will encourage and assist those who seek to lead others to worship the Lord.

John Cox

Feasts and festivals

1. Advent

It is thought that originally Advent had no association with Christmas at all but was 40 days of preparation for those who were to be baptised in January at the feast of the Epiphany. During that Epiphany season not only was the visit of the wise men to the infant Jesus remembered (Matthew 2:1-12), but also Jesus' baptism in the Jordan (John 1:29-34) and his first miracle at the wedding at Cana (John 2:1-11). By the sixth century, Advent was associated with the coming of Christ – not as a baby in Bethlehem but his return on the clouds of glory. The practice of preparing for the celebration of Christ's birth with a period of fasting and abstinence, known as the Nativity fast, first occurred in the Middle Ages.

The length of Advent has varied over the centuries. Since the time of Pope Gregory VII (1073–85) it has been normal in the western Church for Advent to begin on the fourth Sunday before Christmas – the Sunday nearest to St Andrew's Day on 30 November. Previously there had been five weeks of preparation. Advent has also been celebrated for the seven weeks following St Martin's Day on 11 November until Christmas Eve, giving rise to the alternative name of St Martin's Lent. In the Celtic tradition and in the Orthodox Church, Advent begins on 15 November, offering a more obvious 40 days of fasting and in honour of St Philip whose feast day is 15 November. This period also has the name of St Philip's Lent.

Themes for Advent vary but may include: The Patriarchs, the Prophets, John the Baptist, The Virgin Mary, Christ, Judgement, Hope, the Second Coming, the Light of the World and the Great Antiphons' (Wisdom, Almighty God, Root of Jesse, Key of David, Morning star, King of the nations).

Advent Wreath and Candles

The lighting of a circle of candles during the long, dark winter months probably goes back to Norse times. The candles were set around a wheel that represented the earth, and prayers were offered to the god of light. They were used as a sign of hope for the return of the sun and the coming of spring. In the Christian tradition it is generally agreed that the use of a wreath with candles during the Advent season began with the Lutherans. It was part of the preparation for the coming of the one who is the Light of the world.

The wreath itself, made of evergreens, signifies life everlasting, while individual sprays have their own significance: laurel for victory over persecution; yew and pine for immortality, and cedar for strength and healing. The use of holly is especially associated with Christ's Passion since in some traditions the cross is said to have been made of holly, as was the crown of thorns. So together the wreath symbolises both death and suffering and healing and immortality.

The number of candles can vary – either four or five – as can their colour. The use of four candles indicates the four weeks of Advent and also represents the 4000 years that were thought to be the time between creation and the coming of Jesus. Sometimes a fifth candle, representing Christ, is added for use on Christmas Day itself. It is white. Three of the other candles are normally purple or blue, this being a penitential season, with the fourth being pink. The pink candle is traditionally lit on the third Sunday of Advent, known as Gaudete Sunday. The name comes from the first words of the Introit used at the Mass on that Sunday: 'Rejoice in the Lord always; again I will say, Rejoice' (Philippians 4:4). Being halfway through the season of abstinence and fasting, this was a Sunday of joy when there was a sense of relief from the austerities of the fast. This is comparable to the fourth Sunday in Lent when there is a relaxation of the demands of Lenten discipline. That is known as Laetare Sunday, from its Introit which begins with the words, 'Rejoice with Jerusalem' (Isaiah 66:10). Its more common name is 'Refreshment Sunday'.

Churches vary in the meaning they give to each of the candles – for example, expectation, hope, joy and purity.

2. Christmas

In the early Church there was considerable speculation about the actual date, and at one time a date in May was suggested. The December date was first known to have been used in the year 336. It is thought that this date was chosen as a way of countering the celebration of the birth of 'the victorious sun' as advocated by Mithraism, an ancient pagan religion. The Christians saw this day as celebrating not the birth of the sun but the birth of the 'Sun of righteousness' (Malachi 4:2). The choice of 25 December spread from Rome throughout the western part of Christendom. In the East, 6 January was a day of celebrating Jesus' baptism as well as the visit of the wise men (see 'Epiphany' below) and was initially more important than Jesus' birth. By the middle of the fifth century, East and West were celebrating Jesus' birth on 25 December, apart from the Armenian Church which still celebrates Christ's birth on 6 January.

The joyful celebration has popularly been marked by festivities and merrymaking – a legacy of the pagan Roman festivals it replaced. Many of the current customs, such as decorated trees and Christmas cards, are in fact largely Victorian introductions and show the influence of the Queen's German Consort, Prince Albert.

The day following Christmas Day is commonly called Boxing Day. In the Church it is the day when St Stephen, the first Christian martyr, is remembered. Metal boxes would be put out to collect money for the poor on this day. From medieval times it was the practice on this day to give servants and tradespeople a boxed gift, and this may be the origin of the day's name.

On 27 December the Church remembers the young children of Bethlehem who were slaughtered on the orders of King Herod in a vain attempt to kill the infant Jesus. The event is recorded in Matthew 2:16-18 and is known as the Feast of the Holy Innocents.

3. Epiphany

Since the fourth century, this festival, held on 6 January, has in the West recalled the visit of the wise men to the infant Jesus (Matthew 2:1-15).

The word 'epiphany' means 'manifestation' or 'showing forth'. This was originally associated with the baptism of Jesus by John which marked the beginning of Jesus' public ministry. However, the visit of the wise men was also seen as a 'manifestation' since it was understood as the time when the infant Christ was 'shown forth' to the non-Jewish world as represented by the foreign wise men who had come from the East. The day marks Twelfth

Night which has traditionally been a time of dramatic performances and music (mumming and wassailing) and when the Christmas decorations are taken down.

4. Ash Wednesday

This day marks the beginning of the season of Lent when Christians remember the 40 days Jesus spent in the wilderness fasting and being tempted (Matthew 4:1-11; Mark 1:12, 13; Luke 4:1-13). It has no fixed date because it is linked to Easter, the date of which is determined by the phases of the moon.

Lent is a time of fasting and penance, and this has traditionally been marked on Ash Wednesday by the practice of marking the foreheads of worshippers with ashes made by burning the palm crosses of the previous year. Ashes symbolise mourning and penitence.

The day before Ash Wednesday is known as Shrove Tuesday – now more commonly known in Britain as Pancake Tuesday when pancakes are cooked and pancake races are held. Shrove comes from the act of 'shriving', i.e. confession and absolution, which occurred on this day. In some cultures, for example in New Orleans, the period leading up to Lent is known as Mardi Gras. It is a time of festivities culminating in 'Fat Tuesday' (Mardi Gras) when people eat rich foods prior to the start of the Lenten season of fast.

5. Mothering Sunday

This is the fourth Sunday in Lent and is also known as 'Refreshment Sunday' or 'Laetare Sunday' (which comes from the first word in Latin of the Introit for the Mass on that day: 'Rejoice with Jerusalem . . .' Isaiah 66:10). At this mid-point in Lent some relaxation of the traditional penitential observances is allowed – hence the name 'refreshment'.

The origins of the name 'Mothering Sunday' have been associated with various customs, such as mothers being visited on this day, visits made to the cathedral (mother church of the dioceses), or words from the traditional reading from the epistle for this day which includes the words 'Jerusalem . . . is our mother' (Galatians 4:26). In many churches the day is marked by children presenting gifts of flowers to their mothers, and sermons focusing on the theme of mothers – either our own mothers, the act of mothering, Mother Church or Mary, mother of Jesus.

Father's Day is increasingly and variously celebrated, most often on the third Sunday of June.

6. Palm Sunday

This day, at the beginning of Holy Week, recalls the triumphal entry of Jesus into Jerusalem, riding on a donkey (Matthew 21:1-11; Mark 11:1-11; Luke 19:29-40; John 12:12-19). The crowds welcomed him as king, waved palm branches and laid their coats in the road. The blessing of palm branches or palm crosses, and processions mark the day.

In the Middle Ages worshippers would process from one church to another where the palms were blessed and distributed. A representation of Christ – a cross, a Bible or a carved figure – was often set on a wooden donkey and carried in the procession. These days it is not unusual to have a live donkey in the procession. A highly elaborate ceremony for the blessing of the palms was developed in the early Middle Ages in England but it was rejected by Order of Council in 1549 and was never included in the Book of Common Prayer. In 1955 the liturgies of Holy Week in the Roman Catholic Church were revised, and this ceremony was radically simplified.

7. Holy Week

This is the week that leads up to Easter and is traditionally observed as a week of devotion to the Passion of Christ. Churches may hold a daily service (commonly an evening service called Compline) in which the events of the week are particularly recalled.

8. Maundy Thursday
(also known as Holy Thursday)

This is the Thursday of Holy Week when Christians recall the occasion when Jesus had a last meal with his disciples before his crucifixion the next day (Good Friday) (Matthew 26:17-35; Mark 14:12-25; Luke 22:7-38; John 13-17). An evening service of Holy Communion is normally held, during which the minister may wash the feet of representatives of the congregation. In some churches the service concludes with the stripping of the altar, the procession of the reserved sacrament when the consecrated bread and wine are carried in procession from the main altar to a side chapel, and a vigil that recalls the time Jesus spent in prayer in the Garden of Gethsemane prior to his arrest.

The name 'Maundy' probably comes from the Latin mandatum (commandment) and is the opening word of the phrase, 'I give you a new commandment, that you love one another.' Jesus used these words when explaining to his disciples why, at the meal, he had stripped off and taken the position of a slave and washed their feet (John 13). An alternative explanation has been suggested that relates to the traditional ceremony whereby the British monarch distributed money to the poor. An English word 'maund' meant 'to beg'. The Maundy money ceremony still occurs in the Church of England, taking place these days in a different church (usually a cathedral) each year. It is no longer the poor but representatives of the local elderly who receive the 'Royal Maundy', and the specially minted small silver coins are tokens of the alms originally distributed.

9. Good Friday

This day recalls the death of Jesus on the cross (Matthew 27; Mark 15; Luke 23; John 19). In the Catholic tradition it is a day of fasting and devotion, although in some Protestant churches it is a day of celebration. Good Friday and Holy Saturday are the only days of the year when, in the Roman Catholic Church, the Mass (Holy Communion) is not celebrated.

A common pattern of devotion that has developed alongside other liturgical provision is that of the Three Hours service, held between noon and 3pm. It was first introduced by the Jesuits after the time of the Reformation and has most widely been adopted by the Church of England. The Stations of the Cross, usually 14 carvings or pictures depicting the incidents of Jesus' last journey from Pilate's house to his entombment and which hang on the walls of some churches, may be used as the focus of prayer and devotions as worshippers walk from station to station.

It is also quite common these days for churches to organise a 'Procession of Witness' on Good Friday morning in which the faithful process through the town or village carrying a large cross and bearing witness to the crucifixion of Christ. In some places these have become elaborate re-enactments, with costumed individuals taking the parts of the main characters in the events of the day.

10. Holy Saturday (or Easter Even)

This commemorates the resting of Jesus' body in the tomb between his death on Good Friday and the resurrection on Easter Day. It is not usual for Holy Communion to be celebrated on this day, and the day's ceremonies normally take place during the night of Saturday–Sunday. An all-night vigil of prayer has been traditional since the time of the early Church.

The Paschal Vigil is the first of the Easter Services. Traditionally it is held between sunset on the Saturday and dawn on Easter Day and was when people were baptised and received their first Communion. From a newly created fire, the Paschal Candle (a large candle representing the risen Christ as Light of the world) is lit before it is processed through the church where candles held by members of the congregation are also lit as the proclamation 'The Light of Christ' is said or sung. There is then a service of readings, followed by baptisms or the renewal of baptismal vows and a service of Holy Communion. The exact format of the service can vary considerably according to a church's tradition. Sometimes the service of the new fire and Paschal Candle are held at dawn.

11. Easter

'Christ is risen. He is risen indeed!' The Easter acclamation encapsulates the heart of what Easter is about. The present tense emphasises that while Easter celebrates an event in the past, its reality and significance is not locked in history. Jesus not only came back from the dead; he defeated death and lives today.

As important as Christ's saving death is, it is his resurrection that makes all the difference. If Christ has not been raised, Paul tells us, his own preaching has been in vain and our faith is in vain (1 Corinthians 15:14). We are all this side of the resurrection and the Christian faith can only be understood in the light of Easter.

The biblical accounts

While there is richness in the biblical accounts of the resurrection, it is not possible to reconcile them into a single, coherent story. This disturbs some people, and they prefer not to consider such details. For others it confirms their view that the whole thing was an invention. For still others it provides a rich and spiritually enlightening sequence of narratives about what the disciples experienced, their response and the meaning the Early Church came to give to it. The Common Lectionary for Easter Sunday provides St John's account as the main Gospel reading, with the other three Gospel accounts of Easter Day itself as alternatives across the three years. The further resurrection appearances are spread across the Easter season.

What the accounts seek to do is underline the fact that the tomb was empty and that Jesus appeared, alive again, to his friends. Both points are necessary for a convincing account of the resurrection. Without an empty tomb, Jesus remains a corpse. Without the appearances, his body might simply have been moved or stolen – as clearly some people affirmed.

The appearances themselves speak of both continuity and newness. Jesus was recognisably the same person as had been crucified, as the wounds in his hands and feet bore witness. He was recognised, though not always immediately, and he is said to have eaten with the disciples. Yet he appeared in locked rooms and disappeared as mysteriously. The disciples were both afraid and amazed; there was both doubt and faith.

Jesus assured them that he was the Jesus they knew; he assured them of his peace and he commissioned them to preach and to forgive. To the companions on the road to Emmaus he showed how everything that had happened was spoken of beforehand in the Jewish Scriptures.

Easter Day is a day of fulfilment, vindication and new life, and it is the start of the Church's mission to the world. Without it there would be no Christian faith.

In the background to the accounts that run from Maundy Thursday through to Easter Day lies the Old Testament story of the exodus of the Jews from slavery in Egypt, with the killing of the paschal lamb and the escape across the Red Sea. The Easter period, traditionally the 50 days leading up to Pentecost, was a time of various encounters with the risen Christ, by individuals, groups and (according to Paul in 1 Corinthians 15:6) up to 500 at one time. His being alive again was neither a piece of wish fulfilment, hallucination nor group hysteria, nor was it resuscitation. But what exactly 'occurred' remains a mystery – it was the action of God, affirming all that Jesus had done and taught and been.

Unlike Christmas, Easter is not a festival fixed to a specific date in the calendar. It is a moveable feast and its date each year is determined as being the first Sunday after the (paschal) full moon. It can therefore occur any time between 22 March and 25 April. In the Eastern Church, the dates differ because a different calendar is used.

Although it was intended that the Council of Nicea (AD 325) would settle the matter following two centuries of dispute about the dating of Easter Sunday, it wasn't until the sixth century in the Western Church that anything like uniformity occurred. In modern times there have been various calls for a fixed date for Easter Sunday – not least from schools whose spring and summer terms can vary considerably in length depending on how early or late Easter is.

The Easter liturgy

From earliest times, the first and main Easter celebration happened at night between sunset on Holy Saturday and sunrise on Easter Day – days traditionally being calculated to have begun after sunset. Although there are variations in the celebrations of Eastern and Western churches, they all reflect the earliest known liturgy shaped around numerous readings from the Bible: originally 12 from the Old Testament and Matthew's account of the Last Supper to the end of his Gospel.

Current Roman Catholic and Anglican liturgies share a basic common pattern: the Service of the Light, the Liturgy of the Readings (the Vigil), the Liturgy of Initiation (baptism, confirmation and renewal of baptismal vows) and the Eucharist.

a. **The Service of the Light.** The lighting of the paschal candle (see article on page 317) usually takes place either outside the church or at its entrance. It is lit from 'new fire' and not from an existing candle. It is then processed through the darkened church, making three stops when the acclamation 'Christ our Light' or 'the Light of Christ' is made with the response, 'Thanks be to God'. Small candles may be lit for the congregation as it passes, thus gradually filling the church with light. The candle is then put in a prominent place at the front of the church and the Easter Song of Praise (Exsultet) is sung.

b. **The Vigil.** In some large churches this may take place in a crypt. It is basically a liturgy of readings from Scripture and should include among the Old Testament readings the account of the exodus. Psalms may also be used. Before the reading of a passage from Romans and the Gospel reading, the Easter acclamation 'Christ is risen.' 'He is risen indeed,' is said, and the Gloria is sung for the first time since the beginning of Lent.

c. **The Liturgy of Initiation.** It is an ancient tradition for baptisms to be held at the Easter service, with Lent being used as a time of preparation. If a bishop is present, confirmations may also be held. Whether or not there are candidates for either baptism or confirmation, the members of the congregation are invited to renew their own baptismal vows in an affirmation of faith and commitment to Christ.

   The Eucharist then follows with its seasonal prefaces in the Eucharistic prayer and the newly confirmed receiving communion for the first time. In the Roman missal, the instructions indicate that the service should conclude before sunrise.

The use of the Service of Light and the Vigil has increased in the Anglican Church over recent decades, and it is not uncommon for the Service of Light to be held at dawn in the open air prior to the later main Easter Service.

In the Eastern Church, the liturgies properly begin with Vespers around midday on Holy Saturday and continue, these days with a break, with the Paschal Vigil and the Divine Service until the early morning of Easter Day. All the Easter celebrations will have been completed during this time, and no other service is normally held on Easter Day until the Paschal Vespers in the afternoon.

In popular culture there is not the same festivity or commercialisation at Easter as there is at Christmas. But the theme of new life linked with the emergence of spring after the 'death' of winter can still be seen in the gifts of flowers and the pictures of bunnies and chicks. The egg, with its tomb-like shape out of which new life appears, has made it a widely recognised Easter symbol, and chocolate eggs can mark the end of a Lenten 'fast'.

The Easter Garden

While all the Gospel writers indicate that after his crucifixion Jesus was laid in a rock-hewn tomb belonging to Joseph of Arimathea, little indication is given to where it was. Only John mentions that there was a garden where Jesus had been crucified and that the tomb was also in the garden (John 19:38-42). Tradition has identified the site as that which is now covered by the Church of the Holy Sepulchre. Pilgrims visiting the church can see both the pinnacle of quarry rock on which the cross is said to have stood and the tomb in which Jesus' body is said to have been laid.

Proof for the truth of this tradition is hard to come by, and over the centuries the church has had a very mixed history from the time it was first built on the orders of Constantine (c. AD 325), replacing the temple to Aphrodite built by Emperor Hadrian. The church has been destroyed and rebuilt on a number of occasions, captured by Persians and Crusaders and occupied by Christians of different traditions. Archaeologists have variously found evidence to support the tradition and to refute it.

Partly in protest against the identification of the site by Roman Catholics, Protestants have looked elsewhere for the setting of the garden and tomb. Most famously, General Gordon asserted that a rock formation outside the city wall and which might be thought to resemble a skull (Golgotha – the place of the skull – was where the crucifixion occurred – see Mark 15:22) was the true site of the tomb and the garden. Although archaeological evidence suggests that the site was deserted in the first century and therefore unlikely to have been the place for a new tomb, no other site has been suggested as an alternative, and it remains a popular place for pilgrims and visitors – more than a quarter of a million a year.

On Easter Day, many churches display a small garden, often created by children, showing the three crosses of Golgotha and the rock tomb with its stone rolled away. Flowers symbolise the new life of resurrection. Whether garden, empty tomb or Sepulchre Church, it is not the place that is of most importance, but rather the person of the risen Christ.

12. Ascension Day

This day marks the end of the 40 days during which the risen Christ appeared to his disciples (Acts 1:3-11). Jesus withdrew into heaven, witnessed by his disciples. This is said to have occurred on the Mount of Olives, and guides still show marks in the stone that they say are the imprint of Jesus' feet as he ascended to heaven. It is not possible to know what actually happened, and in Luke's Gospel the event occurs at Bethany on the night of the resurrection itself (Luke 24:50-3). Theologically, the accounts seek to convey the truth that Jesus is now at the right hand of God in glory and to make a break between the time when he was physically present on Earth and his departure which led to the gift of the Holy Spirit to assure believers of his continuing spiritual presence with them.

13. Whit Sunday (Pentecost)

The account in Acts (Acts 2:1-13) tells of the disciples all being together on the day of Pentecost. Pentecost was a Jewish festival when the first fruits of the corn harvest were presented, and later commemorated the giving of the Law to Moses. In the Christian tradition it is associated with the gift of the Holy Spirit who descended on the disciples like tongues of fire. The event is also associated with the ability to speak in tongues, on this occasion in languages from all around the known world. It is generally understood to be the birthday of the Church and the start of its mission to take the gospel to all corners of the Earth.

14. Trinity Sunday

This is not a feast celebrating a part of the story of Jesus but a day on which the distinctive Christian doctrine concerning the nature of God is celebrated, and to that extent concludes the round of 'Jesus festivals'. The celebration of this day, a week after Whit Sunday, dates back to the Middle Ages.

The doctrine of the Holy Trinity asserts that in his very nature God is three 'persons' – Father, Son and Holy Spirit – but that the three are one. It is a way of seeking to understand the mystery of God understood in terms of relationship between God as Creator, God as Redeemer and God as Sustainer.

15. Harvest festivals

In the worship of the Church of England these are among the most popular Church festivals, especially in rural areas. They reflect a long tradition of communal acts of thanksgiving for the harvest and the bounty of the Earth that certainly stretches back to Old Testament times and are to be found in many cultures and religions. In medieval England, Lammas Day (1 August) was commonly recognised as a day for thanksgiving for the 'first fruits', and bread baked from the new wheat was solemnly blessed. The present-day customs date back to the revival of this practice by the Revd R. Hawker at Morwenstone in Cornwall in 1843. The gifts of fruit and vegetables are traditionally distributed to the poor, although these days they will often include tinned and packet food. In fishing areas, a Festival of the Sea may also be celebrated.

16. All Saints and All Souls

The Church has long wanted to honour its saints – the unknown ones as well as those who are famous. Since the seventh century, a day has been set aside for this general devotion. Originally it was 13 May. In the eighth century, Pope Gregory III dedicated a chapel in the basilica of St Peter in Rome to 'All the Saints' on 1 November, and Gregory IV ordered that it should be this day when the saints would be remembered.

The virtuous and well-respected Odio, Abbott of Cluny (963–1048), established the practice at Cluny of observing 2 November as a day for commemorating the faithful departed – All Souls' Day. The practice soon expanded to the whole of the Western Church. In the Catholic tradition, a distinction is made between the saints, who are those believed to have acquired the vision of God in heaven (the ultimate destiny of believers), and those who have died but have not yet reached this state of purification. In other traditions, 'saints' means all the faithful people of God, living and dead.

During the season of All Saints and All Souls, many churches hold services in which worshippers have the opportunity to specifically remember those from among their family and friends who have died. Relatives of those who have died in the previous twelve months are especially invited. In hospitals where there is a maternity unit, chaplains may hold services to which parents are invited to remember babies who have died either as aborted foetuses, still-births or neonatally.

All Saints' Day is also known as All Hallows, and the evening before is celebrated in popular culture as Hallowe'en ('All Hallows' evening'). Whether or not this had a pagan Celtic origin is uncertain, but it has come to be associated with various practices such as 'trick or treat', bonfires and apple-bobbing, which may well have their origins and festivities associated with the dead.

Prayers

Opening Prayers

1

Creator God, whose order came from the chaos.
Be with us now.
Creator God, whose light shone in the darkness.
Be with us now.
Amen

2

All that we have are gifts from the Lord,
to him we offer our praise and our worship.
May all we do and all we offer,
be done with a pure heart,
in the power of the Spirit,
and to the glory of God's name.
Amen

3

Lord, as we gather in your name,
fill our hearts with hope.
Lord, as we remember all your promises
fill our hearts with thankfulness.
Lord, as we worship you and praise you,
fill our hearts with love.
Amen

4

Let us worship the Lord and praise his name.
Blessed is the name of the Lord.
Let us praise the Lord and rejoice in his goodness.
Blessed is the name of the Lord.

Let us offer thanks and gratitude for all he has done.
Blessed is the name of the Lord.
Amen

5

Open our hearts and raise our voices, O Lord,
that filled with expectation
we may know your presence and sing your praise.
Amen

6

In the dark of the night and the light of the day,
come to us, O God.
In the cold of loneliness and the warmth of friends,
come to us, O God.
In the struggle of doubt and the joy of faith,
come to us, O God.
In our praise and our prayers,
come to us, O God.
Amen

7

God of the mountains and the valleys,
we come to worship you.
God of the woodlands and the meadows,
we come to worship you.
God of the towns and villages,
we come to worship you.
God of our past and of our future,
we come to worship you.
God of our present,
we come to worship you.
Amen

8

Come to us, O Lord our God,
in the glory of your presence,
come to us, Lord.

Be with us, O Lord our God,
in our time of worship,
be with us, Lord.

Go before us, O Lord our God,
in all that we do,
go before us, Lord.
Amen

9

Let us worship the lord of all the earth,
the Lord of all peoples.
Let us come to the Lord,
he welcomes all to the feast.
Let none be refused, none turned away,
let us join together in praise of our God.
Amen

10

Open our eyes, O Lord,
that we may delight in this new day.
Open our ears, O Lord,
that we may hear the word you would speak to us.
Open our hearts, O Lord,
that we may know your presence.
Open our lips, O Lord,
that we may sing your praise.
Amen

11

God of all goodness,
we come in worship.
God of all beauty,
we come in praise.
God of all truth,
we come in adoration.
Make yourself known to us as we gather in your name.
Amen

12

Glory and splendour surround you, O Lord,
none can outshine you.
Wisdom and judgement are your gift, O Lord,
who can compare to you?
We bring you our offerings of praise and worship,
to set in your presence, the gift of our love.
Amen

13

Let us worship the Lord of sea and dry land,
the Lord of justice and mercy, judgement and forgiveness.
Let us worship the Lord who loves us,
the Lord who loves all people.
Let us worship the Lord.
Amen

14

Proclaim the wonder and mystery of the Lord;
let all the world give praise.
Proclaim the mercy and the love of the Lord;
let all the world give praise.
Proclaim the glory and the majesty of the Lord;
let all the world give praise.
Amen

15

You, O Christ are the Lord;
we worship you.
You, O Christ, are the Messiah;
we worship you.
You, O Christ, are the Son of the Most High;
we worship you.
Amen

16

Spirit of God,
the voice of truth and the breath of creation,
calm our hearts and still our minds,
that together we may know your presence
and draw upon your grace.
Help us to be open to God's Word
and to worship with joy and sincerity.
Amen

17

We are in your presence, God our Father,
you are with us, the Lord of all.
We come to learn: open us to your Spirit,
show us your way, teach us your truth.

Help us to be honest with ourselves
and honest about ourselves,
to listen to each other
and to speak without judging,
that we may grow in understanding,
in trust and faith,
for Jesus' sake.
Amen

18

Lord Jesus, you taught your disciples how to pray;
lead us by your Spirit as we learn to pray.
Help us to quieten our hearts and minds,
that we may know your presence with us
and focus our thoughts on you,
that as we pray for others and for ourselves,
we may do so in accordance with your will.
To you be the glory.
Amen

Confessions

1

Cleanse us, Lord, from all that distorts your image in us,
in your mercy forgive us.
For all that divides us from one another and from you,
in your mercy forgive us.
For our satisfaction with less than the truth,
in your mercy forgive us.
For our dishonesty in thought or action,
in your mercy forgive us.
For worship that is unworthy of you,
in your mercy forgive us.
Amen

2

Lord, for the blindness
which prevents us from seeing your glory,
in your mercy forgive us.
Lord, for the meanness
that restricts our thankfulness,
in your mercy forgive us.
For the failure to honour you as King,

in your mercy forgive us.
Lord, for the pride
that prevents us from admitting our faults,
in your mercy forgive us.
Lord, for our lack of faith,
in your mercy forgive us.
Amen

3

Lord God, we have sinned against you;
we have done evil in your sight.
We are sorry and repent.
Have mercy on us according to your love.
Wash away our wrongdoing
and cleanse us from our sin.
Renew a right spirit within us
and restore to us the joy of your salvation,
through Jesus Christ our Lord.
Amen

4

In you we trust, O Lord.
Forgive our lack of faith.

Your love surrounds our every moment.
Forgive our lack of love.

You call us to your service.
Forgive our disobedience.

You go before us in all we do.
Forgive us when we do not follow.
Amen

5

Loving God,
always loving, always forgiving.
We are sorry for the things we do that hurt you
and hurt others:
for the times when we do less than our best,
when we speak unkindly,
and behave unpleasantly.
Help us to respect ourselves and one another,
help us to look out for others,
as Jesus cared for everyone he met.
Amen

6

In your mercy forgive us, Lord,
For the hurt we do to others by belittling them.
Lord have mercy.

In your mercy forgive us, Lord,
For making fun of others because they are different.
Lord have mercy.

In your mercy forgive us, Lord,
For our anger and our resentment.
Lord have mercy.
Amen

7

For times of despair,
forgive us Lord.
For doubting your promises,
forgive us Lord.
For lacking trust in the love of others,
forgive us Lord.
For doubting your goodness,
forgive us Lord.

For hurting our loved ones,
forgive us Lord.
For ignoring the needy,
forgive us Lord.
Amen

8

For love that has been scorned,
by your love, forgive us, Lord.
For love that has been hurt,
by your love, forgive us, Lord.
For love that has been manipulated,
by your love, forgive us, Lord.
For love that has been betrayed,
by your love, forgive us, Lord.
Amen

9

For times when I presumed upon your goodness,
forgive me Lord.
For times I have cheated and manipulated others,
forgive me Lord.
For taking advantage of those in need,
forgive me Lord.
For thinking the worst of others,
forgive me Lord.
Amen

10

For the sins of today and the sins of the past,
Lord, have mercy.
For the wrongs to others and the love withheld,
Christ, have mercy.
For hard hearts and closed minds,
Lord, have mercy.
Amen

11

Lord, I want to love you above all things,
to put you first in every thought and every choice,
forgive me when I fail.

Lord, I want to obey your every word,
to live by the values of a holy life,
forgive me when I fail.

Lord, I want to offer you all I am and all I have,
to hold nothing back, however precious it might be,
forgive me when I fail.
Amen

12

Lord Jesus, the Light of the world,
illumine our hearts and forgive our blindness.
Lord, have mercy.
Lord have mercy.

Lord Jesus, king of all, and child of Mary,
grant us understanding and forgive our dullness.
Christ, have mercy.
Christ have mercy.

Lord Jesus, Word of Salvation
and bringer of Good News, forgive our deafness.
Lord, have mercy.
Lord have mercy.
Amen

13

Lord, we bring you our best and think it is enough;
Father, forgive us.
Lord, we trust in our deeds but not in you;
Father, forgive us.

Lord, we hide in the darkness, though you call us to the light;
Father, forgive us.
Lord, we are timid in our witness and hide our discipleship;
Father, forgive us.
Amen

14

Keep us faithful, Lord,
and forgive us when we turn from you;
Lord, have mercy.
Make us obedient, Lord,
and forgive us when we go our own way;
Christ, have mercy.
Purify us by your Spirit, Lord,
and forgive our waywardness;
Lord, have mercy.
Keep us in your truth, Lord,
and forgive our lack of integrity.
Christ, have mercy.
Amen

15

Father,
when you call to us and we do not listen;
when we have gone our own way
rather than turn aside to see your burning presence;
forgive us in your mercy.
Father,
when we have approached,
careless that we are on holy ground;
when we have heard you call
and excused ourselves
from the service you have asked of us;
forgive us in your mercy.

Father,

when we have tried to do too much,

and have not trusted others to share the task,

believing we are the only ones who can do it well;

forgive us in your mercy.

Amen

16

God in creation and in the events of history,

forgive me my blindness.

God in the love and care of others,

forgive me my blindness.

God in your Word and in your Son,

forgive me my blindness.

God in the work of the Spirit,

forgive me my blindness.

Amen

17

Lord, when you feel distant and we cannot see your face;

forgive us if we doubt your love.

Lord, when times are difficult and we feel afraid;

forgive us if we complain and turn from you.

Lord, when we want certainty and guarantees;

forgive us, if we forsake faith and mystery.

Lord, when we cannot face the challenge of your call;

forgive us, if we follow the easier way of our own desires.

Amen

18

For times when we have failed to trust in you,

Father, forgive us.

For times we have been blind to the signs of your kingdom,

Father, forgive us.

For times we have been deaf to your promises,
Father, forgive us.
For times we have failed to act on what we know to be right,
Father, forgive us.
Amen

19

For times of self-importance,
forgive us, Lord.
For times of rage and anger,
forgive us, Lord.
For times of unjust suspicion,
forgive us, Lord.
For times of lacking trust,
forgive us, Lord.
For times of compromised integrity,
forgive us, Lord.
Amen

20

Lord, all things come from you;
keep us from boasting of our own ability and gifts.
Lord, you are the giver of wisdom;
keep us from pride in our own cleverness.
Lord, your love is the greatest of riches;
keep us from putting our trust in possessions.
Amen

21

Lord, accept my activity, but forgive my anxiety;
Lord, in your mercy.
Lord, accept my quietness, but forgive my laziness;
Lord, in your mercy.
Lord, accept my trust and forgive my doubting.
Lord, in your mercy.

Lord, accept my giving and forgive my grasping.
Lord, in your mercy.
Amen

22

In our worship, Lord, grant us reverence
and forgive all that is insincere.
Lord, in your mercy,
forgive us.

As we bring you our offering of praise,
forgive us our thoughts of self.
Lord, in your mercy,
forgive us.

Lord in giving our gifts,
forgive all our desire for praise.
Lord, in your mercy,
forgive us.

Cleanse us, good Lord,
that in our worship and our work,
all may be done to your glory.
Amen

23

Lord, you never forget us,
forgive us when we forget you.

Lord, you never stop loving us,
forgive us when our love grows cold.

Lord, you always protect us,
forgive us when we fail to trust you.

Lord, your promises never fail,
forgive us when we break our word.
Amen

24

For all prejudice and jumping to conclusions,
forgive me, Lord.
For blindness to the insights of others,
forgive me, Lord.
For thinking the worst of others,
forgive me, Lord.
For my fear in the face of the unexpected,
forgive me, Lord.
For lack of trust and deafness to your word,
forgive me, Lord.
Amen

25

From pride and the desire for status,
good Lord, deliver us.
From the love of power and abuse of authority,
good Lord, deliver us.
From lies and all falsehood,
good Lord, deliver us.
From false ambition and a cheating heart,
good Lord, deliver us.
Amen

26

Lord, you know us better than we know ourselves,
forgive us all that is amiss.
Lord, we make you promises and fail to keep them,
forgive us, Lord, for our idle boasts.
Lord, you restore us and call us to follow you,
forgive us the times we fail you.
Amen

Intercessions

1

For all who live in exile from their homes,
we pray to the Father;
for all who are in prison,
we pray to the Father;
for all who work to bring liberty of spirit,
we pray to the Father.
Amen

2

Lord of all and King of kings,
we pray for leaders with a vision
for the good of all people;
for those who seek peace, make peace and keep peace;
we pray for the well-being of all your creation
and a responsible stewardship of the world's resources;
we pray for those who serve at great personal cost
and all whose care of others goes unseen.
Amen

3

Lord Jesus,
we pray for all who are in special need:
the hungry and the lonely,
the lost and the forsaken,
the oppressed and all victims
of violence and abuse.
May we be generous in our giving,
sensitive in our helping
and loving in our supporting.
Amen

4

Lord of lords and king of kings,
we pray for all who have the responsibility of leadership
in the nations of the world.
Grant them integrity
in all their dealings and decisions,
and a desire to serve that is stronger
than a desire for personal power.
In Jesus' name.
Amen

5

Lord, we pray for all who lead worship,
that they may be true to your word
and sensitive to the needs of your people;
that all they do may be for your glory
and the honour of your name.
Amen

6

Lord, we pray for all who worship,
that they may do so in spirit and in truth,
open to your forgiveness
and drawn by your Spirit.
Amen

7

Lord, we pray for those who are burdened with guilt,
that they may know your forgiveness
and live to give you thanks.

Lord, we pray for the poor and the homeless,
for the hungry and the unloved,
that we may be generous in our giving.

Lord, we pray for those who suffer and are in pain,
for the dying and those who care for them,
that they may know your presence and your comfort.

Lord, we pray for all leaders
and those who bear great responsibility,
for wisdom in the decision-making
and integrity in their actions,
that all people may be ruled with justice and honesty.
Amen

8

In the name of Christ and in the power of the Spirit,
let us pray to the Father:

That your church may be one
in faith and trust and obedience,
Lord hear our prayer.
That priests and ministers may lead
by their good example,
Lord hear our prayer.
That your people may honour your name
and serve your world,
Lord hear our prayer.
That the leaders of the nations may govern with integrity
for the good of all people,
Lord hear our prayer.
That they may be honest in the dealings
and truthful in their words,
Lord hear our prayer.
That where there is war
they may work for peace and reconciliation,
Lord hear our prayer.
That our families and communities
may be places of well-being,
Lord hear our prayer.

That in our work and in our relaxation
we may find fufilment,
Lord hear our prayer.
That our relationships may be built
on love and mutual respect,
Lord hear our prayer.
That there will be food for the hungry
and shelter for the homeless,
Lord hear our prayer.
That refugees may find a home
and the persecuted asylum,
Lord hear our prayer.
That the sick will be cared for
and the grieving comforted,
Lord hear our prayer.
Amen

9

Lord, hear our prayer
and let our cry come unto you.

We pray for peace among the nations,
remembering especially places of present conflict . . .
for those who long for peace
and those who make peace,
for members of the armed forces and their families.

Lord, hear our prayer
and let our cry come unto you.

We pray for peace in our communities,
for peace on our streets and in our homes,
for those caught up in gangs and for street pastors,
for victims of violence and abuse.

Lord, hear our prayer
and let our cry come unto you.

We pray for peace in the church,
for all who work to end our disunity,
for local and national church leaders,
for ecumenical officers and the World Council of Churches.

Lord, hear our prayer
and let our cry come unto you.

We pray for peace in our hearts,
for love that casts out fear
and hope that dissolves despair,
for forgiveness that overcomes guilt,
and assurance that comforts grief.

Lord, hear our prayer
and let our cry come unto you.
Amen

10

Lord of all power and all wisdom,
we pray for the leaders of the nations;
grant them wisdom in their decisions
and integrity in their actions.
Lord, hear our prayer.

Lord of all splendour and glory,
we pray for all who are wealthy,
that they may use their riches wisely
and for the benefit of others.
Lord, hear our prayer.

Lord of all knowledge,
we pray for all who teach and all who learn,
and for those who have no opportunity to go to school.
Lord, hear our prayer.

Lord of all lands,
we pray for those who travel,
that they be courteous in the journeying
and arrive safely.
Lord, hear our prayer.

Lord of all health and all wholeness,
we pray for those who are sick
and for all who care for them,
remembering those who have no access to medical care.
Lord, hear our prayer.
Amen

11

Heavenly Father,
grant the strength of your grace
to all who find the daily demands of life testing;
the demand of compassion and sympathy;
the demand of decision-making and conflicting choices;
the demand of particular need and the general good;
the demand of what is right in the face of desire;
the demand of your will amidst the insistence of their wishes.

Lord, in your mercy,
hear our prayer.

Heavenly Father,
we pray for all in authority
and for those of whom obedience is required,
we pray for leaders in the nations and in the church,
we pray for all members of the armed forces,
especially for those serving in places of conflict,
we pray for all teachers and lecturers,
for schools, for colleges and universities,
for all who find learning difficult.

Lord, in your mercy,
hear our prayer.

Heavenly Father,
we pray for parents and carers,
we pray for all who work in the National Health Service,
we pray for caring friends and good neighbours,
we pray for those who sit and watch
and those who wait to die.

Lord, in your mercy,
hear our prayer.
Amen

12

We pray for all who seek to reflect the Word of God
in their preaching and teaching;
for all who administer justice and make legal judgements;
for all who seek forgiveness and release from their guilt.
Lord, in your mercy,
hear our prayer.

We pray for all who sail the oceans of the world;
for the sailors of the merchant fleets;
for those who serve in the nations' navies;
for those who fish the seas and work on pleasure cruisers,
that they may travel safely through storm and calm.
Lord, in your mercy,
hear our prayer.

We pray for all who run away
from their sense of vocation;
for all who are confused
by the different demands of their faith;
for all who feel cut off from the love of God.
Lord, in your mercy,
hear our prayer.

We pray for all who are overwhelmed
by illness and disability;
for all who are overcome by despair and hopelessness;
for all whose minds have become confused;
for all who are close to death.
Lord, in your mercy,
hear our prayer.
Amen

13

We give thanks for wisdom and knowledge,
for the insights of past ages
and for the discoveries of today.
We pray for scientists and investigators,
for researchers and technicians,
that the results of their work
may be used for the benefit of all.
Lord of glory,
hear our prayer.

We give thanks for artists and novelists,
for poets and musicians,
whose works shine in our imagination
and dance through our feelings.
May we value their insights
and listen to the voice of our hearts.
Lord of glory,
hear our prayer.

We give thanks for all who help us
in our quest for knowledge,
for those who have taught us
and inspired us to learn.

We pray for teachers and lecturers,
and all who work in schools and colleges,
that they may work with integrity and passion
to lead others to wisdom.
Lord of glory,
hear our prayer.

We give thanks for the generosity of others:
for all who share their time,
their possessions and themselves.
We pray for a generous spirit,
that we might offer the gifts you have given us
for the well-being of those in need.
Lord of glory,
hear our prayer.
Amen

14

Lord, we thank you
that in Christ we can know the light guides our lives.
We pray for all who have lost their way.

Lord, we thank you
that in Christ we are born again with new life.
We pray for all who are dogged by the past.

Lord, we thank you
that in Christ we have the gift of the Spirit.
We pray for all whose lives are lacking vitality.
Amen

15

Lord, we pray for religious leaders,
that their religion may never become simply a rule to keep
rather than a life of trust.

Lord, we pray for leaders of the nations,
that they may not use their power for their own ends
but for the good of all.
Lord, we pray for ourselves,
that we may not lose our wonder
at the mystery of your love.

Lord, in your mercy,
hear our prayer.

Lord, we pray for all who are in need:
for the homeless and the deserted;
for the betrayed and the abused;
for the fearful and the foolhardy;
for the confused and the guilty;
for those whose voice is never heard
and for those whose voice is never quiet.
For the sick and the dying;
for the sorrowful and the grieving;
for all who do not know you
and for those who cannot find you.

Lord, in your mercy,
hear our prayer.
Amen

16

In the light of Christ
we bring our thanks and our prayers to God the Father.

In a world where so many are blinded by the dazzle of power,
we pray for the light of service and humility,
giving thanks for all who lead with wisdom and compassion.
Lord, hear our prayer,
and let our cry to you.

In a world where so many are dazzled by the glitter of wealth,
we pray for the light of generosity and simplicity,
giving thanks for all who give willingly
of their possessions, their time and themselves.
Lord, hear our prayer,
and let our cry to you.

In a world where so many are blind to the needs of others,
we pray for the light of compassion and unselfishness,
giving thanks for the care of doctors and nurses,
of carers and good neighbours.
Lord, hear our prayer,
and let our cry to you.

In a world that suffers from ignorance and the lack of education,
we pray for our schools and universities
and for all who teach,
giving thanks for those who have taught us
and been our example.
Lord, hear our prayer,
and let our cry to you.

In a world of fear and anxiety, of guilt and despair,
we pray for all who suffer
and who are terminally ill,
giving thanks for the gift of health
and the hope we have in Christ.
Lord, hear our prayer,
and let our cry to you.
Amen

17
Lord, we thank you for all the good things of this life,
for enough to eat and for homes in which to live.
We pray for those who have very little,
those who are starving
and those who are homeless.

Lord, we thank you for all who work
in factories and warehouses,
in construction and transport,
in shops and in banks,
at sea and on the land,
for civil servants and government officials.
May they work with honesty and integrity,
courtesy and insight.

Lord, we thank you for all who strengthen our sense of worth
and help build up our self-confidence.
We pray for all who are bullied and abused,
for those who suffer through acts of prejudice and hatred.
May we show respect to all whom we meet
and listen with care
to those whose views differ from our own.
Amen

18

We pray for all who seek to know the Lord,
that none may feel too small or too ignorant,
shut out by their past or shunned for their present.

We pray for all who seek to worship God,
that they may find a place of reverence
and a fellowship of welcome.
May no one prevent their entering,
nor place hurdles in their way.

We pray for all who seek to serve the Lord,
that none may despise their offering,
nor ignore the gifts they bring,
but value and encourage them.
We pray for ourselves

that we may come to God,
admitting our failings
and assured of his forgiveness,
joyful in our praise,
and loving in our service,
that together we may know the unity of the Spirit.
Amen

19

Heavenly Father,
whose goodness flows to all corners of the world,
we pray for leaders of the nations,
that they may be honest in their dealings
and just in their decision;
that the poor are not exploited
nor the vulnerable disadvantaged.
Lord, hear our prayer.

We pray for the churches,
that the integrity of each may be recognised
and diversity of views be valued;
that all may be bound in love
and filled with the power of the Spirit.
Lord, hear our prayer.

We pray for all places of work,
that the contribution of each may be valued,
that honesty of endeavour be rewarded justly
and all find purpose in what they do.
Lord, hear our prayer.

We pray for our homes and families,
that love will overcome differences,
that we may be kept from jealousy and rivalry,
that we may be a blessing to one another.
Lord, hear our prayer.
Amen

20

Let us pray to God.
We pray for all whose lives have been disrupted
by war and violence;
for refugees and those with no country to call their own,
for the dispossessed and the asylum seekers,
for all who have been driven from their homes.
Lord, in your mercy,
hear our prayer.

For all whose lives are torn by domestic violence,
for the abused and the violated,
for war orphans and the children of the streets,
Lord, in your mercy,
hear our prayer.

We pray for all who seek to make peace and to bring peace;
for the Secretary of the united Nations and his staff,
for peace-keeping forces and arms control officials,
for the Red Cross and Red Crescent,
Lord, in your mercy,
hear our prayer.

We pray for all who work to keep homes safe places;
for the Children's Society and Save the Children,
for refuges and safe houses,
for social workers and probation officers,
Lord, in your mercy,
hear our prayer.
Amen

21

For the leaders of the nations:
that they may show wisdom and courage,
that all may live in peace
and share the good things of the earth.
Lord hear our prayer.
For all who govern:
that they may treat all with fairness,
that none may be exploited,
none pushed to the margins or left in poverty.
Lord hear our prayer.
For the leaders of the churches:
that they may teach your word,
guiding your people with holiness
and caring for all with compassion.
Lord hear our prayer.
For our homes:
that they may be places of love,
welcoming to strangers
and hospitable to neighbours.
Lord hear our prayer.
For all who are in need:
for the lonely and the bewildered,
for the sick and the anxious,
for the dying and the grieving.
Lord hear our prayer.
Amen

22

Father God,
we pray for your world,
giving thanks for its wonder and its beauty,
for all that you have given to the human race
to steward and develop.
We pray for all who suffer from natural disasters
and those whose pain calls out in anguish.

Father God,
we pray for your church,
giving thanks for all we have learnt and enjoyed
in its fellowship,
for the faithfulness of its witness
and the wonder of its worship.
We pray for the divisions that tear us apart
and the fears that hold us back for your future.

Father God,
we pray for our family,
friends, neighbours and colleagues,
giving thanks for all the variety of their gifts and abilities,
for all they have meant to us
and all they have brought us.
We pray for all whose relationships are broken or abusive,
for all who are lonely and unloved.

Father God,
we pray for all parents
and those about to become parents,
giving thanks for the wonder
and the mystery of new life.
We pray for those whose child is unwanted
and for those who are unable to have children.

Hear our prayers
and in your mercy
look with compassion
on those who call to you for help.
Amen

23

Let us pray for the Church,
its priests and its ministers,
its elders and all God's people.

We pray for those who serve at the altar
and minister the sacraments,
that they may do so with reverence.
We pray for those who preach the Gospel
and teach the good news,
that they may do so
with understanding and imagination.
We pray for those who pastor the needy
and care for the troubled,
that they may do so with compassion and sensitivity.
Merciful Father,
hear our prayers and let our cry come to you.

Let us pray for the world,
its leaders and governments,
for all the nations and their peoples.

We pray for those whose decisions affect the lives of millions,
that they may be wise in their judgements.
We pray for those who control the wealth of the nations,
that they may be kept from greed.
We pray for those who teach in schools and universities,
that they may put first the needs of their students.
Merciful Father,
hear our prayers and let our cry come to you.

Let us pray for all who are in need,
in body, mind or spirit.

We pray for those without enough to eat
and with nowhere to live.
We pray for those who are ill
and who face operations.
We pray for those who are troubled
by guilt and by mental disorder.
We pray for those who are approaching death
and who grieve for loved ones.
Merciful Father,
hear our prayers and let our cry come to you.
Amen

24

Heavenly Father,
for all whose lives feel empty and unfulfilled;
we pray today.
For all whose work is tedious and uncreative;
we pray today.
For all whom illness and infirmity have robbed of activity;
we pray today.
For all who long for children and are unable to have them;
we pray today.
For all who feel ashamed through failure;
we pray today.
Amen

25

We pray for all who are imprisoned
through the malice of others
and through acts of injustice,
through political intrigue and acts of oppression,
through the wrongs they have done
and the harm they have caused.
Lord, hear our prayer.

We pray for all whose lives are restricted
through guilt and fear,
through illness and disability,
through disadvantage and powerlessness,
through hunger and homelessness.
Lord, hear our prayer.

Grant us Lord,
the skill and the will
to bring freedom to the oppressed,
healing to the sick,
release to the prisoner,
learning to the ignorant,
shelter to the homeless,
hope to the distressed,
Lord, hear our prayer.
Amen

26

Let us pray for the Church throughout the world.
We pray for all bishops, priests and ministers,
for lay leaders and elders,
for evangelists and pastors,
and in particular we remember . . .

We pray for synods, councils and assemblies,
for congregations and for all Christian gatherings,
for study groups and prayer meetings,
and in particular we remember . . .

We pray for church schools and colleges,
for Christian hospitals and clinics,
for all who have left their homes to serve you abroad,
and in particular we remember . . .

We give thanks for all who have witnessed to you,
through their words and their actions,
for all those who died for their faith,
and in particular we remember . . .

Lord, hear us.
Lord, graciously hear us.
Amen

27

We pray for all prisoners:
for those guilty of crimes,
and those who are innocent;
for those who long for freedom,
and those who cannot face freedom;
for those soon to be released,
and those who will never be released;
for those imprisoned by ignorance,
and those imprisoned by guilt;
for those restricted by illness,
and those facing death.
Amen

28

We pray for all who serve in the armed forces:
for those who face danger,
and those who fear boredom;
for those who seek excitement,
and those who have had too much;
for those who give orders,
and those who have to obey orders;
for the injured and the disabled,
for the dying and the grieving.
Amen

Blessings

1

God, Creator and Father, bless you and keep you,
God, Saviour and Friend, bless you and keep you,
God, Guide and Protector, bless you and keep you,
today and for evermore.
Amen

2

God give you joy and gratitude
for all the good things of your lives;
God give you peace in your homes
and where you work;
God give you health and happiness,
enough to live on and the extras to enjoy;
God give you the blessing of love
in the name of Christ
and in the power of his Spirit,
today and always.
Amen

3

God be with you in your departing;
God be with you in your journey;
God be with you in your arriving.
Amen

4

God the Father, whose love created you,
give you his blessing;
God the Son, whose love has rescued you,
give you his blessing;
God the Spirit, whose love sustains you,
give you his blessing;
now and always.
Amen

5

May God the Father, who loves us,
bless us.
May God the Son, who intercedes for us,
bless us.
May God the Holy Spirit, who guides us,
bless us.

God, our Father, bless us from your throne of majesty.
God, the Son, bless us through your cross of sacrifice.
God, the Spirit, bless us through your breath of inspiration.

Go in peace and love, to serve the Lord.
Thanks be to God.
Amen

6

May God our Creator
watch over you and bless you in all you do.
May God our Saviour
forgive you and bless you in all your relationships.
May God our Guide
direct your way and bless you in all your journeying.
Amen

7

God the Father, who calls you to his service;
God the Son, who rescues you from all that binds you;
God the Holy Spirit, who guides and strengthens you;
bless you and keep you, this day and for evermore.
Amen

8

The Lord bless you at your rising.
The Lord bless you at your working.
The Lord bless you at your resting.
And the blessing of God almighty,
Father, Son and Holy Spirit,
be with you today and for evermore.
Amen

9

Go out in the love of the Father;
go out in the joy of the Son;
go out in the power of the Spirit
and go with the blessing of God
resting on you and abiding with you.
Amen

10

Go in the power of God to proclaim his Word.
Go in the love of God to serve all people.
Go in the spirit of God to stand up for truth.
And the blessing of God,
Father, Son and Holy Spirit
be upon you, now and always.
Amen

11

May God travel with you on your journey,
be your companion at every step,
be with you at your setting out and at your arrival,
be present in your greeting and your meeting,
and bless you through friend and stranger.
Amen

12

May the voice of God call to you;
may the Word of God speak to you;
may the Spirit of God guide you;
may the hand of God protect you;
may the love of God dwell in you.
And the blessing of God,
Father, Son and Holy Spirit be upon you,
on those you love and those you serve,
this day and for evermore.
Amen

13

May the power of God strengthen you in his service,
may the truth of God lighten your way,
may the love of God keep your heart pure
and the blessing of God be upon you today and for evermore.
Amen

14

May God the Father bless you with his welcome;
may God the Son bless you with his friendship;
may God the Holy Spirit bless you with encouragement,
today and always.
Amen

15

May the Truth of God fill you with all knowing,
may the Spirit of God fill you with all wisdom,
may the power of God fill you with all loving,
and the blessing of God almighty,
Father, Son and Holy Spirit
go with you and rest upon you,
today and always.
Amen

16

May the glory of God enrich your life;
may the wisdom of God inspire your thoughts;
may the love of God envelop your heart;
may God bless you, all your days.
Amen

17

May the love of God support you in all your fears;
may the mercy of God uphold you in all your troubles;
may the grace of God surround you in all you do.
And the blessing of God,
Father, Son and Holy Spirit,
be with you at all times and in every place.
Amen

18

May the power of God surround you,
may the forgiveness of God uphold you,
may the love of God fulfil you.
May the arms of Christ embrace you,
may the welcome of Christ delight you,
may the love of Christ accept you.
May the blessing of God be with you,
upon you, within you and around you,
this day and for evermore.
Amen

19

May God, who called you into being,
bless you.
May Christ, who calls you to follow him,
bless you.
May the Spirit, who calls you into the future,
bless you.
Amen

20

The Lord bless you with the mystery of his love;
the Lord bless you with the wonder of new birth;
the Lord bless you with the breath of his life.
And the blessing of God almighty,
Father, Son and Holy Spirit,
be with you this day and for evermore.
Amen

21

Go in the strength of God the Father;
go with God's blessing.
Go in the love of God the Son;
go with God's blessing.
Go in the peace of God the Holy Spirit;
go with God's blessing.
Let us go with God.
Amen

22

Father God, creator and protector,
bless us on our way.
Son of God, saviour and friend,
bless us on our way.
Holy Spirit, guide and comforter,
bless us on our way.
Amen

Seasonal prayers

Advent

1

Help us, Lord, to read the signs of your coming,
that our expectations may be true to your purpose,
neither leading us to the disappointment that hurts us
nor to the surprise which we miss.
Come Lord Jesus – we await you.
Amen

2

At this advent time, we give thanks:
for the faith of the patriarchs, we give thanks;
for the message of the prophets, we give thanks;
for the witness of John the Baptist, we give thanks;
for the obedience of Mary, we give thanks;
for the coming of Christ, the Light of the world, we give thanks.
Amen

3

We look for the coming of the Lord of Light,
the Child of Bethlehem,
the giver of freedom.
For the forgiveness of sins, we give thanks;
for release from guilt, we give thanks;
for the freedoms we enjoy, we give thanks.
For all who are in prison, we pray to the Father;
for all who are held in the grip of disease, we pray to the Father;
for all who are constrained by mental illness, we pray to the Father.
Amen

4

Amidst the darkness of winter
we look for the brightness of Christ's light.
To keep us from false teaching and misunderstanding,
may your light surround us.
To lead us in the way of your truth,
may your light surround us.
To overcome the darkness of our fears,
may your light surround us.
To bring us hope in times of doubts,
may your light surround us.
Amen

5

Almighty God,
in your love, look with mercy
on all that is wrong in our lives and in our world;
help us to reject the darkness and to live in your light,
that we may rejoice in the coming of your Son
who is the Light of the world,
the light to the nations.
In your love, root out what is evil,
in your holiness, strengthen what is good,
that we may give thanks for your merciful judgement
and celebrate the wonder of your love.
In Jesus Christ's name.
Amen

Christmas

1

Glory to God in the highest.
Glory to God in the highest.
Peace on earth for all people.
Glory to God in the highest.

Today is the day of joyous news.
Glory to God in the highest.
A Saviour born, the Messiah, the Lord.
Glory to God in the highest.
Amen

2

Through Jesus our Saviour, born in humility,
we ask forgiveness.
Through Jesus Christ, proclaimed by the angels,
we ask forgiveness.
Through Jesus our Saviour, sought by the shepherds,
we ask forgiveness.
Through Jesus Christ our Saviour, worshipped by magi,
we ask forgiveness.
Amen

3

In the power of the Spirit
and in union with Christ,
let us pray to the Father.

We give thanks for the angels' message of peace:
we pray for the peace of the world,
for the leaders of the nations,
for peace keepers and peace makers,
remembering all whose lives are torn by war and violence.

We give thanks for the angels' message of the Saviour's birth:
we pray for all who have never heard the Good News,
for all who seek to share the Good News with others,
for missionary societies
and those who translate the Scriptures,
remembering our responsibility to live the Gospel life.

We give thanks for the love of Mary and Joseph:
we pray for all parents and carers,
for those who bring up children on their own,
for those couples who cannot have children,
remembering all children and young people
who are abused and neglected.

We give thanks for the welcome
of the shepherds and the gifts of the wise men:
we pray for all asylum seekers and refugees,
for all who lack a sense of true worth,
for all who have nowhere they can call home,
remembering all who are strangers in a strange land.

Lord, in your mercy,
hear our prayers and let our cry come to you.
Amen

4

Lord, open our hearts and our ears
that, as Mary listened to the voice of the angel,
so we may learn of your will for us
and hear the message of your love for all the world.
In Jesus' name.
Amen

5

Angel voices fill the heavens,
singing of the one who comes;
may their music fill my spirit,
lift my wonder into worship
for the infant, Lord of all.
Amen

6

Heavenly Father,
we join with the angels
in proclaiming the good news
of the birth of your Son, our Saviour.
May the light of this coming
shine in our hearts,
illumine our path,
and fill the earth.
In his name we pray.
Amen

7

Lord of all time,
who when the time was right
sent your Son, born of a virgin;
grant us the wisdom and the insight
to discern his coming among us.
May we have perseverance
as we grow in grace and in our encounter with you,
that all may be done to your glory
and the fulfilment of your purposes,
through him who came to be our Saviour,
Jesus Christ our Lord.
Amen

8

Lord Jesus,
at your birth you received gifts
of shepherds and wise men;
accept the offering of my obedience and my love
that they may be a fragrant sacrifice acceptable to you.
Amen

9

Almighty God, Lord of all the universe,
at the coming of your Son
the heavens rang with angelic choirs,
telling the good news of his birth;
fill our hearts with the joy of his coming
that we may share the wonder of this special time
and live as those who know its importance.
Amen

10

Special was the message of the angels,
special was the worship of the shepherds,
special were the gifts of the wise men,
special was the love of Mary and Joseph,
but more special than all was the birth of the baby;
to God be the glory.
Amen

11

Show us, O Lord, the meaning of Christ's coming
revealed long ago,
and in our lives now;
that in whatever we have to face,
we may be people of trust and hope.
Amen

12

Lord Jesus Christ, Son of God,
at whose coming the angels rejoiced,
and the shepherds delighted in their message;
grant that we may welcome you with joy
and be blessed by your peace,
now and always.
Amen

13

Come, love, with the angels' voices.
Come, love, in the shepherds' worship.
Come, love, in the wise men's homage.
Come, love, in Mary's obedience.
Come, love, in the gift of the child.
Come, love, in the response of my life.
Amen

14

May Christ, who came in humility
that we might share his glory,
grant us all joy and peace in our hearts,
our homes
and our world.
And the blessing of God, Father, Son and Holy Spirit,
be amongst us and remain with us,
those we love and those we serve,
this Christmas and for evermore.
Amen

15

Immanuel, God with us,
be with us now
and show us the wonder of this mystery.

Son of God, Lord of all,
be with us now
and help us to grow in understanding.

Son of Mary, born as one of us,
be with us now
and fill us with the light of your presence.
Amen

16

May the love of the Father overshadow you,
may the promise of the Christ child dwell within you,
may the power of the Spirit fill you with creative love,
and the blessing of God,
Father, Son and Holy Spirit,
rest upon you and remain with you, now and always.
Amen

17

May the humility of the shepherds,
the perseverance of the wise men,
the joy of the angels,
and the peace of the Christ child,
be God's gift to you.
And the blessing of God almighty,
Father, Son and Holy Spirit,
be upon you and remain with you,
now and always.
Amen

Epiphany

1

Bright star of love,
guide us to where we can see Christ:
in the worship of your church
and in the unexpected places of your world.
Where there is darkness
may we shine with your light,
that all may see your saving grace
and together we may offer you the gift of our lives.
Amen

2

May Christ our Lord,
the Babe of Bethlehem and King of all,
to whom wise men came and bowed in worship,
reveal to you the glory of his presence;
and the blessing of God,
Father, Son and Holy Spirit,
rest upon you and surround you, today and always.
Amen

3

Almighty God,
whose Son our Lord Jesus Christ is King of all,
may all wisdom, all power, all superstition
be brought into the Light of Christ,
submitting to the wisdom of his truth,
the power of his love,
and the fulness of his life.
Amen

Palm Sunday

1

We gather in the name of the Lord, Jesus Christ,
the King of Glory.
We gather as the followers of the Prince of Peace,
the Servant of all.
We gather not knowing what he will ask of us,
not always understanding what he will do in us.
We will follow the One who comes in the name of the Lord.
Amen

2

Lord Jesus,
you set your face to go to Jerusalem
and told your disciples what would happen there.
Grant us a trust like theirs,
that we may follow you
whatever is asked of us
and wherever you may lead.
Grant us through your Spirit,
the knowledge of your presence with us,
to sustain us and guide us,
to encourage us and to challenge us,
that we may witness to your truth and your love
in all we do and say and are.
In your name we ask this.
Amen

3

We hold the palm of acclamation.
May we always be bold
in our witness to you, our King.
We hold the cross of sacrifice,
may we always be courageous
in following your way
of service to others,
whatever the cost.
Amen

4

Lord, you are king, enthroned in majesty,
come rule in our hearts.
Blessed is the king. Hosanna in the highest!

Lord, you are king,
the ruler of the nations,
bring peace to our world.
Blessed is the king. Hosanna in the highest!

Lord, you are king,
worshipped by angels,
accept our praise.
Blessed is the king. Hosanna in the highest!
Amen

5

Lord Jesus,
you entered Jerusalem on a donkey's back,
amidst shouts of praise and triumph;
come to us with your rule of peace,
that we may rejoice in the glory of the cross
and in the triumph of your resurrection.
Amen

6

Heavenly Father,
we have joined in the acclamation of your Son,
echoing the words of the crowds.
Forgive us when our praise grows silent,
when our acclamations give way to apathy.
Forgive us the times we ask for the wrong things
and look only to our own wants.
Forgive us the times when we hide from your demands,
and want your power but not your love.
Go with us through this coming week,
that we may accompany you on your road to the cross
and so discover the joy and wonder of your resurrection.
We ask this in the name of our King and Saviour.
Amen

7

May the Lord of Glory bless you and keep you.

May the Son of David bless you and keep you.

May the humble King bless you and keep you

on this day of acclamation,

through this week of trial and execution

and in the wonder of his resurrection.

Amen

8

May the peace of Christ the King, rule in your hearts.

May the humility of Christ the King rule your lives.

May the glory of Christ the King rule your way.

And the blessing of God almighty,

Father, Son and Holy Spirit,

be with you now and always.

Amen

Maundy Thursday

1

Christ, our Lord and Master,

with towel and water

you show us how to serve.

We worship you.

Christ, our Saviour,

with broken bread and poured out wine

you ask us to remember you.

We worship you.

Christ, our Redeemer,

with prayers and agony,

with dread and in obedience,

you prepare for dying.

We worship you.

Christ, who has taught us the meaning of service,
forgive us the times we think too much of our own importance.
Christ, who wrestled to do the Father's will,
forgive us the times we seek the easy way out.
Christ, who thought of others while in agony on the cross,
Forgive us the times we think only of ourselves.
Amen

2

Father, we give you thanks
for this night of fellowship,
for the presence of our Lord
amongst us and with us.
He is the host,
the head at our table,
and he invites us to join him.
Let us bless the Lord.
Thanks be to God.

Father, we give thanks for our world,
for all its resources and for all its beauty.
We thank you for bread –
for all that sustains us.
We thank you for wine –
for all that delights us.
We remember with sadness
the hungry and the unhappy.
Let us bless the Lord.
Thanks be to God.

Father, we give you thanks
for all who serve you in the church
and in the community.
For those who do the lowly jobs
no one else wants to do.

For those who are busy
when we are at rest.
Let us bless the Lord.
Thanks be to God.

Father, we give you thanks
for freedom,
for peace, for good health.
We remember all prisoners,
all who suffer because of violence,
all who are sick, at home and in hospital.
Let us bless the Lord.
Thanks be to God.
Amen

3

Father,
on this night of meeting with his disciples
Jesus was betrayed.
We pray for all whose loyalty is being tested
and who will tonight be tempted
to betray friends, loved ones or themselves.
Grant them your strength
and grant us grace
when we are tempted to deny you.
Lord in your mercy
hear our prayers.

Father,
on this night your Son commanded his disciples to love
but suffered rejection himself.
We pray for all who feel themselves rejected and unloved
and for those who feel that their lives are useless
and who are in despair.

May we be bearers of love and hope
to those around us
who look to us for care and support.
Lord in your mercy
hear our prayers.

Father,
on this night they came with soldiers
bearing arms to arrest your Son.
We pray for all victims of injustice,
persecution and war.
We pray for members of the armed services
who fight on our behalf
to maintain peace and justice.
We pray for the injured and the maimed,
for the terrified and the grieving,
for all who work for reconciliation and peace.
Lord in your mercy
hear our prayers.

Lord Jesus,
on this night before your crucifixion,
we pray for all who will die this night.
For those whose lives will end
in violence or accident
and for those who will slip peacefully into their final sleep.
We pray for those who watch and wait and grieve.
Lord in your mercy
hear our prayers.
Amen

4

God our Father,
you have invited us to share in the supper
which your Son gave to his Church
to proclaim his death until he comes again;

may he nourish us by his presence
and unite us in his love.
For his sake we ask this.
Amen

Lord, you are with us in this sacred meal;
you share fellowship with us and call us to follow you.
Nourish us through the gifts of your body and blood;
they speak of your self-giving love and death for us.
Grant us the courage and the faith
that we may follow you in the way,
taking up our cross
and looking for the coming of your kingdom.
In your name we ask this.
Amen

5

Watch and pray.
The Lord is in distress of soul,
torn between his own desire
and the will of the Father;
torn between escape
and the demands of his own integrity.
We watch and pray.

Watch and pray.
The Lord is betrayed with a kiss.
With swords and with cudgels
they make the arrest.
He has not hidden from them
and he does not resist.
He is to fulfil his destiny
and the work of God's saving plan
foretold in Scripture.
We watch and we are afraid.

Good Friday

1

Come, let us watch and wait a while
here in the shadow of the cross,
let us bring our fears, our guilts, our troubles,
and lay them where love was crucified.
Where forgiveness is shown to all,
let us declare our love and our thanks,
and praise the Lord our Saviour.
Amen

2

By your bruised and bloodied body,
forgive us, Lord.
By your thorn-crowned head and spear-torn side,
forgive us, Lord.
By your nail-pierced hands and nail-pierced feet,
forgive us, Lord.
By your cross and cruel throne,
forgive us, Lord.
By your sacrifice and loving gift,
forgive us, Lord.
By your triumph and your victory,
forgive us, Lord.
Amen

3

Look mercifully upon us, Lord,
as we come to this time of your Passion.
Reveal again to us
the meaning of your suffering and your death,
that as we hear the story of your self-giving love
we may know the cost of our forgiveness
and the depth of your compassion.
In your dear name we ask it.
Amen

4

Forgive us, Lord,
for all the times we have denied you,
through the fear of embarrassment
or fear of ridicule,
through the weakness of our love for you
and the care we have for the opinion of others.
Forgive us, Lord, and look on us in mercy.
Amen

5

Your silence spoke of innocence
and the mockery revealed your majesty.
Give us eyes to see your glory
in the humility of your self-giving.
Give us grace
to respond to your love revealed in your suffering;
our salvation declared on your cross.
Amen

6

Lord Jesus Christ,
your way of love became the way of the cross.
As you walk in obedience to the Father,
give us the faith and the courage
to follow you who are the way,
walking always in the path of your truth
and under the guidance of your holy and life-giving spirit.
Amen

7

Lord Jesus Christ,
your outstretched arms
offer us love and life.

Give us grace to accept your love
and to offer ourselves in your service.
Forgive what is false in us
and by your love nurture us in holiness.
For your dear name's sake.
Amen

8

Son of God, victim and victor,
your work is finished,
and the cost of our salvation is revealed in full.
We bring you our repentance and our thanks,
the love of our hearts and the commitment of our lives.
To you be praise and honour, now and always.
Amen

9

Jesus Christ,
crucified Lord and King of all,
show us the mystery of your suffering and death,
that the defeat of the cross
may become the throne of victory, that its humiliation
may become the place of glory,
and that love may rule
both in heaven and in our hearts.
We ask it in your dear name.
Amen

10

Go with us, Lord, from this place of your Passion,
that in hope and expectation
we may look beyond the tomb
and meet again to celebrate your resurrection,
for through your death we come to new life.
Amen

11

Most merciful God,
who by the death and resurrection of your Son Jesus Christ,
delivered and saved the world,
grant that by faith in him who suffered on the cross
we may triumph in the power of his victory
through Jesus Christ our Lord.
Amen

12

Crucified Christ, go with us,
forgiving Christ, go with us,
forsaken and trusting Christ, go with us,
into the waiting time, Christ, go with us.
Amen

13

Lord Jesus Christ,
whose love for us
was shown in the agony of the cross,
may we never take your love for granted;
but filled with love for you
may we seek to serve with courage and compassion,
the world for which you died.
Amen

14

Loving Lord,
who on the cross showed care both for your mother
and for John, your beloved disciples,
make us compassionate for the plight of others,
and loving to those in need,
for your name's sake.
Amen

15

May Christ, our crucified Lord,
draw you to himself,
fill you with all hope
and with the assurance of sins forgiven;
and the blessing of God almighty,
the Father, the Son and the Holy Spirit,
rest upon you and remain with you,
this day and for evermore.
Amen

Holy Saturday

1

God of hope and inspiration,
send out your light and your truth
that we may walk in the way of your Son;
bearing our cross in service and obedience,
and living in the power of your resurrection.
Amen

2

Lord, you lead us from the darkness of your death
into the glorious light of your resurrection.
May we leave the path of sin and death
and follow in the way of eternal life.
May we leave the darkness of the night
and rejoice once more in the coming of the new day.
Amen

Easter

1

Lord of all, you are the life of the world.
You are the resurrection and the life.
Lord of all, you are the life of the church.
You are the resurrection and the life.
Lord of all, you are our life and our joy.
You are the resurrection and the life.
Amen

2

Risen and triumphant Lord,
we confess the weakness of our faith,
have mercy on us.

Lord of new life,
we confess that we have lived in our own strength,
have mercy on us.

Lord of all truth and light,
we confess we have been blind to your glory,
have mercy on us.
Amen

3

Lord Jesus Christ, you endured the cross for us,
revealing the costly love with which you forgive us.
Lead us from the place of sin and death
to the glory of your resurrection,
that we may rejoice in your light
and walk in your way.
Amen

4

God in whom we live, you raised your Son to new life,
may this Easter garden be a blessing to all who visit it.
May it witness to the power of your love to overcome death,
And may we be filled with resurrection joy.
Amen

5

Great and all-loving God,
we praise you for this day
when you raised your Son to new life.
Grant us the ears to hear the message of resurrection,
grant us the eyes to see his risen presence,
grant us the voices to tell the good news to all,
grant us the feet to follow in the way of our risen, living Lord.
Amen

6

Risen Lord,
who appeared to Mary in the garden,
and called her by name,
so that she saw you and believed;
grant us the eyes of faith
and hearts to believe,
that we may proclaim
the glory of your resurrection life,
by word and deed.
Amen

7

Risen Christ,
help us to love you more;
fill us with courage to follow in your way,
to spread the good news of your kingdom,
to witness for justice and truth
and to care for the poor and the marginalised.
To the glory of your name.
Amen

8

God the Father,
who through the resurrection of our Lord Jesus Christ,
has granted us hope and new life,
give you all joy and peace in believing;
and the blessing of God almighty,
the Father, the Son and the Holy Spirit,
be upon you and remain with you,
now and always.
Amen

9

In the power of the Easter hope,
let us pray to the Father.

That our risen Lord may fill us
with the joy and the glory of his resurrection life,
we pray to the Father;
hear our prayer.

That the Church throughout the world
may proclaim afresh the good news of Easter,
we pray to the Father;
hear our prayer.

That our homes and our communities
may be renewed in love and trust,
we pray to the Father;
hear our prayer.

That all may be good stewards
of the resources of the earth
and share with those who do not have enough,
we pray to the Father;
hear our prayer.

That the peace of the risen Lord
may rule in the hearts of all people,
we pray to the Father;
hear our prayer.

That he may comfort those who are in distress,
and grant healing to the sick,
we pray to the Father;
hear our prayer.

That through his resurrection
the grieving may find hope
and the departed new life,
we pray to the Father;
hear our prayer.
Amen

10

We give thanks for the love of God seen in Jesus:
for the teachings of Jesus,
that lead us to new understanding and truth.
We pray for all who teach
and search for truth.

We give thanks for the love of God seen in Jesus:
for the humility of Jesus,
that shows us the way of service.
We pray for all who work
for the good of others.

We give thanks for the love of God seen in Jesus:
for the welcome of Jesus,
that embraced the outsider and the unloved.
We pray for all who have dropped out of society
and those who do not conform.

We give thanks for the love of God seen in Jesus:
for the self-sacrifice of Jesus,
that brought forgiveness and promised hope.
We pray for the guilty and the despairing.

We give thanks for the love of God seen in Jesus:
for the resurrection life
and the opportunities of new beginnings.
We pray for those who face endings and for the dying.
Amen

11

Risen and living Lord,
who entered glory only by the path of suffering,
help us to trust
in the mystery of your passion and resurrection,
that in serving you,
we may be strengthened in times of hardship
and sustained through the darkness of doubt.
Travel with us in the way,
and may we know your presence
in the breaking of the bread.
Amen

12

Go in the love and peace of the risen Lord.
Go with the blessing of the risen Lord.
Go to live and serve in the power of the risen Lord.
Amen

Pentecost

1

Come Holy Spirit,
and surprise us with your presence.
Come Holy Spirit,
and inspire us in our worship.
Come Holy Spirit,
and fill our hearts with praise and gratitude.
Amen

2

Holy Spirit of God,
forgive us when we have failed
to respond to your prompting.
Forgive us when we have failed
to bring your comfort to others.
Forgive us when we have ignored
the guidance you have given us.
Forgive us when we have avoided
the challenges you present to us.
Forgive us in the name of Jesus
and in the love of the Father.
Amen

3

Come, Holy Spirit,
hover over us and turn our chaos into creative order;
come, Holy Spirit,
speak to us and teach us your truth;
come, Holy Spirit,
overshadow us and protect us;
come, Holy Spirit,
enable us that we may do God's will;
come, Holy Spirit,
and build in us obedience
that we might be faithful disciples of Jesus Christ,
the Son of God our Saviour.
Amen

4

Heavenly Father,
pour upon us your Holy Spirit,
that we may witness to your love in Christ
with boldness and conviction.
Teach us how to share the gospel with others,
making its message of loving forgiveness
accessible to all,
that none may be excluded from your kingdom.
Amen

5

Wind of the Spirit blow through the dryness of our lives
and stir them into new life.
Fire of the Spirit blaze through your church
and set it alight with a passion for God's mission.
Breath of the Spirit inspire our leaders
with a deep desire for truth and for justice.
Guiding and enabling Spirit
show us the way into God's future.
Amen

6

Holy Spirit,
move amongst us with the freshness of a wind
and the attraction of a flame.
Inspire us to speak with boldness and imagination
that we may tell the Good News
so that it can be heard and understood by all.
Guide us and all your church
in the adventure of mission,
reaching out to those longing to hear good news;
supporting those burdened by guilt or by anxiety;
freeing those imprisoned by addiction or fear;
healing those wounded in spirit and troubled in mind;

feeding those hungry and thirsty for the truth;
comforting those overcome by pain or by grief;
transforming those who have lost all hope.
We ask this in Jesus' name.
Amen

Trinity

1

Let us worship the Father whose loving created us;
let us worship the Son whose suffering saved us;
let us worship the Spirit whose guiding directs us.
Let us worship God, Father, Son and Holy Spirit.
Amen

2

God our Father,
too often we have disobeyed you and gone our own way;
have mercy on us.
God the Son,
too often we have denied you and forsaken you;
have mercy on us.
God the Holy Spirit,
too often we have ignored you and rejected you;
have mercy on us.
Amen

3

Creator Father, you made us and sustain us,
we delight in you.
Saviour Son, you redeemed us and rescued us,
we delight in you.
Holy Spirit, you inspire us and strengthen us,
we delight in you.
Holy Trinity,
Creator, Saviour, Inspirer,
we delight in you.
Amen

4

Help us, good Lord, to respond to the mystery of your love:

the love that creates and sustains us;

the love that saves and transforms us;

the love that comforts and challenges us.

Help us, good Lord, to know the mystery of your being:

the one who is Father of all people;

the one who is Saviour of all people;

the one who is Inspirer of all people.

Help us, good Lord, to trust in the mystery of your promises:

the promise to welcome us;

the promise to forgive us;

the promise to comfort us.

Help us, good Lord, to respond, to know to trust in the mystery

of the Three and the One.

Amen

5

When we cannot understand,

help us, Lord, to trust.

When we feel confused,

help us to have faith.

When we are plagued by doubt,

help us, Lord, to love.

When we have travelled far from you,

help us, Lord, to find the way back.

For you are our God,

Father, Son and Holy Spirit.

Amen

Transfiguration

1

Draw us, Lord,
to the vision of your glory,
that we may worship you
with joy and with gratitude.

Draw us, Lord,
to the mystery of your suffering,
that we may worship you
in penitence and obedience.

Draw us, Lord,
to the urgency of your mission,
that we may worship you
with passion and expectation.
Amen

2

Forgive us, Lord,
when we see but do not understand;
when we hear but do not comprehend;
when we speak but do not communicate;
when we long to stay but do not move on.
Amen

3

Father God,
lead us to that mountain place
where we may perceive the glory of your Son,
shining with divine splendour.
In trust and obedience to his word,
and following in the way of the cross,
may we reflect that glory in our lives
in service of others
and in worship of you.
Amen

Harvest

1

Come and worship the Lord of all.
Give praise to God the creator of land and sea.
Rejoice in the product of field and farm,
of orchard and vineyard,
of garden and allotment.
The corn is cut, the wheat is gathered,
fruit has been picked
and vegetables harvested.
Let us give thanks to our generous God.
Amen

2

All the world is yours, O Lord,
its fertility and its fruitfulness.
You have made us stewards
of your generous gifts.
Forgive us for not respecting your creation,
for exploitation and destruction.
Forgive us for squandering the abundance
and for not sharing it with all.
Forgive us our greed and selfishness
and our lack of compassion for the poor.
Amen

3

Praise be to God,
for all who work to bring us the harvest of the land
and of the soil,
for farmers and horticulturists,
for nursery men and growers of herbs,
for fruit and vegetables, cereals and wine.
Praise be to God.

Praise be to God,
for all who care for herds and flocks,
for shepherds and stockmen,
for vets and farriers,
for slaughtermen and butchers,
for packers and processors.
Praise be to God.

Lord, all that we have comes from you;
all that we offer is already yours.
Accept our praises and thanksgiving
and cleanse us from all unworthiness.
Amen.

4

We pray for all who work at sea:
for those who fish along our coasts
and in the great oceans;
for those who spend long days on oil rigs,
and on large tankers;
for the crews of the merchant fleets of the world,
and those who work on luxury cruisers;
for pilots and navigators;
for life boat crews and the rescue services;
for the men and women of the navy and the coastguards.

We pray for them in times of danger
and in times of boredom;
we pray for them amidst the storms
and when all is plain sailing.

As we pray, we give you thanks for all they do.
Amen

5

We thank you, Lord,
that through your goodness
and the efforts of countless men and women,
we enjoy the good things of the harvest,
now and throughout the year.

We pray for those who have little and who go hungry;
for the farmers waiting amidst drought for the rains to come;
for the overworked and the exploited;
for those who have been driven from the land
and those whose crops have failed.

We pray for all who work to make trade fair;
and for those who seek to end child labour
and slavery.
We pray for migrant labourers in our farms and factories,
and all who work the land so that we are fed.

To the God of the harvest we bring our thanks and prayers.
Amen

All Saints and All Souls

1

Let us join with all the saints, and say:
Salvation belongs to our God
who is seated on the throne, and to the Lamb!
Blessing and glory and wisdom
and thanksgiving and honour and power and might
be to our God for ever and ever!
Amen

Revelation 7: 10,12

2

Let us join with all who have gone before us in the faith
as we worship God.
We bring our praise and our thanksgiving
to the throne of the King of all.
We bring our confession and intercessions
to the crucified, risen and ascended Lord.
We raise our voices in songs of adoration
in the power of the Spirit of the Living Lord.
With saints and angels praising you we say,
Holy, holy, holy is the Lord.
Amen

3

We are invited to the banquet of God's love
and join with saints on earth and in heaven
as we sing the praises of our Lord.
Let us raise voices in joy and in thanksgiving
and proclaim all that God has done for us.
Amen

4

Blessed are the pure in heart.
Lord, forgive us our sins.
Blessed are the humble and meek.
Lord, forgive us our pride.
Blessed are those who hunger after righteousness.
Lord, forgive us our selfishness.
Blessed are the merciful.
Lord, forgive us our failure to forgive others.
Blessed are those who suffer for faith's sake.
Lord, forgive us our lack of courage.
Blessed are your saints.
Lord, forgive us our failure to follow their example.
Amen

5

Heavenly Father,
we thank you for the example of the saints:
for their teaching and their wisdom,
for their courage and their faith,
for their witness and their service.
Grant us grace and the power of your Holy Spirit,
that with them we may follow the way of Christ
in whose love we are held as one,
the living and the departed.
Amen

6

We remember with love and with gratitude
those whom we love and who have gone before us
through death to your new life.
Grant them rest and peace
in the transforming power of your resurrection life.
Amen

7

Lord Jesus Christ, King of glory,
as we follow your way in the journey of discipleship
may we know we are not alone.
You lead us on our way
and with us go all your saints, known and unknown:
witnesses to the Gospel,
servants of your love,
martyrs in the faith,
encouraging us,
praying for us,
guiding us.
For all your saints we give you thanks.
Amen

General Prayers

Ambition

O God, direct our ambitions
to your service and the service of others.
Give us, we pray, insight into ourselves,
and an understanding of your will for us,
that whether we are raised up
or brought low,
all may be done to your glory.
Amen

Numbers 12

Anger

Lord, in your mercy protect us from ourselves;
help us when resentment grows and anger overwhelms us;
keep us from bitterness and hurt pride;
from dark thoughts of revenge and plans to retaliate;
keep us from dwelling on the hurts
and forgetting the good things.
Lord, in your mercy accept us as we are
and by your grace help us become what you would have us be.
In Jesus' name.
Amen

Baptism

Almighty and merciful God,
Father of our Lord, your only Son,
draw us from the darkness and confusion of ourselves
that, trusting in you,
we may live in your light
and become the people you would have us be,
born from above, through water and the Spirit.
Amen

Beauty

Lord of all beauty,
grant me the eye to look carefully and deeply,
to see what lies in your giving
beneath the surface of things;
to delight in the great and intricate beauties
of your creation,
and to see in others the beauty of their true humanity.
In Jesus' name I ask it.
Amen

Bereavement

1

Father God,
from whose love nothing can tear us away,
we pray for all who grieve and are saddened
by the loss of family or friends.
Uphold them when they feel low,
strengthen them when they feel weak,
make yourself known to them
when they feel you are far away.
We ask this in the name of your dear Son.
Amen

2

Heavenly Father,
strengthen our faith in times of doubt
with its promise of the good news
that death is not the final word.
Help us to remember those we miss
but not to cling on to them
so that we do not accept their parting.
Give us the courage to move on,
without forgetting;
for you can transform this sadness,

and grant us the way forward
in hope and trust.
In Jesus' name, who died and rose for us.
Amen

3
We give thanks for those we remember today,
for all that they meant to us:
their example, their love and their friendship,
what they taught us and what they shared with us.
Lord, we give you thanks.

We remember all who have gone before us in the faith:
those who kept the faith in times of darkness;
those who faced persecution and imprisonment;
those who passed on the good news
and who inspired us;
for the unknown saints of God.
Lord, we give you thanks.

We give thanks for your Son Jesus,
for his life and teachings,
for his love for the ordinary and the outcast,
for his dying and his rising,
that have revealed to us
your forgiveness and your gift of new life.
Lord, we give you thanks.

We give you thanks for the delights of the past
and for the gift of shared memories.
We thank you too for the future,
for its new possibilities and opportunities.
Give us the courage to face changes,
and your presence to ease the loneliness.
Lord, we give you thanks.
Amen

4

May God give us comfort in our sorrow
and delight in our thanksgiving;
amidst the sadness of death
may we know the hope in Christ of resurrection.
Amen

5

Heavenly Father, we give you thanks for the life of your servant
(Name);
for the friendship shared and for the memories of good times.
We rejoice in (his/her) life and for the joy it brought.
Let us bless the Lord.
Thanks be to God.

Lord Jesus Christ,
you know our sadness and share our feelings of loss;
grant us the faith to trust in your power to give new life,
to discover the light of your resurrection hope
and to know your presence with us
in both darkness and light.
Let us bless the Lord.
Thanks be to God.

We celebrate (Name's) life:
for all (he/she) achieved in ways known to many
and in ways known only to a few;
for friendship shared,
and times spent together;
for laughter and delight
and for challenges faced;
for just being (himself/herself).
Let us bless the Lord.
Thanks be to God.
Amen

6

Holy Spirit,
in whose power we join in thankfulness today,
fill us with the joy of past memories and of future possibilities,
and draw us together in the continuing bond of friendship
within the fellowship of God's company.
Let us bless the Lord.
Thanks be to God.
Amen

7

Heavenly Father,
we pray for all who are anxious
and who seek comfort in their grief.
Grant to them the assurance of your love,
that knowledge that all who live and die
are in your care,
and faith in the reality of new life,
promised through the death and resurrection of your Son.
Amen

Call

1

Lord of all,
grant me the discerning eye
to see what you would have me do;
grant me the listening ear
to hear what you are calling me to;
grant me the willing heart
to respond faithfully and obediently;
that I may serve you in all I say, and think and do
for the good of others,
and to the glory of your name.
Amen

2

Almighty God,
you call us to serve you
as partners in your loving and saving purpose;
strengthen the gifts you have already given us;
develop in us those gifts that we shall need;
and direct our gifts in the service of all,
through Jesus your Son our Lord.
Amen

3

Lord, you call us to your service.
May we be prompt in our response
and will in our obedience.

Lord, you invite us to share
in your work of love.
It is not a burden to serve you but a joy;
it is not a hardship but a privilege.
We will follow you.
Amen

4

Heavenly Father,
whose voice we do not always recognise
and whose words we do not always want to hear,
grant us the gift of your Spirit
that we might discern your will
and have the courage to trust in you,
whatever the message.
Amen

1 Samuel 3:1-18

Comfort

1

God of all mercies,
you make nothing in vain
and love all that you have made.
Comfort all who grieve,
and console them
by the knowledge of your unfailing love,
through Jesus Christ our Lord.
Amen

2

Hand of God, hold me and protect me.
Touch of God, calm me and give me peace.
Kiss of God, love me and heal me.
Finger of God, direct me and guide me.
Amen

Commitment

Lord Jesus,
you are the Way we would follow,
the Truth we would know,
the Life we would experience
and the King we would serve.
Enable us by your Spirit
to fulfil our intention,
to be steadfast in our loyalty,
and courageous in our actions.
Amen

Courage

Almighty and all-loving God,

hold us close amidst the problems that beset us;

grant us trust and courage,

that unafraid we may overcome those things that daunt us,

and with you beside us we may

overcome what threatens to overwhelm us.

We ask it in the name of your Son, our Saviour.

Amen

Judges 7:1-23

Duty

Loving Lord,

when duty is the best we can manage,

grant us your grace,

turning obedience into love

and love to adoration,

that with joy we may do what is asked of us,

in Jesus' name.

Amen

Fairness

Loving Father,

in whose love we are all treated with equal fairness,

help our preferences not to become favouritism,

nor our ambition to become arrogance.

Watch over us and be with us,

that we may know your presence

however our future works out.

Amen

Genesis 37:2-11

Faith

Heavenly Father,
ever present, ever caring,
grant us the insight and the faith
that turns belief into trust,
and knowledge into obedience;
that we might walk in your presence
and trust in your love,
now and always.
Amen

Exodus 3:1-15

Forgiveness

1

Heavenly Father, in whose patience
we are given the time to mature in your love,
forgive those things that distract us
and lead us from the path of your will;
help us to follow in the footsteps of your Son,
the Light of the world.
Amen

2

Loving Father,
forgive the weakness of our love
and the waywardness of our lives.
In your mercy
forgive and restore us,
transform us and empower us,
that through your love
we may be more loving
to others and to ourselves.
Amen

Future

Dear Lord,

so often the future feels as though it is out of our control.

Keep us from despair or anger,

from being complacent, anxious or paralysed.

Give us the wisdom to see what we can do

and the courage to do it,

trusting that the future is in fact in your hands.

In your mercy we ask this.

Amen

Genesis 41:1-14,25-41

Generosity

Lord God, your generosity overwhelms us,

it shines out with love and goodness

from the wonders of creation

and the mystery of the cross.

Grant us your generous Spirit

in all we do and all we are,

that depending solely on you

we may grow in the way of holiness

through Christ your Son our Lord.

Amen

Glory

Glory to God, who in his Son has come as one of us.

Glory to God, for the gift of his love, his light and his truth.

Glory to God, for the grace of his presence

within and amongst us.

Amen

God's purposes

Almighty God,
in whose purposes your Son was born in humility
that he might live and die to bring us to new life,
help us so to direct our lives
that we might fulfil the purpose you have for us,
and so give you the glory.
In Jesus' name we ask it.
Amen

God's Word

1

Come Holy Spirit
and open to us the treasures of God's Word.
Grant us a readiness to listen
and an openness to learn;
that through the riches of your gifts
we may better understand the needs of the poor
and the good news to be proclaimed.
We ask this in the name of Jesus
who came as a light to the nations.
Amen

2

Come, living God, in the power of your Spirit!
Open our eyes
as we read your Word.
Open our ears
as we listen to the voice of your prophets
and to one another.
May we be challenged by your judgements,
forgiven through your mercy,
and granted hope for our futures.
Amen

3

Come to us, Lord, in the stillness
and quieten our hearts and minds.
Speak to us through your Word
and the words of one another.
Teach us by your Spirit,
with insight and understanding,
and fill our hearts with the love
you have shown us in your Son.
To you be the glory, now and always.
Amen

4

You speak to us through your Word
and we seek to learn your will.
Help us to understand the Bible,
its message and its meaning.
Through it may we learn of your activity
in the world, among nations, in communities
and in the hearts of men and women,
that we may grow in understanding,
in trust and in faith.
For Jesus' sake.
Amen

5

Lord, we thank you for the gift of your Word,
that through the pages of the Bible
we may hear you speak to us.
But we especially thank you for the gift of your Son,
the Word, bringing us love and mercy,
forgiveness and salvation.
To you be praise, now and always.
Amen

6

God and Father of our Lord Jesus Christ,
grant us the gift of your Holy Spirit
that we might discern the truth of your Word,
always open to new insights that you reveal to us,
tested by the love and teaching of your Son.
Amen

Good News

1

Spirit of God rest upon us,
Spirit of God move amongst us,
Spirit of God stir within us;
that we might hear the Good News,
that we might live the Good News,
that we might proclaim the Good News.
Amen

2

Lord of all blessings,
we give you thanks
for the gift of your Son
and the Good News of the gospel;
in the power of your Spirit
may we witness to your love,
bringing hope to the despairing,
forgiveness to the guilty,
healing to the sick,
and freedom to the imprisoned.
In Jesus' name we ask it.
Amen

Gratitude

Lord God, giver of all things
help me to grow in gratitude –
giving thanks for the gift of life itself;
thanks for the people I meet and work with,
for friends and family,
and those I so easily take for granted;
thanks for the world around – created, made;
for opportunities and challenges,
for the delight of successes and the lessons of failure;
for the gift of health and the challenge of pain,
and above all things for the love you have shown,
the guidance given, the forgiveness offered.
All is thanks in Jesus' name.
Amen

Guidance

Guide us, Lord, by the light of your Spirit
as we seek to discover more of your truth.
Grant us courage to continue
when we are unsure of where the path leads.
Strengthen our trust in you and one another
amidst the questions and the doubts.
Bring us to the place of your disclosure
that we might offer thanks for all that you give us.
Delight us with the surprise of your presence
and lead us out to witness to your love.
In Jesus' name.
Amen

Healing

1

Heavenly Father,
whose Son touched the diseased and unlovely,
and held the dying and the grieving,
grant a gentle and healing touch
to all who nurse the ill,
to those who care for the marginalised
and those who comfort the lonely and the hurting.
In Jesus' name.
Amen

2

Come, Lord Jesus, with your healing power,
and mend the broken fragments of our fractured world:
the peace between nations torn by violence;
the rights of individuals denied by oppression;
the love between people destroyed by selfishness;
the wholeness of spirit disrupted by sin.
Help us to remove the burden of oppression from others
and to take on your yoke to direct our lives
and to give rest to our souls.
Amen

Holiness

Holy God, you come to us
in your Holy Son and through your Holy Spirit.
We approach you in awe and penitence,
for the place of our meeting is holy ground.
Grant us to grow in holiness
through obedience and love,
and so fulfil your will for us.
In Jesus' name.
Amen

Hope

1

May the God of all hope
fill you with all joy and peace in believing,
so that by the power of the Holy Spirit
you may abound in hope.
Amen

Based on Romans 15:13

2

O God of hope, fill us, we beseech you,
with all joy and peace in believing,
that we may abound in hope
by the power of your Holy Spirit,
and show forth our thankfulness to you
in trustful and courageous lives;
through Jesus Christ our Lord.
Amen

Based on Romans 15:13

3

Heavenly Father,
grant us faith in your unending love
and in the power of your promises;
when the future appears bleak, give us hope
and thankful hearts for all you do for us.
Amen

4

Heavenly Father,
we pray for all who live without hope;
for those trapped by poverty and ignorance;
for those without home or country;
for children who are terrified,
and adults who despair.

Grant to them the inner vision
that gives them hope
and the support of others
that turns hope into a reality.
We ask this in Jesus' name.
Amen

5

Fill us, Lord, with your hope,
that the anxieties of the world may not overcome us.
Fill us, Lord, with your love,
that the fears of the world may not defeat us.
Give us a vision of your possibilities
for the world and for all people,
that we may know your presence with us,
and fulfil our responsibilities as your servants.
Amen

Humour

Heavenly Father,
keep me from taking myself too seriously
and others not seriously enough;
help me to delight in the fun of others
and to welcome the joke of your unexpected word.
May my humour never be hurtful or cause offence
but lighten the moment by raising a smile.
In Jesus' name.
Amen

Justice

1

Look, O Lord, with compassion upon all
who suffer from the injustices of our world;
who suffer exploitation
through the greed of others,
those who are victims with no opportunity for redress,
those whose rights are ignored and overridden.

Grant to all who administer the law
and exercise authority
a clear sense of justice;
and in all my dealings guide me
by your Spirit of justice and truth.
In Jesus' name.
Amen

2

Almighty God,
Sovereign Lord of sky and land,
river and seas,
in your holiness you turn your face from evil
and in your love you have mercy on all;
grant us a burning desire to see justice prevail
and hearts on fire with love for all.
In Jesus' name and for his sake.
Amen

3

Almighty God,
we pray for all who are falsely accused
and wrongfully imprisoned;
for all prisoners of conscience
and those persecuted for their faith.

Grant to all judges and legal authorities
a strong sense of justice,
that they might exercise their powers wisely and with mercy,
not bowing to outside pressure or inner prejudice.
We ask in the name of our Lord,
who, though innocent, was condemned and executed.
Amen

Leaders

Lord, you are sovereign of all the earth,
so rule in the hearts of the world's leaders
that, guided by your wisdom
and obedient to your truth,
they may govern wisely,
maintain justice
and serve the well-being of all.
We ask it in Jesus' name.
Amen

Light

1

Glorious God, your light shines in our lives
to guide us into truth and love;
enlighten our hearts and minds
that we may welcome the coming of your Light
and overcome in us the darkness that hides your truth.
In Jesus' name.
Amen

2

Lord of light,
guide me in times of darkness,
enlighten me in times of ignorance,
comfort me in times of fearfulness,
sustain me in times of desolation,
by the light of your Word,
the presence of your Spirit,
and the power of your merciful love,
for your name's sake.
Amen

3

When all feels dark around us, grant us your Light;
when all is silent within us, grant us your Word;
that in the promise of your being with us
we may know the comfort of your presence
and rest secure in the knowledge of your ceaseless love.
Amen

4

To keep us from false teaching and misunderstandings,
may your light surround us.
To lead us in the way of truth,
may your light surround us.
To fill us with understanding of those whose sight is impaired,
may your light surround us.
To overcome the darkness of our fears,
may your light surround us.
To bring us hope in time of doubt,
may your light surround us.
Amen

5

Almighty God,
in your love, look with mercy
on all that is wrong in our lives and our world;
help us to reject the darkness and to live in your light,
that we might rejoice in the coming of your Son
who is the Light of the world,
the Light to the nations.
Amen

6

Lord God,
who brought light out of darkness,
shine in our hearts,
that we may forsake the ways of darkness,
and live in the light of your truth.
May Christ open our eyes to the wonders of your glory
and the mystery of salvation.
Amen

7

Lord, giver of light and life,
come to us in the midst of our darkness,
and banish our despair.
Lord of forgiveness and freedom,
come to us burdened by our guilt,
and make us dance with joy.
For you are our Saviour and our Redeemer.
Amen

8

Christ the Light of the world,
scatter the darkness from your path
and open your eyes to his truth and glory.
And the blessing of God Almighty,

Father, Son and Holy Spirit,
be with you now and always.
Amen

Love

1

All loving God,
whose message of love sounds throughout creation,
open our ears to your meaning
amidst the noise of our busy lives;
heal our deafness,
that we may hear afresh
the good news of the coming of Christ;
enable our speaking
that we may tell of your praise.
Amen

2

Closer than the beat of my heart
is your love, O Lord.
Sweeter than the ripest fruit
is the taste of your presence.
More pleasing than the finest perfume
is the gift of your Word.
Come and fill my sense,
that I might delight in you.
Amen

3

Almighty God,
you have shown us in your Son that you are Love;
pour your love into our hearts
that we may abide in you and you in us
and love others as you have loved us;

that your purpose of love might be fulfilled
to the glory of your name.
Amen

4

In your love, root out what is evil,
in your holiness, strengthen all that is good,
that we may give thanks for your merciful judgement
and celebrate the wonder of your love.
In Jesus Christ's name.
Amen

5

Loving Father,
in your love you made us;
fill us with your love.
Loving Christ,
in your love you died for us;
fill us with your love.
Loving Spirit,
in your love you sustain us;
fill us with your love.
Loving Trinity,
you are creating, saving, enabling love;
fill us with your love.
Amen

6

God of love,
help us to be more loving;
help us to love you more fully
and to be more loving to our neighbours.
In the name of the Father who loves us in creating,
and of the Son who loves us in his dying,
and of the Spirit who loves in her guiding,
one God, one love.
Amen

7

Lord, God, Father of our Lord Jesus Christ,
when we are tempted to run from you
out of fear or guilt,
grant us a vision of your continuing love
that in whatever place we find ourselves,
we may know your presence,
receive your forgiveness,
and offer you our worship.
Amen

Genesis 28:10-19

Motives

Dear Lord,
before we judge the motives of others,
give us the courage to examine our own.
Not everything we do is entirely right,
seldom do we do totally wrong things.
Forgive what is wrong, develop what is right,
and give us the insight
to tell the one from the other.
In Jesus' name.
Amen

Obedience

Lord of all creation,
you have made us to love you and be loved by you,
grant us the wisdom to follow your commands
and to live in the way of obedience.
Keep us from all false ambition
and guide us in our choices.
When we go wrong give us the grace to admit it,

not seeking to place the blame on others
nor excusing ourselves at their expense,
through Jesus Christ your Son, our Lord.
Amen

Peace

Father God, you gave yourself to us in your Son
that we might know your love and your forgiveness;
help us to accept your offer of peace
that we might then walk in the path of peace
following the way of the Prince of Peace
and be people of peace.
Amen

Petition

1

Heavenly Father,
give us your spirit of insight,
that we may see your working
amongst us and within us.

Heavenly Father,
give us the courage
to stand up for what is right,
and to resist what is wrong.

Heavenly Father,
give us the humility
to admit our failings,
and the strength to ask for forgiveness.

Heavenly Father,
grant us the grace to be forgiving,
especially when that is difficult.
Amen

2

Be with us Lord,
in the power of your Spirit,
that we may read your Word with understanding,
and speak openly and graciously.
Help us to grow in faith
and to act with justice.
In Jesus' name.
Amen

3

Heavenly Father,
grant us the voice of praise
and a heart of thanksgiving.
Grant us the humility to acknowledge our sins
and the grace to receive your forgiveness.

May our eyes look up to you
and out to the world,
that in loving you
we may also love our neighbours.

Turn our prayers for the poor into action;
make our concern for justice
more than mere words,
so that in all that we do
your name may be honoured
and your kingdom come.
Amen

4

May the love of God be with us.
May the peace of Christ be with us.
May the light of the Spirit be with us,
now and always.
Amen

5

Be with us, Lord,
to forgive and transform us.
Stay with us, Lord,
to comfort and to challenge us.
Go with us, Lord,
to strengthen and encourage us,
in the power of your love
and in the light of your truth.
Amen

6

Lord, our God and King,
enthroned above the heavens
and within our hearts,
you show us the way to our full humanity.
Grant us the humility to be obedient
and the courage to do your will.
In Jesus' name.
Amen

7

Fill our hearts, good Lord,
with a desire to know you more fully.
Strengthen our wills, good Lord,
to make right choices.
Grant us, good Lord,
the will and the perseverance
to persist in doing good.
Amen

8

Father of all,
whose messengers tell of your loving promise,
grant us the openness to recognise your voice,

the wisdom to understand your guidance
and the strength to do your will.
We ask this in Jesus' name.
Amen

9

Lord God,
give me a heart that longs to know you better,
a mind that seeks to discover your truth,
and a life that is devoted to your service;
that my actions may help to establish your kingdom,
my words may speak of your love;
and my thoughts reflect the splendour of your glory.
In Jesus' name.
Amen

10

Christ our Saviour, friend and brother,
stand with us in our times of trouble,
hold us when we stumble and are anxious,
give us courage for our fear
and boldness to speak out with faith.
We ask this for your dear name's sake.
Amen

11

Lord, when we go far from you,
seek us out and find us.
Lord, when we feel guilty and cannot face you,
seek us out and find us.
Lord, when we are hurt and confused,
seek us out and find us.
Lord, when we don't know the way to go,
seek us out and find us.
For you are our risen Lord.
Amen

Possessions

Lord of all riches,
teach us to use our possessions wisely,
for the service of others
and not simply for ourselves.
Make us generous and keep us from greed,
that the good things of this world
may be shared with justice and fairness
to the good of all.
We ask this in the name of our Saviour Christ,
who though he was rich, humbled himself
and gave himself for us.
Amen

Prayer

Almighty God,
you are Lord of all and worthy of all praise.
Teach us how to pray
and guide us by your Spirit,
that all our words and thoughts
may be directed by your will
and to the glory of your name.
Forgive us our self-centredness,
but give us a concern for others
and a love for you,
in Jesus' name.
Amen

Prejudice

1

Lord, whose care is for all the people of the world,
keep us from the prejudice that divides one from another,
that looks only at the surface of things
and through our fear fails to see our common humanity.
We ask this in Jesus' name,
who came to save all.
Amen

2

Lord and Creator of all,
in whose eyes all are of equal worth,
the object of your all-embracing love;
keep us from the prejudice that divides people
by race or gender, age or colour,
religion or culture.
May we see others through the eyes of Christ,
valuing them as we ourselves wish to be valued,
knowing that they are heirs to the same grace,
and through faith granted the same Holy Spirit.
In the name of Christ our Saviour, who died for the sins of all.
Amen

Presence

1

Heavenly Father,
give us the eyes
to see your presence all around us,
ears to hear your voice
amidst the hubbub of our world,
and hearts willing to obey your call
to act for you;

that people may be freed from fear,
from hurt and guilt.
We ask it in the name of Jesus Christ,
our rescuer and redeemer.
Amen

2

Grant us, O Lord,
the spirit of expectation;
the open spirit that looks for your presence
and listens to your voice.
Come to us in the beauty
and the solemnity of worship,
in the joy of song and the excitement of drama.
But most of all, make yourself known
in the bread that is broken
and the wine that is poured.
For you are our Saviour.
Amen

School

1

Heavenly Father,
we thank you for our gifts of mind and body,
for imagination and creative skill.
We thank you
for the encouragement of parents and carers,
teachers and governors,
helping young people to grow and develop.
We thank you
for the joy of working together,
and the delight of shared success.
Amen

2

We give thanks to God
for the opportunities we have to learn
and for all that school means to us.
We give thanks
for all the members of the community
who help at school,
for those who raise funds,
and for the governors.
Amen

3

We pray for all who find school difficult
and for those who have no schools to go to.
We pray for children in schools in other countries
where they have few books
and none of the advantages we enjoy.
We pray for the people of this community,
and especially for the elderly and the lonely,
the sick and the unemployed.
Amen

Sensitivity

Lord, grant us sensitivity and understanding
towards those less fortunate than ourselves.
May we never belittle them nor despise them
but through encouragement and support,
build their self-esteem and sense of worth.
In Jesus' name.
Amen

Spirit

1

Lord, you give strength to the weak
and wisdom to the innocent,
grant us the gift of your Spirit
to be bold for truth
and courageous for justice,
that your kingdom may come on earth
and your will overcome all that is evil.
In Jesus' name we ask.
Amen

2

Spirit of God, Spirit of Wisdom,
fill our hearts with knowledge of your love;
inspire our minds with knowledge of your truth;
guide our feet in the way of your holiness;
that all we are, all we think, and all we do
may be in the name of Christ our Lord.
Amen

3

Mysterious God,
you reveal yourself to us
in the wonder of our physical word;
you have proclaimed your message
through the Word of Scripture;
you have come to us in the person of your Son;
grant us grace that knowing you as Spirit
we may worship you in spirit and in truth.
Amen

Suffering

1

Heavenly Father,
we give thanks for the knowledge and skills of medical science,
but know that pain and suffering continue,
leaving us with so many questions.
Amidst our uncertainties,
may we find comfort
in the knowledge of your undying love
and your presence in all suffering.
Through Jesus Christ
who gave himself for us on the cross.
Amen

2

Gracious Father,
grant that in all our sufferings for the truth
we may learn to love even our enemies
and to seek forgiveness for those who would hurt us,
looking to him who was crucified for us,
Jesus Christ, our rescuer and reconciler.
Amen

Testing

1

Walking to the altar of offering,
Isaac bore the wood for his burning.
On his way to execution,
Jesus bore the cross piece for his nailing.
In your mercy, Lord, do not ask too much of me
for I am fearful of too much sacrifice.
Yet in the time of my testing
grant me courage and trust
in your providing.
Amen

2

Heavenly Father,
Righteous Lord and Mighty Saviour,
when we are tempted
to follow the impulse of our desires,
strengthen our resolve to do what is right,
that we may neither offend your laws
nor hurt our neighbours.
Amen

Thanks

1

For the forgiveness of sins,
we give thanks;
for release from guilt,
we give thanks;
for the freedoms we enjoy,
we give thanks.
Amen

2

For all that is good and just,
for all that is true and beautiful,
for all that is forgiving and loving,
we give you thanks and praise,
in Jesus' name.
Amen

3

We give you thanks, good Lord,
for all who rule with wisdom and lead with integrity;
for all who care for the needy:
for their family,

their neighbourhood,

their country,

the world.

We give you thanks, good Lord.

We give you thanks, good Lord,

for all who bring shelter to the homeless,

food to the starving,

justice to the dispossessed,

health to the ailing,

knowledge to the ignorant,

insight to the prejudiced.

We give you thanks, good Lord.

We give you thanks, good Lord,

for all who bring relief to refugees,

a welcome to the alien and the immigrant,

hope to the despairing,

friendship to the lonely,

comfort to the grieving,

the light of your gospel where it is unknown or ignored.

We give you thanks, good Lord.

We give you thanks, good Lord,

and pray that you will make each one of us

a bearer of your gift of fulness of life

by word and deed,

to all places and all people,

to wherever it is needed.

We give you thanks, good Lord.

Amen

4

God of all joy,
fill us with praise and thankfulness
when life is going well.
God of comfort,
hold us in your love
when life is hard.
God of believing,
shine in the darkness
when doubt overwhelms us.
God of our progressing,
be with us
in our journeying.
To the ever-present, ever-loving God,
be thanks and praise
at all times and in all circumstances.
Amen

5

Lord, we thank you for one another,
for the variety of gifts and insights each one brings.
We thank you for all who love and support us,
for those who value us and give us worth.
We thank you that you have called us into being,
called us to be your friends.
Be with us and hold,
guide us and challenge us,
love us and forgive us.
In Jesus' name.
Amen

Trust

Lord,
when I can no longer fathom out
the meaning of your being in my head,
hold me in the mystery of your love.

Give me courage to risk trusting,
even when I don't fully know,
that I may grow in love for you and for others
within the mystery of your purposes.
In the name of Jesus
who reveals the mystery of your kingdom.
Amen

Truth

1

Lord of all truth,
who has given us the Spirit to lead us into truth,
help us to be attentive and gracious
as we listen to those whose views differ from our own;
give us courage
to explore new possibilities, new perspectives,
and so enlarge our understanding
of ourselves, of others, of our world and of you.
In Jesus' name.
Amen

2

Grant us, O Lord, the courage to speak the truth,
and not to lie simply to avoid embarrassment
or from fear for our safety.
When truth is painful for others to hear,
let us speak with courtesy and care,
that they may be held in our love.
Keep us faithful and not fearful,
that you may be glorified;
in Jesus' name and through the power of the Spirit.
Amen

3

Give me the courage, Lord,
to stand up for your truth as I see it.
Give me the humility, Lord,
to know I do not have all the truth.
Give me the wisdom, Lord,
to find your truth in the insight of others.
Give me the joy, Lord,
of sharing your truth with all.
Amen

Wisdom

Almighty God,
source of all knowledge and all wisdom,
help us to journey from being gatherers of data,
to seekers of meaning,
and then to become storehouses of wisdom.
Amen

Wonder

1

Lord God, the vastness of the universe overwhelms me;
the numbers are too large for my imagination to hold,
too complex to get my head round.
Yet the smallest thing too is a marvel and a message,
speaking of what is beyond our comprehension,
beyond thought.
Grant me the eyes and a heart
open to the wonder of your creation,
and fill my heart with praise.
Amen

2

Heavenly Father,
you reveal yourself in the wonders of nature
and in the person of your Son;
grant us eyes open to the mystery of your light
around us
and hearts that respond to your love within us;
and in these holy places may we worship you.
Amen

World

Almighty God, this is your world,
full of beauty and wonder,
a created order that is both amazing and terrifying,
a world that delights us and puzzles us.
Help us to see your activity in your world
and to bear the stewardship of it
with responsibility and with care.
In Jesus' name.
Amen

Worship

Purify our hearts, O Lord,
and fill them with your love;
purify our minds, O Lord,
and fill them with your truth;
that in the power of your Spirit,
and through the name of your Son,
we may offer you worship
that honours your name
and lives that give you the glory.
Amen

Worth

1

Lord, help me to know the worth you give me –
the worth that is my true value:
neither inflated as when I think too highly of myself,
nor so low as when I feel I am worthless.
Help me to so value others,
that they may see the love you have for them,
who came and gave yourself for us all.
Amen

2

Lord, you have no favourites
but call each one to be your child,
granting to all your love without distinction;
help us to give worth to all we meet,
that none might be despised,
none cheated or excluded.
We ask it in the name of your Son who died for all.
Amen

3

Grant Lord,
to all who are elderly,
patience with the young,
and to the young,
grant respect for those who are older.
For those whose life has been fulfilling
give grateful hearts
and to those who feel they have failed,
grant the peace of your forgiveness.
In your love
may we all know that we are loved
and have worth.
We ask this in Jesus' name.
Amen

4

Almighty God,
who rules on high and is above all things,
from you we have our value and our worth,
in you may we find the wholeness and the healing,
which is our salvation.
Help us to overcome the fear
that inflates our self-importance,
belittling the worth of others.
Through Jesus Christ our Lord.
Amen

5

Lift us up, good Lord,
when we fall.
Forgive us, good Lord,
when we fail.
Hold us, good Lord,
in our weakness.
Guide us, good Lord,
in our wilfulness.
Guard us, good Lord,
in our fearfulness.
Enable us, good Lord,
in our powerlessness.
Above all, good Lord,
love us and give us worth.
Amen

Thoughts and Reflections

1. Good news to the poor

The Christian message is summed up as 'gospel' or 'good news'. Jesus, we are told, came to proclaim good news. The disciples and apostles preached good news. The Church is committed to share good news.

But what is the good news? Saint Mark begins his Gospel with these words: 'The beginning of the good news [gospel] of Jesus Christ, the Son of God' (Mark 1:1). Ask Christians today and some will say that it is the good news of forgiveness and salvation that God offers us through the life, death and resurrection of Jesus: that, in fact, Jesus is the heart of the gospel.

Others will see the heart of the good news in the way Jesus directs our attention to the needs of the poor and in God's continuing concern for the disadvantaged and outcast. For them, the heart of the gospel is more to do with social action than with personal salvation.

Neither aspect is actually likely to be seen as exclusive; it is more a matter of emphasis. Each will see in Jesus the key to the good news – what he did and what he said. Without reference to Jesus and what he did, social action can become merely a programme of good works without any specific reference to God. But without the application of faith in concern for social justice, belief in Jesus can become a matter of individual piety.

But if that is the case, what was the good news that Jesus preached during his earthly ministry? He is certainly reported as having told his disciples that he would undergo great suffering, be rejected by the religious authorities, be killed and on the third day be raised (see Luke 9:21-22). The disciples didn't want to face such a possibility, and Peter told Jesus off for saying such things, receiving a rebuke for his pains (Mark 8:31-33). But it was only later, when members of the early Church reflected on all that had happened to Jesus together with their experience of forgiveness and new life found in Jesus, that his death and resurrection were seen as central to the good news that they would proclaim to the world.

Jesus, however, did not preach a gospel so centred upon himself. He was not himself the heart of his good news. Jesus' preaching and teaching were

145

more about the kingdom of God and the forgiving and saving work of God. He may well have seen himself as the agent in bringing that kingdom close, but it was God's action rather than his own that filled his message. Because the early Church was convinced that Jesus was, in fact, key to this action of God, they changed the emphasis and placed Jesus at the heart of the good news of the kingdom and of salvation.

Since the coming of the day of the Lord that Jesus looked for has yet to happen, this aspect of the good news has given way to a much more Jesus-centred gospel in which the cross has been a particular focus. This is interesting when one considers that the first depiction of the cross was, in fact, in a piece of ironic graffiti by a pagan and didn't appear until 300 years after the actual event.

Luke, unlike Matthew and Mark, avoids using the noun (good news) but does use the verb (to tell good news). Originally, the word was used about telling good news of victory, and this, of course, fits well with the interpretation of the cross that sees it as Christ's victory over sin and death. It was this emphasis on the promise of eternal life that so attracted Roman citizens, especially the poor, away from paganism to the new Christian faith. The Roman gods promised victory in battle and expansion of the empire. For the middle class and 'aristocracy', this could mean wealth and status, but it had little general benefit for the poor. The distinctive element of the new Jewish sect centred on Jesus was that it offered a life beyond this, a life where the injustices of this life were made good. Even the brutal suppression of Christians under Diocletian could not stop the spread of Christianity because the threat of death did not outweigh the promise of eternal life.

In the original version of the Isaiah passage that Jesus read in the synagogue at Nazareth, the good news was preached to 'the oppressed' but Luke has changed this to read 'the poor'. He seems to have had a special concern for the poor and the disadvantaged, and he mentions them more than the other Gospels do. He appears to have meant those who were literally poor. In his version of the Beatitudes (Luke 6:20-23) is the straightforward statement, 'Blessed are you who are poor, for yours is the kingdom of God.' By comparison, Matthew says, 'Blessed are the poor in spirit, for theirs is the kingdom of heaven' (Matthew 5:3). In the Psalms, 'the poor' or 'the needy' (the word being the same in the Hebrew) can also mean those who are humble (e.g. Psalm 9:18), oppressed (e.g. Psalm 35:10) or weak (e.g. Psalm 72:13).

We see here something of those same twin emphases noted above – on the one hand the spiritual aspect is emphasised; on the other there is social understanding. It is still with us and can be seen either as a theological difference or one of temperament (or perhaps a mixture of both). There are some, notably among the evangelical wing of the Church, who emphasise the fact that a person without Christ is spiritually impoverished and that preaching the good news of Christ's forgiveness and new life is to offer inner riches with eternal significance. Others emphasise the Christian imperative to work for the good of the poor through social action as a way of proclaiming the kingdom value of justice. This apparent divide is, of course, often blurred, and it is noteworthy, for example, that among some young evangelical voters in America, there was support for Barack Obama precisely because of his concern for social justice.

Proclamation is not only a matter of preaching words. It is also action – doing something individually and socially that makes a difference to the lives of the poor. Such action is to make people free, not dependent; to make them more able to make choices and take advantage of opportunities, but not to tie them into a culture of dependency. The importance of freedom is a constant theme in the message of the prophets and is to be understood through a rich diversity of meanings, mundane and spiritual.

2. Release to captives

Although we often speak of Jesus Christ almost as though these were his forename and surname, more strictly we should speak of Jesus the Christ (or Jesus who is the Christ) – Christ meaning 'the anointed'. It describes his status as the one anointed by God, and his role as the kingly figure who would be his people's saviour. 'Messiah' also means 'anointed' (see Daniel 9:25-26; John 1:41).

As well as the anointing there was the positive 'sending'. Prophets were often reluctant to speak the words they felt they had been given to proclaim. Their message was often hard and unpopular, but they were impelled by their sense of a vocation through which God sent them as messengers, as his voice to his people. They were appointed by God and came, as it were, from the presence of God. We see this in the account of Isaiah's call:

> Then I heard the voice of the Lord saying, 'Whom shall I send, and who will go for us?' And I said, 'Here am I; send me!'
>
> *Isaiah 6:8*

Jeremiah came to understand that he had been consecrated even before he was born and appointed as a prophet to the nations. Yet he felt inadequate to the task:

> Then I said, 'Ah, Lord God! Truly I do not know how to speak, for I am only a boy.' But the Lord said to me, 'Do not say, "I am only a boy"; for you shall go to all to whom I send you, and you shall speak whatever I command you. Do not be afraid of them, for I am with you to deliver you,' says the Lord. *Jeremiah 1:6-8*

Jesus, too, was understood as having been sent by and from God:

> But [Jesus] said to them, 'I must proclaim the good news of the kingdom of God to the other cities also; for I was sent for this purpose.'
>
> *Luke 4:43*

> 'The works that the Father has given me to complete, the very works that I am doing, testify on my behalf that the Father has sent me.'
>
> *John 5:36 (see also John 17:3, 8, 23)*

The sending of Jesus can be understood as part of the continuing outgoing activity of God which is at the heart of the nature of God – what has been called the *missio dei*. All mission originates with God – it is his initiative. And just as Jesus was 'sent', so he sent his disciples: 'See, I am sending you out like sheep into the midst of wolves; so be wise as serpents and innocent as doves' (Matthew 10:16; see also Matthew 28:19; John 17:18).

One of the tasks that Isaiah understood he had been anointed for and sent to do was to proclaim liberty and release. Jesus adopted this as one of his tasks.

A distinction can be made between those who are captive and those who are prisoners, although there is inevitably some overlap. In the Old Testament, 'captive' nearly always refers to those who have been captured and taken into exile; this is certainly in the mind of Isaiah as we find it in chapters 40–55 where the setting for the prophecies is the people's exile in Babylon. In older translations such as the King James Bible, the word 'captive' was used, where in more modern translations the term is usually translated as 'exile' or 'taken into exile' – e.g. Jeremiah 24:1, 43:3. We can note, however, that when nations other than the people of God are mentioned, the word captivity occurs more frequently – e.g. 'Woe to you, O Moab! The people of Chemosh have perished, for your sons have been taken captive, and your daughters into captivity' (Jeremiah 48:46).

The passage in Isaiah 61, however, speaks of captives at a time when the exile was over and the people had returned to their homeland. Captivity may therefore have come to be associated with any form of oppression. Prisoners may be considered in a more general way – as those who were 'bound' or 'incarcerated'. No distinction is made between those who were imprisoned as the result of an actual or perceived wrongdoing and those who had been imprisoned unjustly or on broadly 'political' grounds. Joseph may have been put in prison on a charge trumped up by Pharaoh's wife, but there is no suggestion that other prisoners, including the chief cup-bearer and chief baker, had been unfairly imprisoned.

Exactly who the 'prisoners' were in Isaiah's prophecy is not exactly clear. Exiles were not normally put in prison so it is unlikely that they are being referred to. In Isaiah 42:6-7, the Lord speaks to his Servant:

> I have given you as a covenant to the people, a light to the nations,
> to open the eyes that are blind, to bring out the prisoners from the
> dungeon, from the prison those who sit in darkness.

It has been suggested that 'prison' is being used here in a metaphorical sense and refers to the darkness and ignorance in which foreign nations are bound through their paganism. If this is how Jesus (and the Gospel writers) understood such passages, then the release he is referring to is freedom from the grip of sin. However, the story of the imprisonment of the apostles (Acts 5:17-26) and Peter's imprisonment (Acts 12:1-17) indicate that God's power was also understood to extend to those who were literally in prison.

3. Sight to the blind

By the age of 46, John Milton was completely blind. It is generally agreed that it was around this time that he wrote the poem 'On his blindness', in which he sought to come to terms with his blindness and the demands of God. He concluded that while many rush all over the world to serve God, 'They also serve who only stand and wait.' His most famous poems, 'Paradise Lost' and 'Paradise Regained', were written in his blindness and at a time when he was impoverished.

Milton certainly suffered as a result of his blindness, but he found a way both of coping with it and of not allowing it to prevent his work as a poet. Not everyone has that opportunity, nor what he called 'patience', and blindness can be devastating. Statistically, blindness or serious sight impairment increasingly affects people in their later years.

In the UK, one in nine of those over the age of 60 are currently living with sight loss, and by 2050 the total number of people with sight loss is expected to reach four million. This is a serious figure, not least when it is estimated that 50 per cent of sight loss can be avoided.

In developing countries the statistics are far, far worse, and the social and economic effects of blindness are also proportionately more severe. Of the 285 million people globally suffering from sight impairment, 90 per cent live in the developing world.

In times of less advanced medical help and when the causes of blindness were less known and less treatable, blindness was a serious problem. Little wonder that it was among the social and personal ills that Isaiah saw that the Lord had called his people to rectify. In his account of the event at the Nazareth synagogue, Luke inserted the recovery of sight to the blind into the list of tasks that the 'anointed one' was to fulfil as outlined in the prophecy of Isaiah in chapter 61. Later in his Gospel, Luke gave accounts of Jesus indeed curing the blind (Luke 18:35-43; see also Mark 8:11-26).

In the light of these accounts it is likely that Luke and the other Gospel writers saw blindness and its cure in realistic, though miraculous, terms. In Mark's understanding it was one of the manifestations of evil against which Jesus battled. But both Luke and Mark understood blindness in spiritual as well as simply physical terms. The context of both the healing of the blind man at Bethsaida (Mark) and of the man at Jericho (Luke) indicates that both Mark and Luke understood physical blindness as a metaphor of a failure to understand on the part of either the Jewish religious leaders or the disciples.

The crowds had come out to listen to Jesus' teaching. Realising that they had come without any food, Jesus instructed his disciples to collect what they could. From seven loaves and a few small fish, he provided enough for the crowd of 4000. This aroused the attention of some Pharisees and they engaged Jesus in discussion, asking him for a sign as evidence of his authority.

In Mark's account, Jesus refuses to give them a sign, and he gets in a boat to cross to the other side of the lake. While making the crossing, he warns the disciples about the 'yeast of the Pharisees' – a saying that confuses the disciples, who think he is referring to the miraculous feeding they have just witnessed. Jesus remonstrates with them: 'Do you still not perceive or understand?' he asks. 'Are your hearts hardened? Do you have eyes, and fail to see?' He reminds them of the number of loaves they had and the number of basketfuls of scraps they gathered up. The seven and the twelve were obviously significant, but the disciples still did not understand.

They arrive at Bethsaida and a blind man is brought to Jesus. His friends beg Jesus to heal him. Jesus 'anoints' his eyes with mud and spittle and at first the man sees men looking like trees walking about. After a second 'anointing', he sees everything clearly. Gaining sight can be a gradual process; so, too, is gaining insight (Mark 8:11-26).

If the blindness of the religious leaders was their failure to realise the significance of Jesus as the 'anointed prophet', the disciples' failure was more specific: they could not see that the only way he would be able to fulfil his divine commission would be through suffering, death and resurrection. When, according to Luke, he told them he would be mocked, maltreated, flogged and killed, 'they understood nothing about all these things; in fact, what he said was hidden from them.' As they continued their journey to Jerusalem, they came to Jericho where a blind man sat at the roadside, begging. He addressed Jesus as the Son of David and asked him to have pity and to restore his sight. Jesus did no more than tell him, 'Receive your sight,' and he was immediately cured. The Word was sufficient to bring sight, to give insight (Luke 18:31-43; see also Matthew 20:17-34; John 8:30 - 9:12). Metaphors drawn from blindness or sight impairment do not only occur in religious texts. They are found in everyday conversation. We talk of going down 'blind alleys' when a path of action leads nowhere. A 'blind date' brings two people together who have never met before. A 'blind plant' is one that produces no flower. People who not only fail to see the truth that is being presented to them but constantly refuse to do so are characterised as 'none so blind as those who won't see.' In the 1962 song 'Blowin' in the wind', Bob Dylan asks the questions, 'How many times must a man look up before he can see the sky? How many times can a man turn his head and pretend that he just doesn't see?' Jesus warned his followers that it is vital to ensure that the truth – the 'light' – that guides their lives is truly light and not darkness:

> Your eye is the lamp of your body. If your eye is healthy, your whole body is full of light; but if it is not healthy, your body is full of darkness. Therefore consider whether the light in you is not darkness. If then your whole body is full of light, with no part of it in darkness, it will be as full of light as when a lamp gives you light with its rays.
>
> *Luke 11:34-36*

The use of blindness as a metaphor for failing or refusing to see truth has led some blind people to feel that this can lead to a subtle, even subconscious, form of discrimination or prejudice by which people make assumptions that blind people are in some sense less able or intelligent. However, not all metaphors from blindness have negative connotations. We speak approvingly of 'blind justice' in the belief that judgements made purely on the basis of appearances can offer poor justice. This reminds us that people spoke approvingly of the fact that Jesus knew what was in a person's heart and did not judge by appearances. 'Blind trust' is more ambiguous.

Kittens and puppies are born blind (and deaf) as this protects their developing optical systems both from damaging particles and the bright light that could damage their delicate photosensitive receptors The fanatical Saul was blind for a period after his challenging and life-changing experience on the road to Damascus. At one level, this might be understood as a result of the bright light that confronted him, but at another, the blindness represented the period of transition from one set of convictions to another, from one way of seeing the world to another. His 'healing' through Ananias after a period of three days was followed by his baptism. 'And immediately something like scales fell from his eyes, and his sight was restored. Then he got up and was baptised, and after taking some food, he regained his strength, (Acts 9:1-19). The response to a sudden revelation has often been described in a similar way.

4. Freedom to the oppressed

The literal meaning of the phrase translated 'let the oppressed go free' is 'to send away in freedom those who have been broken in pieces.' As a metaphor, it is powerful but not entirely logical, as it does not make explicit that those broken should first be mended. It does, however, have a dramatic and dynamic quality that is perhaps lacking in the associations with oppression.

Oppression speaks more of a heavy burden weighing down the victim, a burden that has to be carried while the normal act of living goes on. It is restrictive and, to those who are oppressed, the promise of freedom would certainly be a welcome release.

Oppression is a chronic, long-term condition, and in the struggles for power and empire there have always been those who have suffered oppression. It was true in Isaiah's time, in the days of Jesus and is still true today. Slavery is perhaps its most obvious general manifestation, where entire races are subjected to a state of oppression and where there is little hope of freedom.

Exile has its own characteristics, and those who are driven from their own country as refugees are oppressed by their loss, even if attempts are made to alleviate their desperate state. For others, oppression can arise simply as a result of their gender, their colour, their race, their sexual orientation or their economic condition.

Human society, no matter how apparently enlightened, too often treats some of its members in ways that are experienced as oppression. The Declaration of Human Rights has provided nations with a yardstick by which to measure how well they behave towards their citizens, but a declaration is not enough. There is a constant need for human rights to be monitored and for pressure to be brought upon those who are failing to promote such rights.

Oppression is not simply a passive withdrawal of people's rights; it is the active constraining of their freedoms. This is what is conveyed by the image of the yoke. The oxen have no right to decide which way to turn but must follow the direction of the driver exerting pressure through the yoke. It is both a weight and a means of limiting freedom of choice. To be released from that is to enjoy a greater physical freedom and, metaphorically, a greater moral and spiritual freedom as well. That a yoke ensures that a task may be fulfilled does not alter the fact that it also restricts.

Right up until the middle of the last century, yokes could be seen being used by farmers carrying pails of milk from the cowsheds, or taking buckets of feed to their stock. The yoke helped to distribute the weight of the load across the shoulders, but the wearer had little freedom to do much else. A yoke has the power to limit a person to a functional task – and people are more than that. This is why it can convey the notion of oppression – for an individual as well as for large groups of people, or even for a whole nation.

Paradoxically, when Jesus promised that he would offer rest to those coming to him who are weary and carrying heavy burdens, he did so by inviting them to take on his yoke – 'For my yoke is easy, and my burden is light' (Matthew 11:28-30). To be directed by Jesus is to discover our true selves and therefore the freedom to be ourselves. Saint Augustine reflected this in his prayer: 'Grant us so to know thee that we may truly love thee, and so to love thee that we may fully serve thee, whom to serve is perfect freedom.' (Frank Colquhoun (ed), Prayer 1592 in *Parish Prayers*, where it is given as 'after St Augustine', (Hodder and Stoughton, 1967)).

Poverty is a kind of oppression and restriction in itself. It is not simply that it limits choices and the ability to purchase things, but it is also oppressive in that there often appears to be no way out from under its burden. It weighs heavily upon the human spirit; it depresses. At its most severe it means that there is nothing else a person can do but put all their energies into survival. And that is not what we mean by living, nor by freedom.

Oppression can be the result of the actions of others. It can result from the conditions of one's environment. Long-term drought produces the oppression of famine. But the constant fear of flooding can also feel oppressive – as people in the west of England experienced in the repeated floods of 2012. Hopefully this was a temporary 'oppression', although the uncertainties of climate change bring their own kind of anxious weight for many people, not least those living in low-lying regions.

There is also oppression that arises from within oneself – the oppression of obsession or addiction, the oppression of guilt and anxiety. These can be debilitating, restricting and a burden from which the sufferer longs to be free.

The effect of a more immediate, dramatic event can feel less often like oppression and more like being broken into pieces. The experience is reflected in the way it is described. People say, for example, 'I was shattered.' We speak of being 'broken-hearted' and of 'just going to pieces.' Our worlds can 'fall apart' and our dreams end up 'in tatters'. All of these speak of a loss of the wholeness we had experienced or had hoped for. What had appeared to fit well together is wrenched apart. The unity is broken, the harmony disturbed.

This is in many ways a description of the world of human relationships, for all that it is also loving and creative. Things jar and split apart. There are broken relationships at the personal level and alienation in society and between nations. Secular explanations for this condition would no doubt look to such things as the fight for resources and the struggle for power, each rooted in our genetic make-up and surviving primal instincts. The person of religion looks into the heart and the spirit.

In the Jewish/Christian tradition is the story of the brokenness that came about through disobedience and which is described in the story of Adam and Eve. Other faiths have their own stories and myths that seek to cast light on the mystery of our human brokenness. The Christian faith may have sometimes overemphasised the wickedness of humanity, but it has never hidden from its reality. The hope of freedom from such brokenness is, for the Christian, not to be found in greater moral endeavour, nor in reforming programmes and renewed structures, necessary and helpful though these may be, but in the transformation of the human heart through the forgiveness, grace and empowering of God.

Nevertheless, where oppression and brokenness can be seen as the result of human activity, either by individuals or institutions, freedom may also be brought about by human endeavour. There are peacemakers, and those who work for the reinstatement of refugees. Groups seek to monitor human rights and to bring about change where those rights are abused. Agencies seek to relieve famine and to develop local resources. But such moves towards restoration and renewal only come about because there is a desire, a will, to find the possibility of new wholeness and transforming freedom. Such a will, such action, arises from hearts that are themselves more in harmony with the wholeness that God seeks and enables, whether or not he is recognised. Experience of exile that was experienced by the Jews of Isaiah's time as oppression and brokenness. But internally there had already been the oppression of injustice and the burden of deprivation, made worse by a lack of compassion in society. It was against this that prophets like Amos (see Amos 5:21-24) and Isaiah of Jerusalem had spoken, and it was a message taken up by Jesus in the parable of the sheep and the goats (Matthew 25:31-46).

Those who are people of the kingdom, who have, as it were, placed themselves under the rule of God's way of justice and love, are the ones who show compassion to the needy. Those whose lives are governed by self-concern and an indifference to justice are those whom Jesus believed were far from the kingdom.

Some have seen Jesus' message of forgiveness as a spiritual understanding of 'freeing the oppressed'. As far as the Gospel writers are concerned, it was in his healing and ministry of exorcism that they saw the oppressed being freed, the broken made whole. An example of this is found in the account in Luke's Gospel of the woman who had been crippled for 18 years. In curing her, Jesus declares, 'Woman, you are set free from your ailment.' Later he asks the Pharisees, who objected to her being cured on the Sabbath, 'Ought not this woman, a daughter of Abraham whom Satan bound for eighteen long years, be set free from this bondage on the sabbath day?' (Luke 13:10-17). So Luke may well have understood this healing as an exorcism.

At a personal and interpersonal level, at a national and a global level, experience forces us to admit to the brokenness of human relationships and that oppression is a present reality, not simply a historical aberration. Both are part of the darkness that the Light of the world came to dispel.

5. Prophets and Prophecy

Wikipedia lists over 65 prophets in the Bible, not counting the false prophets. In doing so it defines prophecy in a particular way. 'Biblical prophecy,' says Wikipedia, 'is the prediction of future events based on the action, function, or faculty of a prophet.' Popular opinion would give that general assent. But prophecy is actually a little more complicated and interesting than that – 'forth-telling' rather than simply 'fore-telling'.

It is true that you cannot read any of the books assigned to prophets without coming across frequent predictions about what is going to happen in the future or, more strictly, what God is going to do in the future. But to focus only on that aspect of the prophets' message is to miss much else that is valuable.

The role of the prophet

Clues to the particular role of the prophets are found in the early words associated with the title of 'prophet', which give hints about their origins. Prophets were 'called' people, who had insight into the events around and into the ways of God (they were 'seers'); they 'spoke out' the Word of the Lord, having received inspiration through the 'spirit' or 'breath' of God. Some of them, especially among the earlier ones, also experienced states of 'ecstacy'. Although often highly critical of the worship of the sanctuaries and cultic centres with their plethora of sacrifices, there was often a close link between prophets and the Temple. This can be traced, for example, through their use of Psalm forms in their prophecies – psalms being typical of the worship at the Temple.

Having been called by God, the prophet was understood to be in a special relationship with God, sharing in the mystery and power of the supernatural order through the gift of the Spirit of God upon him. He was therefore someone to be both feared, because of this special power, but also someone whose advice was to be sought. The account of the call of the prophet into this relationship is often very powerful and highly significant, providing deep spiritual and psychological insights into the character of both the prophet and his prophetic role (see Isaiah 6, Jeremiah 1:4-10, Ezekiel 1:1-4, 13).

The faith of the prophets

The roots of the prophets' faith is to be found in God's activity on behalf of his people in the Exodus from Egypt, in the Sinai **Covenant** through which he committed himself to them and they to him, and in the gift of the Law summarised in the decalogue given to Moses. This set of events was the foundation upon which their faith in God and their understanding of the people's obligations was built. The revelation of what God had done, was doing and would do arises from this. It was in God's action that his righteousness and justice were to be found – not in legal or ethical abstractions. It was from their conviction that God's holiness and righteousness were unique and his sovereignty was exclusive that the prophets could proclaim Yahweh as **the only God** and that the events of history were ultimately in his hand. Because they believed God alone was **King** they had the courage and the fortitude to face and challenge the kings of their day – Samuel with Saul, Nathan with David, Amos with Jereboam, Isaiah with Ahaz and Hezekiah.

The Kingship of God meant that for the prophets God was also the righteous **Judge**, condemning not only the people's religious disobedience but also their moral failings. The destiny of all the nations was in his hands. The punishment exacted on the people was often severe, and at times appeared to bring them close to the point of extinction, but the prophets always saw God's actions in relation to the Covenant which was his gift and to which he was faithful no matter what the people might do. Therefore they saw God not only as Judge but also as **Redeemer, Saviour.**

Although the balance varies with the different prophets there was always a sense that however dark the message of doom might be there was also the glorious hope, dependent upon God alone, that the purpose of God was for his Covenant to persist and for his rule to prevail. The prophets did not believe that the final word of God was one of destruction. The purpose of God was blessing (see especially Isaiah 40–55), although judgement might be needed to achieve it. The invasions and the exiles were brought about by God to bring the people to their senses, summoning them back from the foreign gods that were nothing but idols. God, the prophets believed, would ultimately act in mercy, but the people had to respond to him in repentance and with renewed faithfulness. To that extent it was up to them. Turning again to God would bring about a future that was peaceful, just, and glorious; in which the whole of creation would be renewed. God might well use the rulers of this world, such as Cyrus, to fulfill his purpose, but the people were to rely on God alone, not on alliances with rulers of Assyria, Babylon or Egypt. God was King, not them.

Through the message and the experience of judgement, runs the bright light of a future hope that became the inspiration which would never leave the people, even when they failed to live up to God's expectations. God, the prophets believed, would never forsake the promises he had made in the Covenant.

It is worth noting that the Covenant is **a corporate agreement** – it is between God and the people as a whole. God's activity, as understood by the prophets, was shaped by this. Both judgement and redemption were seen therefore mainly in terms of what happened to the people as a whole corporate body rather than individually. The prophets' concern with what the king did reflects this. He was seen as the representative of the whole people – if the king was faithful and just that was, by and large, how the people were viewed. If he was disobedient, followed other gods or sought security in alliances with foreigners rather than putting his trust in God, then not only was he condemned but judgement would fall on the whole nation. Jeremiah does speak of an individual's responsibility and the way in which judgement would fall upon the wrongdoer and not on his descendants, but the main thrust remains corporate in a way that has a different emphasis to the theology of the New Testament. There the redeeming work of Christ through the cross and resurrection is affected through the faith of the individual – although as a member of the Body of Christ the corporate aspect is not entirely absent.

6. The Word of the Lord – Isaiah

The picture that many people have of God through the Old Testament is the God of wrath and judgement. He went out to war alongside his people and not only did he ensure the enemy was defeated but he commanded that everything and everyone was to be put to the sword. To show that he was the one with the power he wiped out cities, killed a nation's firstborn children and used the forces of nature to exact punishment on those deemed to be in the wrong.

It is not only those who are anti-religion that have found accounts of such activity so off-putting that they have dismissed the Christian faith for ever. It is not difficult to see why some people suggest that the God of love that Jesus speaks of, the New Testament God, is very different from the one they find in the Old Testament.

It is easy, of course, to dismiss such views as simplistic or reactionary, failing to take into account the whole of the Old Testament. The Psalms, for example, are full of references to God's mercy (or steadfast love), although it is true that most often in pleading for God to show his mercy the Psalmists believed that this would best be achieved by God refusing mercy to the petitioner's enemies!

The great claim of Psalm 145 is not always easy to see in practice:

> The Lord is gracious and merciful,
>
> slow to anger and abounding in steadfast love.
>
> The Lord is good to all,
>
> and his compassion is over all that he has made.
>
> *Psalm 145:8, 9*

Some account for all this has to be given by those who believe God to be a loving God, open in his invitation to all, unconditional in his forgiveness, overwhelmingly generous in his graciousness. This is especially true in a season like Advent when judgement is a common theme and the voice of the prophet is often heard with the prediction of a coming day of wrath and punishment.

A changing understanding

While it may be true that God does not change, our understanding of him certainly does. Humankind, like individuals, has to develop spiritual maturity and insight It doesn't come fully grown. Whatever one makes of the idea that human beings were created perfect (as in the Genesis account) our experience teaches us that we've had and still have a lot of growing up to do, not least spiritually. But God doesn't just leave us to discover things about him the best we can. He reveals himself to us in creation, in action and most significantly through his Word. It would appear that this revelation too is gradual. As we explore and respond to what God has revealed, more is revealed to us. Even if we say that Jesus is the full revelation of God we know that we don't fully understand all that that means. Much of it remains a mystery that we have to explore, trust, lay ourselves open to if we are to grow in our discipleship.

From tribal God to God of all

An early understanding of God, reflected in the name he was known by at the time, saw him as a tribal god, interested only in the fortunes of a small group of people. He was a god of war. Key events like the Exodus and the giving of the Covenant at Sinai 'enlarged' the people's understanding. From being a tribal deity, God was seen to be the God of the whole people, a people he had specially chosen. He was their God just as other nations had their gods. It was the people's belief that he was the greatest and the strongest and that he showed this by defeating their enemies. But he was also a righteous and a just God – not arbitrary, not simply governing by power. In his care for his people he made demands upon them, demands of holy living and faithful obedience.

Most significantly he was a God who had not only created all there was, but also played an active part in the events of history to fulfil the purpose that people came to see was a saving purpose. The desperate events of invasion by foreign powers and of exile in foreign lands taught them that God was not constrained by geography. He wasn't just God of Palestine and the Temple, but he was present with his people wherever they went. He was God of all people and he was the only God – all the others were but man-made idols. And if he was the only God then his choice of Israel to be his people was not simply for their sake, it was so they could be his witnesses, his servant to all the nations, the bearer of God's light to all peoples, that all might repent and receive mercy.

Such a description is of course very simplistic and there was no straight line of development. Then, as now, the people's understanding of the God they worshipped twisted and turned, took a pace forward and then slipped back. Depending on the circumstances, one aspect of God tended to be emphasised rather than another – judgement or forgiveness.

The prophet's task

One of the tasks the prophets felt most keenly was the demand placed upon them by God to call the people back to the faith and trust they had first shown at the Exodus and in the Wilderness, when they committed themselves to God in the Covenant relationship in response to his commitment to them. It was their failure to live up to that agreement that called down judgement upon them. In the turmoil of the international scene, the prophet saw the judgement of God upon the people. The political events that threatened Israel, and which led to invasion and deportation, were understood to be an appropriate punishment for their wrongdoing.

What is surprising amidst all this disaster was the Word of the Lord that brought promise and hope (see Isaiah 40–55 in particular). A depressed and deported people, living in a strange land with strange gods and a foreign culture, were given a Word of the Lord that promised a restoration more glorious than they could have imagined or ever felt they deserved.

The prophet spoke out in loyalty to the message of judgement he was given, but he was equally obliged to be true to the message given to him of God's saving purpose. It was this that in the end dominated and fired all that the prophet declared.

God's action in history

How far we see the events on the international scene as involving the action of God will vary. The Christian faith believes that God fulfils his purposes through or in reaction to the choices, decisions and actions of men and women. He is a God who does not leave his creation to its own devices, even though he gives it the responsibility of free will.

In the 'spiritual economy' of God, judgement may be seen as the eventual consequence worked out in the lives of individuals and of nations when they act wrongly. But, underpinning this judgement, there is the purpose of God to bring people through that experience to an awareness of what has gone wrong and to a change of direction (repentance) so that they may enjoy the promise of forgiveness, restoration and renewal. A saved people is God's desire, not a destroyed people.

The prophets had the insight to see that vision of promise, they had the ears to hear that Word of hope, even in the darkest situations. Through this revelation given to them they believed that the God of the Covenant would remain faithful. In holiness he would judge but in mercy he would forgive, and both his holy judgement and his merciful forgiveness would serve the purpose of a loving God, to save.

7. Worship and Justice

'You don't have to go to church to be a Christian,' is, or used to be, a fairly common response to an enquiry about whether a person went to church or not. Nowadays people are perhaps more prepared to come out with a straight Yes or No.

'I'm not fanatical about it,' the person goes on. 'I don't go in for all that religious mumbo-jumbo.'

And here, of course, is the rub. Worship is seen to be off-putting and to involve 'religious mumbo-jumbo'. You can be a perfectly good Christian without all that, thank you very much. But can you?

It all depends – on quite a number of things. It depends on what you think being a Christian is all about and whether doing religious things is, in your opinion, what makes a *good* Christian.

Worship is key

A very good case can be made for saying that worship, in one form or another, is a key feature to the life of a religious believer. At its most basic, worship is precisely what it says: it is 'worth-ship'; the honouring, the expression of worth offered to one's god. Whatever value worship may have for the worshipper, it begins with focussing upon God – with praise and awe, wonder and delight. It proclaims the mystery and the majesty of God. In words and music, action and symbol, it seeks to take the worshipper out of the mundane into the sphere of the transcendent. In that presence the gap between the holy God and the sinful worshipper leads to confession and the request for forgiveness. The penitent becomes the petitioner, asking for himself and for others the good things God has to offer, drawing upon the Word and the Spirit of God. By act and by symbol a connection is made between the worshipper and the worshipped and for the Christian this is most dramatically realised in the act of Holy Communion. The grace of God is given to nourish and strengthen the believer's faith and spirit.

In public worship this is a corporate event, not simply something the individual does. In attending worship, individuals identify themselves with the whole body of believers. The communion is not solely with God, it is also with one another, building up the life of the congregation, the church. In worship there is giving as well as receiving, there is confession and forgiveness, there is thanking and asking, there is a coming together and a going out. Being part of the Body of Christ may be possible on your own, but it is both a whole lot more difficult and less likely to be sustaining than coming together with others to express the faith in worship. For many it does not make best sense to say we can be a follower of Christ if we never worship God in the company of other believers. Certainly the prophets would not have understood the concept of being a child of God except as part of the worshipping people of God. They may complain bitterly that the people worship other gods, but not to worship at all would have been unthinkable. It was a duty, an obligation; it's what constituted being part of the people of God.

Being religious is not enough

Does attending worship make you a good Christian? Yes, it can, but not necessarily. It might certainly make you a very religious person, if by that we mean a person absorbed in the practices associated with belief: prayer, fasting, reading the Scriptures, receiving Communion, singing hymns. You could be 'religious' in that and still not be the kind of person God wants you to be.

This was one of the sharpest complaints the prophets had about the people of Israel. The people were very good at being religious – they were great on sacrifices and offerings, at going to the Temple and the sanctuaries, at making prayers and singing psalms. But that was where it stopped. And for God this was not enough. To be God's people, worship was not enough. What mattered was what went on in the marketplace and not only what happened in the Temple. God didn't just want a nice offering, a psalm well sung, a prayer well said – he wanted honesty in trading, integrity in matters of the law, just dealings with foreigners, generous compassion for the vulnerable and the disadvantaged. In fact if this did not happen, said the prophets, the sacrifices and the rituals were all a waste of time, worse than useless. The holy God demanded a holy people – and holiness is more to do with how we behave with integrity towards others than it is to do with being religious.

Have your cake and eat it

Those who complain that the Church has forgotten its spiritual purpose and been too ready to take up issues of human rights, social justice and the plight of the poor would do well to listen to the prophets. Their message is as relevant today as it ever was. What the prophets don't say is that being honest is all that matters. Ultimately, they wanted to have their cake and eat it – they believed God wanted his people to be just and honest but also to worship him. But worship was not worth having if it did not lead to moral, just, righteous lives. Yet without worship of the true God the people could go equally astray.

For the prophets, whether the people found the worship accessible, relevant, meaningful (all these modern obsessions) was not an issue, but clearly it is today. Part of the skill of modern liturgists is to be able to devise worship that is both contemporary and evocative, in language that speaks to the spirit without becoming mumbo-jumbo or banal.

It is not a matter of being a better Christian if you go to church or don't go to church – it is more a matter of 'by their fruits you shall know them'.

8. A new leader

At the beginning of 2011, Tunisia and Egypt grabbed the headlines with their popular revolutions that had the potential to change the political face of the whole of the Middle East. The protesters wanted radical change not only to the way they were governed but who was at the top. For weeks President Mubarak of Egypt held on to power while the people occupied Tahrir Square and Western diplomats encouraged him to leave. One of the problems was that there was no obvious strong, charismatic, popular leader whom all the opposition parties would support.

In troubled Pakistan, struggling to control its own dissidents and having to deal with Afghanistan on its border, there were also voices for change. One spokesman opposed to the current government spoke of his pessimism for his country, lacking as it did, he said, a clear leader.

When, in February 2011, Liverpool city council decided to opt out of the government's Big Society initiative after only 20 weeks, a member of the North West Baptist Association said that, while it was too early to know if the initiative was working or not, what was really needed was not necessarily more money but leadership. 'We need to know the direction we are to be taking,' he said.

There seems to be the same call everywhere – we don't want more bureaucracy or more management, we don't want corrupt and greedy dictators, we want good leadership.

There is nothing new about that. Ever since the time of Saul, Israel had had kings as their leaders. That in itself had been controversial and the biblical account reveals the ambivalence around having a king – a leader who could tax the people, have a standing army, make alliances with foreign powers. Samuel was distinctly uncertain about it. Was not God the people's king? (See for example Psalms 93, 95, 97, 99.) But by the time of the prophets, monarchy had long been established. The question was whether or not the king was good.

The good king

The king represented the sovereignty of Yahweh and he also represented the rights, concerns and aspirations of the people themselves. Two qualities marked out whether a king was 'good' or not – his loyalty to God and his commitment to justice. Time and again in the historical accounts of the books of Kings and Chronicles the formula of 'he did what was evil/good in the sight of God' is used as a summary of a king's reign. A king who encouraged the worship of 'foreign' gods was typically described as evil. Those who were faithful to Yahweh were described as good.

A prophet like Isaiah of Jerusalem, who appears to have had a close association with the royal court, spoke out against the king when he failed to trust God and instead looked for political support from other countries, especially Egypt. Isaiah was also outspoken in his criticism of any failure of justice, especially where that concerned the king's failure to support the rights of the poor or the vulnerable.

The model for the good king was David. As a man, David certainly had his failings, not least in the affair with Bathsheba, but he was faithful to God who enlarged his territories. In showing his approval of David, God promised him a successor for ever. When the fortunes of the nation were at their lowest, the prophets gave hope to the people through the promise of a new leader descended from David. Such a leader would follow in the great king's footsteps, re-establish the people in their faith and rule with justice. On the one hand the prophet expected such a hope to be realised in the near future, played out on the national political scene. On the other, this was also the work of the Lord, an act of his compassion and mercy to save his people.

Faithful and just

The theme of justice is a strong thread running through so much of the Old Testament understanding of what was expected of the nation's rulers. It was a justice that showed a special concern for those who had least power, least voice to make their own case – the widows and the orphans, the poor and the foreigner. The king was to stand up for them. The 'bias to the poor' was a key theme in the Church of England's report 'Faith in the City', having a significant impact upon urban policies and action by Church and state. But it was not a new concept. It was rooted in the Scriptures and in the message of the prophets. Its foundations were not social policy but theology. The king was to be just, with this kind of justice, because this was the way God exercised justice. God has a 'bias to the poor'.

It is perhaps only in most recent times with the concerns about global warming, the disappearance of hundreds of species in the natural world and the rise of public awareness of 'green' issues, that we have recovered a sense of the interconnectedness of our world. Political and global commercial decisions have their repercussions for our environment. Lifestyles and values have their impact upon the natural world. Deforestation on an enormous scale for commercial advantage has its effect on climate across the globe. Loss of habitat means species disappear and the bio-diversity of our world decreases. These things are linked together and it matters.

The prophets already understood the world in this interconnected way. Faith and values affected politics and trade; justice not only made for a good society, it affected the natural world. It was not sentimentality that led Isaiah to speak of the lamb lying down with the wolf, the kid with the leopard. It was a deep sense that in the age of the new leader, called and blessed by God, the life of the nation and all the world would be renewed. And it would happen in the lifetime of the near future.

In times of desperation it is understandable that there is a call for new leadership. In places where there has been dictatorship, the call is for a leader of the people's choice. In democracies the election system has its own way of changing the leadership of a nation. There is the hope that change will mean improvement. It only does so if leaders use their power and influence in ways that arise from values and a vision that are large enough to go beyond individual well-being to the well-being of nations, and ultimately our world.

That was Isaiah's vision. He was clear that such values had to be founded in a faith in God and God's ways.

9. The Word made flesh

When Princess Diana died there was criticism of the Queen because, for whatever reason, she did not immediately join the mourning crowds. People felt she had in some sense failed to share in their grief.

When the hurricane Katrina devastated New Orleans, President George Bush was similarly criticised for failing to make an early visit to the ruined city.

At times of tragedies that affect the whole country there is a desire for heads of state to show their care and concern not only for those immediately suffering but also for the nation's sadness by being present; being with those who hurt and grieve.

It was no different in Isaiah's time. With enemies threatening all around, with leadership uncertain, people complained that God was absent. It was as though God had hidden himself away from the people. 'In over flowing wrath for a moment I hid my face from you' (Isaiah 54:8). The people cried out for God to be with them, to show his face (see Psalms 13:2; 27:9; 44:24-26; 102:2).

In such a situation, during the reign of Ahaz, Isaiah came to the king with a promise and a sign that God would indeed be with his people in their distress (Isaiah 7:10-17). He pointed out one of the young women in the court. She is pregnant, he said, and her baby will have the name Immanuel, God is with us. The name had the power to achieve the promise it conveyed. This was a sign both of hope and also of warning. Hope if the people trusted God – he would be with them to save them. But warning if they didn't trust the God who was with them – there would be invasion. Even the promise that by about the age of three the child would be eating curds and honey held both hope and threat. It could mean that all would be well, there would be plenty and he would eat the food of the gods. Or it could mean that there had been invasion, that there would be deprivation and he would eat the food of the desert. To have God with you was not some magical solution to the people's problems. They still had their responsibility to 'trust and obey'.

The promise of a child, born of a young woman and who would be called Immanuel is taken up in the Gospel account of the birth of Jesus. Joseph was told by God in a dream not to be afraid to take Mary as his wife just because she was pregnant. And according to Matthew this happened to fulfil what Isaiah had said: 'Look the virgin shall conceive and bear a son, and they shall name him Emmanuel' (Matthew 1:22, 23). Joseph was also told that the boy's name was to be Jesus, an Aramaic form of the Hebrew name Joshua, which means 'salvation'. Here too in the birth narratives we have the belief that the name that is given to a child not only shows what he will be like, but will enable him to achieve what the name indicates. Jesus, as 'God with us', saves.

The famous passage from Isaiah 9, 'For unto us a child is born . . .', looks like a proclamation following the birth of the baby that is promised in chapter 7. The use of this as a Christmas reading certainly indicates that that is how the Church has understood it. In fact it is more likely that this was a hymn sung at the accession of the king, at which point he became God's adopted son. The names for the king given here were also believed to have the inherent power of ensuring the way the king ruled – with incomparable wisdom and statesmanship, victorious in battle, a father to his people, bringing them peace and security.

In fact no such king appeared for Israel, but the powerful and visionary words of Isaiah continued to inspire the people's hopes. The great kingly figure, following the footsteps of David, became the way they described the Messiah, the anointed one, the Christ – the special agent of God through whom God's rule, his kingdom, would be established.

The followers of Jesus believed that this hope had been fulfilled in him. 'You,' said Peter to Jesus at Caesarea Philippi, 'are the Messiah, the Christ' (Mark 8:27-30). So Jesus is the one who has been anointed by God (Messiah), the one who saves (Jesus), the one through whom God is present with us (Emmanuel); who being a descendant of David will establish God's kingdom.

Whatever use has been made of Isaiah's words it is worth remembering that when they were spoken Isaiah had no long-term perspective in view. He was talking about events of the time, seeing in them signs of what he believed God was doing for and with his people. It was only as the years progressed, as Jewish spirituality sought to make sense of these unfulfilled promises, that the way of expressing such hopes took on a more symbolic and futuristic style with amazing visions of the future. Such a tradition clearly influenced writers like St John the Divine in writing down his Revelation. But more telling, and in many ways more mysterious, is that tradition from Isaiah of the God who expresses himself in the here and now, who makes himself known in the everyday. Most significant of all for Christians is the key belief that God came into our world, took on our humanity, was 'enfleshed' (Incarnated) in the person of Jesus.

Here is the greatest mystery, the greatest source of hope – that in Christ God made himself known to us, lived amongst us, died and rose for us. We believe in the almighty God who is very down to earth.

10. For all the world

The Abrahamic religions – Judaism, Christianity and Islam – all declare that there is only one God. Western philosophy agrees, on the basis that by definition God is supreme and this is compromised if there is more than one god. But other religions, like Hinduism, do have a number of gods and the same was true of ancient middle-eastern religions. A popular way to get round all this is to speak of there being just one God but with all the religions being different paths to the same God. However, even a fairly rudimentary knowledge of other faiths soon leads one to conclude that there may be only one God but the way he is described by the various religions is sufficiently different to make it look as though they are speaking of different gods.

At a time when many parts of our country have multi-cultural, multi-faith communities this kind of discussion is not simply an academic exercise. It raises significant concerns for social cohesion and for education – especially if any of those faiths adopt a proselytising stance towards the others. At the time of the prophets the existence of a multiplicity of faiths presented real and significant problems. In the faith of Israel the Lord God, Yahweh, was ethically and spiritually demanding – more so than the gods of the nations around them. In part this was because Israel's God was not visible. He was not like the 'graven images' that other faiths had. 'No one has ever seen God' (1 Timothy 6:16; 1 John 4:12). Yahweh was also very demanding, expecting total loyalty and a style of life that reflected his righteousness and holiness. If people expected the benefits of having Yahweh as their God, they had to pledge themselves to him. This mutual agreement was enshrined in the Covenant – a binding mutual commitment of God to his people and of the people to God. This was a foundational belief for Israel in its religious life and for Israel as a nation. It was this that the prophets constantly called the people to honour.

Among the prophets, Isaiah is perhaps most significant in the development of the belief in one God (monotheism). No doubt this understanding of God had been growing over the centuries but there was still the strong view that while Yahweh was Israel's God, each of the nations had their own gods. Yahweh was, in his people's view, the top God, King of kings, Lord of lords. But the prophets increasingly took this a stage further. Yahweh was not simply superior, he was the only God. They didn't arrive at this conclusion by logical reasoning or abstract debate, but through an ever-greater assurance that the one they worshipped, the one who had called them to speak for him, was the one who was sovereign over all and the creator of all. He wasn't battling with other gods in the events of history – he had sole command. The rulers of other nations were, in the end, doing his bidding, fulfilling his purposes. Most typically this is seen in Isaiah's understanding that the Persian general, Cyrus, was acting as a servant of Yahweh: 'He is my shepherd, and he shall carry out all my purpose' (Isaiah 44:28).

Just as Yahweh was the sole Lord of history, he was also seen to be the only creator: 'I am the first and I am the last. My hand laid the foundation of the earth, and my right hand spread out the heavens; when I summon them they stand at attention.' (Isaiah 48:12,13, see also Isaiah 40:28.) Beside this God, the gods of Babylon and Assyria were mere man-made idols. 'All who make idols are nothing, and the things they delight in do not profit; their witnesses neither see nor know' (Isaiah 44:9, see also 44:10-20). Those who worshipped such gods were deceiving themselves. They 'have no knowledge – those who carry about their wooden idols and keep on praying to a god that cannot save' (Isaiah 45:20).

It was this conviction, the overwhelming certainty about the sovereignty of Yahweh, the God of the Covenant, that led Isaiah to assert the exclusive claim of Yahweh to be God. It gave force both to his message of God's judgement upon the people Israel and all peoples, but also to his message of God's saving purpose for Israel and for all people. The prophet could thus speak of the light of God being made splendid in Israel and attracting all the nations to it. Not only would the other nations recognise the presence of Yahweh with his people, but they would acknowledge his sovereignty and bring their gifts and their wealth to the City of David, to Zion, to Jerusalem. It was an amazing message, declaring the reversal of fortunes of a captive people. It would be achieved, not by human effort or by Israel deserving it, but through the purpose and action of the one true God. The conviction was powerful, but in the event things did not work out as Isaiah had declared. There was more invasion than there was homage, not because God was not sovereign but because the people failed to do his will.

Nevertheless, this vision remained, and its fulfilment is symbolised in the Gospel accounts of the visit of the Eastern astrologers bearing gifts to present to the Christ Child at Bethlehem. The nations are there at the start of his life, acknowledging the revelation of God in the person of Jesus.

While, in the first instance, Jesus' mission was to the Jews, it came to be understood in terms of God's action for all people. The gospel was to be proclaimed to Jew and also to Gentile. The salvation made possible through the cross and resurrection was for all. 'Go therefore,' said the risen Christ, 'and make disciples of all nations.' (Matthew 28:19.) It was a message that was underlined in the experience of Peter and his vision of the many creatures in the sail cloth (Acts 10:9-16). His words to Cornelius made this clear: 'I truly understand that God shows no partiality, but in every nation anyone who fears him and does what is right is acceptable to him' (Acts 10:34,35).

The insights of the prophet are echoed and 'fulfilled' in the gospel. The one God is creator, redeemer and enabler of all.

11. Christmas Eve – expectation

The problem for youngsters on Christmas Eve is not the keeping awake but the getting to sleep. The excitement of what is anticipated and expected overwhelms any desire to fall into temporary oblivion. The days and weeks of preparation have all been leading up to this – and they just can't wait. The letters of wishes went off to Santa, and mum and dad have been told as well just in case: the new iPod, the latest PlayStation game, the first grown-up make-up kit, enough food to burst and crackers all round.

But expectations are strange creatures – projections into the future of our dreams and hopes, what we think will make us happy, be the best thing possible. They take on the flesh of actuality. But our imaginations can get things wrong. The reality can be disappointing and leave us dulled of spirit and wondering why things turned out less than we had hoped, had all but touched. Equally the actuality can go beyond our wildest expectations, take us into realms we had never thought possible, offer delights we had never even thought of, provide surprises that make the heart race.

Much of what surprises us most comes precisely when we had not expected it to appear, had not been able to anticipate the timing or even the nature of what occurs. It is not necessarily that the signs were not there, simply that we had not been alert enough or had read them wrong. More difficult are the times when expectations are clear enough but the delay dulls the edge of our attention, frustrates us enough to make us falter in our preparations. Indeed, all the preparation may have been done long before but with expectations unfulfilled such readiness has been set aside, we have got on with other things. The Jews had long heard about a coming Messiah. The prophets had called them to prepare their hearts and their lives for his coming but delay had dulled their sense of expectation. When he did come, the majority failed to acknowledge him, the authorities rejected him – just a handful recognised him: the unexpected Lord.

Early Christians were convinced that, with the resurrection and the gift of the Spirit, the Christ, the Lord, would return as promised. But the years went by and their expectations faltered. The Gospel report of Jesus' warnings about this were read out to congregations to remind them not to be taken by surprise or unprepared: their behaviour and their lives were to be as those fully awake, expecting Christ's return.

The weeks of Advent offer the opportunity to spend time making preparations, not just for the festivities but for the 'long expected Jesus, born to set thy people free', and preparation for ourselves to welcome him anew. Advent gives us time to think afresh just what our expectations are – our expectations of him and of ourselves. Do we expect too much? Are our expectations of God too small? Whichever way, we can be sure that if we have made ourselves open to his coming, there will be surprises, some things we did not anticipate. If we have stayed alert, there will not be disappointment but fulfilment for:

Hark the glad sound! The Saviour comes,
the Saviour promised long:
Let every heart prepare a throne
and every voice a song.

Philip Doddridge (1702–1751)

12. Christmas Day – the presence of God

Although sceptical scientists pour scorn on ever being able to evaluate the reality of a 'sense of God', there are far too many examples of people having this sense for it simply to be dismissed. In times of danger, loneliness, ecstasy; during prayer, a country walk, reading a poem; as a regular occurrence, a one-off experience, something known now and then – countless men, women and children have been convinced that God has been with them in quite a specific and immediate way. For some it has been awesome and terrifying, for others comforting and reassuring. It has awoken faith, challenged lives, reassured the doubtful, called to new service. It is personal, specific and precious.

Luke tells us that when the angel Gabriel visited Mary to tell her that she would be a mother, he greeted her with the words, 'The Lord is with you.' This has become the basis for the liturgical greeting at worship expressed both as a prayer – 'The Lord be with you'– and as a statement of fact – 'The Lord is here.' It reminds the worshipper that at the heart of faith and worship is the reality of God who is present to us and for us. While never less than mystery and beyond all we can know, God is close to us, makes himself known to us. We sense his presence. This greeting among Christians helps to define the nature of who we are and the God we worship – we are a people whose God is with us, a God who is not aloof and unconcerned but who can be personally known in our lives.

The festival of Christ's Nativity is certainly something we can enter into very personally and with a sense of awe and intimacy. But it is also a public event, celebrating the activity of God on the grand scale made real in the local, the specific, the personal. The cosmic dimension is there in the chorus of angels appearing to shepherds on a Bethlehem hillside – a great announcement that this birth in the local village is for 'all people'. It is there in the arrival of astrologers from the East. For this is not just a family event. It is not even only within and for the family descended from David or the people of God, but is for the Gentile world as well. Its representatives are there at the beginning. The birth of Jesus has a large spatial context. It is also an event on a large time-scale. It is not a chance happening but, as Matthew was at such pains to point out, happened in accordance with the promise of God declared by the prophets centuries before.

The time of waiting is over, the promise fulfilled, the Light has come.

> We hear the Christmas angels
> the great glad tidings tell:
> O come to us, abide with us,
> our Lord Emmanuel.
>
> *Phillips Brooks (1835–1893)*

13. Ash Wednesday – Fast

In an age obsessed with happiness, personal choice, self-gratification, the notion of self-denial can feel strange, alien even. No doubt going without the odd chocolate or glass of wine can do no harm, but whole days or weeks of denial appear odd if not plain stupid.

Yet such denial has, in the experience of many, been a means of gain – physical, emotional, spiritual. To go without is good for you! And it is not just a puritanical spirit that says so. Far from being some kind of perverted self-harming it is, experience tells us, self-enhancing. It is one aspect of that wider truth that we shall only find our true selves if we lose them.

But there is something of a paradox here. For while, through some act of self-denial, benefit can be gained, such benefit is limited if one simply focuses on what has been given up. To be beneficial, self-denial is only ever a means, not an end. It is a way, or part of the way, by which we may look for something much more important, be it health, wholeness, truth, or salvation. And while, as Jesus taught us, such acts or regimes of self-denial should not be displayed as though they were virtuous acts to be paraded to others, nevertheless their outcome should in some way be seen in the way we behave.

Traditionally, fasting is seen as the denial of basic needs – abstinence from food and drink and sex. But the story of Jesus' time in the wilderness suggests other acts of denial that are worth considering as we set out on this time of Lent.

Following his baptism, Jesus, we are told, was led by the Spirit into the wilderness, the desert. He took himself away from the daily hurly-burly and social contact with others. He withdrew from the normal comforts and provisions of life. He went in solitude to a lonely place, fasted and prayed and in doing so opened himself up to the risk of temptation and the possibility of spiritual insight. Building on all that had gone before in the previous thirty years, all his experiences, his learning, his relationship with God, he used this time of deprivation to discover and explore the heart and the foundation of his mission. Without food he learnt where his inner-sustenance was to be found; amidst danger and risk he discovered where his true security lay; without company he discovered where his deepest loyalty resided.

For most of us there is not the opportunity, let alone the will, to go off into a desert place for nearly seven weeks. But there are ways by which we might explore something of that experience within the coming weeks. To do so may not be easy, may actually be inconvenient, yet could be worth the effort – a time to fast.

Jesus withdrew to a fast from socialising. He left the daily contact with others, their demands but also their delights. He withdrew to be alone and in that space discovered the difference between solitude and loneliness. Loneliness is anxious-making, the self left alone, unattended, unrelating. In solitude the space is occupied, not by a lone self feeling lonely, but by the self-awareness of the presence of others – of God, of those who love us and whom we love, those whose needs concern us, those whom we need for our fullness.

> Solitude is genuine only when it is inhabited.
> And the best way not to have people in your way
> is to let them into your heart.
>
> *Alessandro Pronzanto, Meditations on the Sand,*
> *St Pauls' Publications, 1982 p.18*

> Solitude separates only to unite.
>
> *Brother Daniel-Angel cited by*
> *Alessandro Prozonto, op cit p.16*

Try to find space away from others for a while each day, and in that space to journey into the depths of who you are. For in doing that you will also journey towards God and to journey to God we discover that we are together with others.

Jesus withdrew to a fast from sounds. He left the demanding voices and the gossiping voices, the chatter of friends and the complaints of crowds, the noise of streets and shops. He withdrew to quietness and discovered there the risk and the depth of silence. So often we seem to see silence as a threat. Few TV programmes ever risk silence. Teenagers live with their ears filled by technologically provided messages and music. Congregations stir uneasily when a time of silent prayer lasts more than a few seconds. A fast from sound could help us to discover the value of silence – to listen to our hearts and the voice of God, to hear the meanings that all the hullabaloo has hidden from us. A time each day of risky, rewarding silence.

Jesus withdrew to where he had nothing, to a fast from possessions. One of the values of self-denial is the discovery of what one really needs as against what one wants and has. It's not that to have things is wrong or to want things is wrong – but to spend a time without the things we have, to spend time not considering what we want, is to discover more deeply the value of those things we need. It sets us in a place from which to get a better perspective of what we have – a place that is not populated by eager sales-people, skilful advertisers, visions of what we ought to have rather than what we need to have. A time each day in which we withdraw from having and acquiring to consider those things that are our deepest needs, and the needs of others.

Jesus withdrew from safety to a place of fasting in which he discovered his security. Our education system urges teachers to ensure that children are, among other things, safe. Of course we do not want them to be unsafe. But in a blame culture, keeping safe means keeping from risk. It is of course a futile exercise and it is not for the fullest well-being of children, nor indeed of adults. Safety is not the most important thing – security might be. Secure enough that risk can be encouraged – risk intellectually, emotionally, physically, socially and spiritually. Amidst the dangers and the struggles of the desert Jesus came to know where his true security lay – in the promise and love of the Father. During Lent it is worth examining what it is that we dare not risk simply because we want to be safe.

The demands of the wilderness, the place of fasting, are considerable and we may only feel able to step, as it were, a short distance into such a place.

There are always others who have gone that way before us. Their guidance may help. But whether we travel far or short, if travelled seriously, with expectation and perseverance, the journey will yield its rewards.

14. Palm Sunday
(Matthew 21:1-11; Mark 11:1-11; John 12:12-16)

There are people whose entry into a room will turn heads. It may be on account of their reputation, their celebrity rating or just personal charisma. Sometimes it is their own heads that get turned. Making a big entry can be dramatic, good for publicity, or just the way things turn out. By all accounts Jesus' arrival in Jerusalem at the start of what we have come to call Holy Week was a big entry. The preacher from Galilee was acclaimed as king.

In the technique of telling Bible stories with groups of children, known as Godly Play, each session concludes with the leader saying: 'I wonder how so-and-so in the story felt . . . I wonder how you would have felt.' We might well wonder what was felt on the day of procession and acclamation, on that Palm Sunday. What was Jesus feeling? What did the disciples feel? How did the crowds feel about it all? How do we feel?

The disciples were geared up for something. Jesus had made it plain on a number of occasions that he was heading for Jerusalem and that his visit on this occasion would be critical. They had been dismissive of his talk about suffering at the hands of the authorities and Peter had earned a stern rebuke for his reaction to such ideas (Matthew 16:23). They didn't understand what Jesus was saying (Luke 18:34) but they knew that Jerusalem would be special. Some of the followers had left, perhaps fearful of what would happen, not wanting to get involved in anything too political.

The atmosphere among the disciples became more charged. They were meeting crowds on the road going up to Jerusalem for the festival (Tabernacles or Dedication) and Jesus seemed to be making arrangements of his own. Their heads would have been increasingly full of sayings and stories from the Jewish Scriptures and their expectations were rising. Their journey had taken them from Jericho and along the road to Bethany where

Lazarus lived with his two sisters, Mary and Martha. It was a place of special personal significance for Jesus and his friends. As they came to the Mount of Olives they were aware that this was a place of national significance – a place of Messianic promise; the place where, it was said, would be the general resurrection when God established his kingdom of the new age.

Jesus had sent two of their number to a village with instructions about getting a donkey for him to ride. That was unusual in itself – Jesus normally walked everywhere. The excitement was mounting and they felt that this was going to be the great moment. Their leader was more than just a rabbi; he was the people's leader, the one they had been looking for, the one who would bring in God's new age. They got carried away with it all. As they put their cloaks on the donkey they led the shout of acclamation: 'God bless you, you come as King, in the name of the Lord.' This was what Jesus meant to them, this was what he deserved – the acclamation as leader, as king.

The crowds, too, were caught up in the excitement of the festival. They had cut branches from the trees to take into the city and once the shout went up about a king they waved them and laid them down in front of this figure who was being acclaimed as king. Some of them (according to John) had been amazed by what Jesus had done at Bethany in bringing Lazarus back from the dead, and they added to the shouts of acclamation. Did they know what they were shouting? Was it more than a bit of hysteria in the excitement of the moment? It may well have seemed real at the time but once they got into the city with its narrow streets and the watchful eyes of the soldiers, it all fizzled out. They had to be careful. The Romans were touchy at festival time and brought in extra troops to man the garrison. A man on a donkey wasn't really going to achieve that much. Perhaps he wasn't the king they had shouted for after all. When the Messiah really came he would come with an army and with power.

Jesus, we might imagine, saw all this very differently. Through his times of prayer and struggle he had come to believe that God required him to go to Jerusalem and face whatever that would bring. He knew he had stirred up opposition among the authorities. He had become convinced that it would involve suffering and no doubt his death. He believed he had no choice if he was to be obedient to his Father's will.

That he was a leader, he did not shrink from. That in some way the new age was indeed being brought in, he did not doubt. He knew he had a special role in that. But he had such a different view of the nature of his leadership, the type of kingdom that would be established. The people wanted a powerful leader to overturn the regime of Roman power and to restore Israel's stature as a nation, its independence, its power. Their vision was in the end too narrow, too parochial, too self-seeking. They had not learnt the lesson of the prophets that being God's people was a privilege for service, not for dominance. The Servant of God was for the freeing of all nations, not just the Jews. Jesus was key to the Big Story of peace, not to the skirmishes of power. He was indeed the one coming in the name of the Lord – in the name of a God of reconciliation and of peace, and to achieve that would be costly. When Jesus came to Jerusalem his entry turned heads, but when he failed to live up to expectations, they turned away again.

15. Confrontation – the cleansing of the Temple (Matthew 21:12, 13; Mark 11:15-19; Luke 19:45, 46; John 2:13-22)

The church council's discussion about the proposed book stall at the back of the church aroused heated debate. There were those who felt that while it was reasonable for the church guidebook to be on sale, it was totally inappropriate to be selling cards and CDs, mementos and all kinds of knick-knacks. Others had no such qualms. Indeed they wanted the recently closed-down Post Office to be relocated to the back of the church. One member brought the discussion to a stop by asking: 'What would Jesus do? Surely he would have thrown out all this buying and selling?' Reference was made to the incident of the cleansing of the Temple. It simply extended the argument. Someone suggested that Jesus was against the dodgy dealings of the traders and there was no intention to cheat anyone by unfair practices at the bookstall. Others pointed out that if there had been no traders selling animals and birds that had been passed as acceptable for sacrifice by the priests, no one would have been able to worship. It was the same with the money: only the Temple coin could be used for the tax so everyone had to exchange their normal coinage. If Jesus was trying to stop all such trade he was in fact as good as saying that there should be no Temple worship. Someone suggested that it was the priests who made such rules and raked in the profits that he was against. The interjection that in that case the church would have to get rid of priests didn't advance the discussion!

Another member suggested that Jesus was against the way all the commercialisation had got out of hand. It was making the Temple into a business and Jesus was protesting that true worship should be spiritual without all the business of animal sacrifices. She did have to concede that he didn't seem to have complained about the sacrificial system anywhere else. However, she gained support from one of the younger members who pointed out that in John's Gospel Jesus had talked about worship being in spirit and in truth and that the time would come when people would worship the Father neither on Mount Gerizim nor in Jerusalem (John 4:19-24). Perhaps, she suggested, he was trying to reform the worship of the Temple.

This didn't satisfy the Sunday School leader. He felt that would have meant there should have been no Temple at all and if Jesus was really making an effort to end Temple worship, then why wasn't he arrested on the spot? In any case, how could he do that with just a whip and a few followers? The minister felt compelled to point out that Jesus had been accused at his trial of saying that he would destroy the Temple and suggesting that he could rebuild it in three days. The fact that no one had agreed about exactly what Jesus had said rather undermined this. It might have been that he had simply predicted the fall of Jerusalem and the end of Temple worship, as happened 40 years after his death.

The oldest member asked to speak. 'I wonder,' she said, 'if what really matters is that first we get our worship right and then worry about the bookstall later. How far is our church really a place of prayer? Are we really a welcoming place so that anyone, whatever their background, can come amongst us and worship without us making them feel awkward, in our way almost? I have to admit I don't like it when someone sits in my usual place and sometimes I let it show. The Lord said that his house should be a house of prayer and for all nations. I think that means anybody and everybody – including the travelling folk who have just moved into the village.' A number of people started looking at their feet. The chairman brought the discussion to an end!

16. Preparation – the costly ointment
(Matthew 26:1-13; Mark 14:1-9; Luke 7:36-50; John 12:1-11)

The concluding climax of a symphony often draws together the whole intention and meaning of the piece, but earlier passages, themes and developments will provide significant clues along the way. So it is here with the woman's anointing of Jesus. This apparently simple, though unusual, event provides an insight into the heart of the gospel and the meaning of what will happen on Good Friday and Easter Sunday.

Both Matthew and Mark report Jesus as promising that an extravagant act of anointing him with perfumed ointment would be recalled 'wherever the good news is proclaimed in the whole world'. Whether these were words actually spoken by Jesus or were insertions by later tradition, they imply a connection between her act and the message of the gospel. Taken as a whole, the four accounts of the event that appear in the Gospels reveal key ideas about the person of Jesus and the meaning of his death and resurrection.

The event reveals the woman's faith in Jesus as King and as the Messiah. This is highlighted in the accounts that speak of the woman anointing Jesus' head. Kings were anointed with oil on their accession or enthronement. In the Holy Week sequence this anointing takes place in close association to the Triumphal Entry into Jerusalem, when Jesus is hailed as King, and confirms it. Further, anointed is the very name of the Messiah, the Christ. Jesus is believed in as the one whom God has called to be his special agent in the establishing of his kingdom – the anointed one. It was not only the inner circle of disciples who would come to this faith.

The good news that Christians proclaim includes the message that the one who is Lord of all and the bringer of the kingdom has in fact appeared in the person of Jesus. God made a decisive move, one that was awaited and looked for by the Jews who failed to recognise the moment when it came, and one that was also promised as part of God's inclusion of all people within his benevolent rule. To catch God's moment in our own lives and experience requires attention to the guidance of the Holy Spirit and a 'holy' imagination to see the presence and work of a God who so often surprises us with the unexpected.

In the kingdom Jesus was bringing in, the relationship with God that had been broken by humankind's sin was mended. God did something decisive through Jesus. At the heart of the gospel is a message of forgiveness, of reconciliation, of a transformed relationship made possible by Jesus. This theme of forgiveness is significant in the account of the woman's anointing of Jesus' feet in Luke, and also present in John.

To offer ointment to guests to pour on their heads was not merely a way of refreshing them, notably before a meal, but also a way of showing them respect. It was an act of honouring. But it was not only the living who were anointed. It was the custom, prior to burial, to anoint the body of a dead person; failure to do this was a cause of distress to relatives and friends. It is not an uncommon experience for grieving relatives to bewail the fact that they left things unsaid or not done. And once the loved one has gone the opportunity has gone for good. Loving things unexpressed. Intended acts of kindness never carried out. Grasping the opportunity while we have the time is important – even if in doing so we flout convention or cause embarrassment to others.

All four Gospels see the woman's anointing, of either the head or the feet, as a symbolic anointing of Jesus' whole body. They make it explicit that this is associated with Jesus' impending death. It was an anticipatory act. It also highlights the gospel truth that God's forgiveness, though freely offered, was costly – a cost revealed in Jesus' giving of himself through the crucifixion. The victory of the cross over sin is a key aspect of the good news, but it came at a terrible price.

It can be all too easy for us to take our forgiveness for granted; often we neither express our gratitude for our renewed relationship with God nor acknowledge the cost of that forgiveness. Forgiveness is not simply a matter of dealing with past wrongs; it is the springboard for transformed lives. Through forgiveness we are no longer locked into past events but are given hope for the future. Forgiveness releases us from the guilt, the burden and brokenness that the past can bring into our present. Forgiveness releases us and makes it possible for us to move on in our relationship with God and in our relationships with one another.

Mark, Matthew and John all set the anointing in close proximity to the events of Good Friday. John, in particular, takes this further and relates it also to the resurrection. For Jesus, who is anointed as the King and the Christ, the one who is anointed in generous gratitude for forgiveness, and whose death and burial is anticipated, is also the one who raised Lazarus and who declared himself to be the resurrection and the life. The gospel message is not only about sins forgiven; it is also the promise of transforming, resurrection life. This was the faith that Mary, Lazarus' sister, had come to. This was the faith that the preaching of the gospel called people to. This is the faith that we travel with as we journey through Holy Week. This is the faith we are called to share with others.

17. Betrayal
(Matthew 26:3-5, 14-16, 20-25, 47-50; Mark 14:1, 2, 10, 11, 17-21, 43-46; Luke 22:2-6, 21-23, 47, 48; John 13:21-32, 18:1-6)

That Judas was one of Jesus' close circle of friends is both undeniable and an embarrassment to the Gospel writers. There is no reason for them to have invented him or made up the shameful part he played in the Passion of Christ. It was a fact to be reckoned with and some account had to be given for it. It was only a little worse than having to face the fact of Peter's denial and allow that a place in the narrative of Holy Week. It reminds us that the Christian story is a very down-to-earth story that is full of human failings as well as divine victory.

John Le Carré once wrote that betrayal can only happen when you love. If that is true, then Judas no less than Peter will have loved Jesus. It is, of course, speculation, just as is any attempt to discover what motive Judas had for the betrayal of his master, his rabbi, his friend. There is no more than a hint that it was out of greed – out of that love of money that is said to be the root of all evil. Luke can do no better than to suggest that it was

185

a kind of possession that overtook Judas: 'Satan entered into Judas.' The implication is the same – Judas was given over to evil. In *Star Wars* terms, he went over to the dark side. He abandoned the one who was 'the light of the world' and sided with the enemy. He not only joined the other side; he was prepared to use his knowledge of Jesus' whereabouts to hand him over to the authorities. His would be the hand of betrayal, his would be the kiss to give proof of identity.

Judas was a companion of Jesus – one who shared bread with him. As they met for the Passover meal he reclined near to Jesus, even possibly in the place of the distinguished guest – the place Peter might have expected for himself. Certainly he was close enough to Jesus and John for their conversation not to be heard by the whole gathering. We don't know whether it was supernatural foreknowledge or just perceptive understanding of a man's character, but Jesus was not surprised by the fact of betrayal. At the shared meal during which, on this Passover occasion, hands were dipped into the common dish, Jesus revealed that he knew what Judas was up to. Some form of arrangement had already been made with the Jewish authorities and whatever it was that Judas had to do he now had to do it, and quickly. Jesus, who was about to be handed over, still had a controlling hand on events. What was happening was understood to have been foretold and part of the divine strategy.

There is a necessary tension in the Gospel accounts. On the one hand the writers believe deeply that what was about to happen was by God's action, his plan, his intention. They do not see the Passion as some ghastly catastrophe that overtook a hapless Jesus, determined by the efforts of paranoid and despotic rulers. That would empty it of its theological heart whereby it is Jesus' and God's self-giving that is at the centre of events. A search of the Scriptures reveals that the hints and clues are already there, set out beforehand. What was about to happen had to happen. But on the other hand, that did not excuse the acts of those who betrayed, and shamed, and scourged, and crucified the Son of Man. The perpetrators still had to bear their responsibility. They made their choice; they weren't forced into it. They remained human beings, not robots in some divine puppet theatre. That Jesus would be handed over may have been in accordance with what had been written, but it was still 'woe' to him who carried out the act of betrayal.

If we are feeling very honest, and perhaps being a bit hard on ourselves, we might well admit that there is something of Peter in us – that ability to back down in our acknowledgement of Jesus when the going gets too embarrassing, too rough. We might be caught out by a conversation at the pub or in the office when to admit to being a follower of Jesus is to be the object of ridicule or simply to be written off as an irrelevance. We hide our light under a bushel and hope that no one will see it. It may be denial but it's not betrayal. Betrayal is something altogether different. Who would like to think of themselves as a Judas? The very phrase is degrading.

Yet perhaps we are more like Judas than we imagine or would care to admit. If betrayal is to hand over the things of Jesus to the realm of 'evil', then is not every prejudice, every unjust act, every act of revenge or retaliation that is carried out in the name of our religion, an act of betrayal? It is not seen as that, of course. We claim that we are standing up for the truth, that we are being beacons of the light, maintaining the standards of the gospel, and yet we can do so in ways that Jesus would never have recognised as belonging to his way. We may admit that in the past Christians have done terrible things in the name of their religion: crusades, inquisitions, witch-hunts. But we delude ourselves if we think there are no contemporary betrayals. We share the bread of Christ and fail to share with the poor. We sit by his side but fail to make room for others of whom we disapprove. We greet him with a kiss and denounce those whose love of Jesus takes different forms. And the responsibility is ours. We have gone out into the night.

18. The Last Supper
(Matthew 26:17-19, 26-30; Mark 14:12-16, 22-26;
Luke 22:7-23, 39; John 13:1-17, 31b-35)

The table is prepared

We don't have to have an excuse to have a meal together, of course, but it's quite common for a meal to be the way we mark an event – just think of regimental dinners, works dinners or wedding receptions. To understand what is really happening you need to know more than just what is on the menu. So it is with this meal – this Lord's Supper, this Eucharist, this Mass, and especially on this occasion when we recall the last supper that our Lord had with his friends.

Jesus' friends thought they knew what the meal was all about. They had been brought up to know about it and to look forward to celebrating it on a visit to Jerusalem at the time of the feast. They may well have heard the youngest son ask the head of the house why it was they were sharing this meal, what it all meant. No Jewish family would have been in doubt about the meaning of the meal that Jesus is said to have shared with his friends.

For generations, Jewish people celebrated Passover as a way of recalling their origins as a people of slavery and a people whom God had rescued. At the meal the family would recall the story of how their ancestors had gone to Egypt during a time of famine, how they had become enslaved by the powerful pharaohs and been driven into forced labour to satisfy the desire for grand palaces and mighty tombs. And they would hear of Moses, the boy rescued by Pharaoh's daughter and brought up at the court, and how he had become a spokesman of the Hebrew people in their plight. Through Moses and his brother Aaron, God brought plagues upon the Egyptians and then made arrangements for the Israelites to leave Egypt in a great act of rescue – an Exodus.

The Passover meal each year was a time not only for recounting the story of God's wonderful act of rescue but also for showing through the very meal itself something of the meaning of the story. They would break bread to remind them of the crusts that were all an enslaved people had to eat. The bread was unleavened, made without yeast because it was made in a hurry on the night of escape. The sauce that they dipped their crusts into was like the clay from which the bricks were made. And, most important of all, there was the whole lamb whose sprinkled blood had been spread on the lintels of the doors to show that this was a Hebrew home when the angel of death swept through the land of Egypt. Prayers were said and psalms were sung as the people's history and the events of the Exodus were recalled.

This was the meal Jesus and his friends were sharing that evening. They knew that this was the reason for coming together. What Jesus was to show them was a different meaning, one they didn't really grasp at the time –

that this was the final Exodus and a new Passover. This was the night of a rescue even greater than that of the Hebrew people from Egypt. Jesus had called them together for the ultimate Exodus meal.

As the table is prepared we are called to prepare our hearts and minds to discover anew the meaning of this meal – the Lord's Supper, the Last Supper, the Exodus meal.

Washing the feet

Water in the Exodus story was involved in warning, in rescue and in judgement.

Pharaoh, we are told, did not easily give in to Moses' request to let the Hebrews go. They were, after all, a significant workforce, part of the pharaonic economy not only financially but also part of what kept the power and memory of the pharaohs before the people. They were part of the workforce that built the great palaces. Big buildings are statements of wealth, power and status. They always have been. These days it's not individuals so much as corporate businesses that create the biggest, the tallest, the grandest buildings to show how important they are.

Moses had warned Pharaoh that there would be trouble. Pharaoh did not heed the warnings and Egypt suffered a whole series of plagues – flies, locusts, frogs, boils, hail. And to set it all off Moses had struck the water of the Nile with his staff and it had turned to blood. It stank. Pharaoh paid no attention to the warnings.

The water of the Red Sea was a boundary between the fertile delta of Egypt and the desert to the north. Rivers are so often territorial boundaries – between countries, between counties, between villages. There are plenty of examples around Kent; which side of the Medway you are born on, for example, determines whether you are a Kentish man or a Man of Kent. So it was significant for the Hebrew people to get across this stretch of water – it was not only a boundary but also an obstacle. The story of the parting of the water was yet further evidence for the Hebrew people that their exit from Egypt was no mere running away but was rescue by the hand of God. The parting of the water that had made the Israelites' escape possible was now reversed and the sea became water of judgement upon the Egyptian armies. The Exodus was an act of God's power – rescuing his people from the pagan people. And in time he would lead them to a promised land.

Jesus' act of washing the disciples' feet was more than a piece of domestic hygiene. It was a deeply symbolic act. It was, of course, a sign of humble service. Washing feet was the job of the lowliest servant in the house and, as *Upstairs, Downstairs* on TV decades ago taught us, the hierarchy of servants is every bit as detailed and rigid as the hierarchy of masters and mistresses. Jesus was setting an example to his disciples of the true nature of his kind of leadership – the servant leader, rather than the status leader. But his words to Peter make it clear that there is something more to this than getting the dust of the day off your feet. Washing is both a judgement upon dirt and uncleanness and a cleansing and renewal of the one washed. The washing Jesus gave is a sign of the forgiveness that he offers. It was a sacramental act –in John's terms, a kind of baptism. The Israelites passed through the waters from the slavery of sin to the freedom of the promised land, the freedom of the kingdom. What we have here is a sign by Jesus that he was the one through whom the promises to Israel were finally being fulfilled – a promise of Exodus, of forgiveness.

It was an Exodus act in an Exodus meal.

Bread

Bread and wine were part of the highly symbolic Passover meal. The Israelites ate unleavened bread because on the night of the Exodus there was no time to wait for the dough to rise. It was a matter of urgency. This was fast food Hebrew- style because there was no time to be leisurely about it. Crusts of bread were broken as a sign of the small broken pieces of bread that the slaves of Egypt were given – never a whole loaf for oneself. One is reminded of images on television of scraps shared by desperate refugees, of little fistfuls of bread or meal crammed into the hungry mouths of children in the camps of the desperate.

The bread on the table at the Last Supper would have been unleavened, and Jesus would have broken it as was done at every Passover. But in breaking this bread, at this time, in his way and with his words, Jesus did more than repeat the Passover story – he was creating his own new Passover story. For what this broken bread was now to symbolise was not the broken bread of slavery but the broken body of release, of exodus. Although the disciples could not take it in, he was showing them that he would be broken. 'This is my body that is for you.' He would not be broken as a failed victim but as the one through whom God would achieve the final act of exodus for his people – to bring them out of all the slavery of their past wrongs, their times of idolatry and disobedience. In and through Jesus, God would bring about his final act of rescue for Israel and for all.

Wine

Four cups of wine were offered and drunk at the Passover. It was the third one, when the meal was over, that Jesus took and reminded the disciples of the promises God had made to the Hebrew slaves that he would rescue them. It was called the cup of blessing, and with it thanks were offered to God for all his blessings. Jesus offered thanks not just for the blessings of the past but for those to be achieved through him on the cross. It was the wine of thanksgiving, Eucharist.

Just as his body would be broken for them, so his blood would be poured out for them. It is the language of sacrifice. The blood of the lamb sprinkled on the doorposts meant life for the Hebrew people when the angel of judgement swept across Egypt. My blood, Jesus told his friends, is God's way through which life will be offered, new life, life that leads us out of the past and into the final promised land of God's kingdom. Jesus shared the cup and told them all to drink of it. It was a cup of fellowship. In sharing it with Christ they would share in the benefits of his death. But they would also share in his life of service and obedience and, if necessary, share his cup of suffering.

When we eat and drink in the context of this account of Christ's self-offering, we share in the new life that his broken body and poured-out blood make possible. We join in fellowship with him and with one another, and we join in a commitment to follow him, whatever the cost.

19. At the foot of the cross

The feet of Christ (Mark 15:1-24)

We stand, as it were, before the cross and look on Christ. We come with heads bowed, drawn by him yet fearful and uncertain of what we shall discover here. We hardly dare look up. It is painful. Slowly, gradually, we do look up – to see his feet, his hands, his head. And these will be the focus of the three meditations – the feet, the hands, the head of our crucified Lord. Each will speak of mystery and strange paradoxes we cannot resolve, only hold together and know that here lies truth somewhere beyond our glimpses and our yearnings, and we would not want it any other way.

We stand, then, before the cross, and as we look up we see the feet of Christ. The shock of it. That they are nailed down. Six-inch spikes. Sharp, rigid iron, splitting flesh and bone. Fixing him there. Pinning him down. The Gospels in their accounts spare us the horror of the physical suffering. It was real nonetheless. That anyone could think of doing such a thing to another human being! The pain and the horror – they too are real. Yet thousands suffered that way, and cruelty in the name of law and order still persists throughout our world. Tortures have not ceased. Daily, almost, we are made aware of them through our newspapers and the television. These feet of Christ stand torn and bleeding where many have stood, and still stand. He is pinned to the common lot of our suffering.

That is mystery. But not just in suffering. That Christ should share in all our common experience, the one who went about amongst us – that, too, is mystery. He went about and walked the streets and the hillsides, the pathways and the hallways of our common life. And he walks with us still, if we would be aware of it. Journeying feet, the feet of a man on the move, a pilgrim and a wanderer, the feet of one who went about all over the place – he did not settle for a sedentary life.

He went to the places of ordinary people, to the bad places where the respectable do not go, to the bad places where sickness and madness and death make entry uneasy. He went to the places of celebration and joy, the places of prayer and retreat, the places of power and religious controversy. The feet now so cruelly pinned down, restricted, fixed, are the feet of a man who went freely to share common cause with men and women. He was the one who walked so freely where his destiny led him. He brought freedom to others so that they could make their way where before they had been unable. For some, like the paralytic, this was literally so – and in their new-found freedom they leapt and jumped for joy. For others he brought freedom from the disgrace of sickness, from the shackles of guilt, from the oppression of mental illness. Freedom to walk in new ways, freedom to walk tall. Freedom to walk along the path he trod, though they had no idea it would lead to such a desperate place as this. Freedom to run away, to leave, to desert, to go another way. The freedom to be human – to make choices and to walk in the way of those choices.

Jesus, who was so much his own man, treading the path he chose, was also the one who walked the way of obedience, the path of God's choosing. He took the road he was called to take. Having freely given that obedience he could walk no other path – he would tread it to the end, even along the Jerusalem streets and into the quarry beyond the wall, to Skull Place. Freedom is not anarchy, the liberty of the Gospel is not running around just where we want. True freedom is obedience to walk the paths of God, to follow the Way, the path of Jesus. As we look on those torn and bleeding feet, shall we be surprised if our own path is sometimes hard, with no guarantees of ease or safety?

It could have been different, of course. He need not have come this way at all. He could have ducked out at any time. Once he knew the authorities were out to get him he could have turned around and gone off quietly to grow hollyhocks! No fuss, no fluttering of the imperial feathers. There were certainly some who would have preferred a quieter life, less confrontation, a different route. At the end, when he set his face to travel up to Jerusalem, it put the wind up some of his followers. Some left then. Later all would run away.

There were some who glimpsed where it was leading; they feared for him yet also caught something deeper. They would offer all they could to honour that. The woman who brought her jar of expensive ointment and broke it over him, who washed his feet with her tears and wiped them with her hair. She caught something of that mystery which bound this free man to go this way. Her act of love and honouring pointed to the mystery of his dying pathway, a death of so much more significance than just a criminal's bad end. So, too, did his act of love, as he took the towel and bowl of water and washed his disciples' feet. The way of obedience is the way of service, and the servant does whatever is needed.

That God should be this involved; that in Jesus he should come to walk with us; that God the totally free should be bound by his love to submit to whatever we do to him; that God should be discovered here, cross-tied, nail-pinned – that is mystery. That we can find the way of freedom here at a place of submission, of obedience – that, too, is mystery.

To stand here and know our part in driving in those nails is to admit the power of our inhumanity. That we come here and meet with God is to know the cost of his forgiveness. At the feet of Christ the two meet – and this is a saving mystery.

The hands of Christ (Mark 15:25-32)

As we stand at the foot of the cross we look up and see at the cross-beam his arms outstretched, his hands spread wide.

The surrealist artist Salvador Dali painted a number of religious paintings, but the best known must be his picture of the crucifixion, looking not from below, from our point of view as it were, but from above, from God's viewpoint. One small detail is easily missed in that picture. There are no nails pinning the Christ to the cross. The fingers cast shadows but there are no nails. It's not how it was, of course, but Dali conveys a truth. It was not what the soldiers did to Jesus that put him and kept him on the cross. It was not Pilate's judgement or the religious leaders' scheming which finally got him where they could control him. At the final count, Jesus was there because he had to be there – not by his own desire, particularly. Certainly not by some masochistic death wish. He was there because he had to be – love demanded it. Wide-armed, all-embracing, all-offering love. Jesus would have stretched out his arms any day of the week to embrace others – the sad, the guilty, the sick, the outcast, the accused, the dying. Love's outstretched arms. This surely was his way, his message, his sign of the loving Father whom he served. But love so open is vulnerable, open to attack, unshielded. Arms that stretch out to all and sundry end up torn and nailed by those who cannot face such openness, those who cannot believe in such generosity, those who fear such appealing open-handedness. They feel threatened by such giving. Love's outstretched welcome, encompassing all, gets pinned to a cross in this world of ours when it won't back down, draw in, limit its embrace to what is reasonable, legal and respectable. But Jesus was not reasonable. He would not make the law his final arbiter. He cared little for respectability – either social or religious. He showed love – unstinting, unconditional, all-honouring, demanding love. Such love was bound to come to this end. It was Jesus through his giving that put him on the cross much more than any nails beaten through his wrists and into wood.

He took children in his arms when others tried to send them away. He wanted all to have that same childlike delight in the open embrace love offers, the warmth of a generous cuddle. It is we who make God too serious, too sombre, too stand-offish for us to receive his cuddle. We are not childlike enough, and such loving embarrasses us when what it wants is to embrace us.

These hands were the giving hands – the caring hands willing to touch the untouchable, to hold the unhealthy, to embrace the unacceptable. Hands to hold us.

And yet this is only half the truth. Do not let go of it, this loving, giving care of Christ – it is shown to us on the cross in those arms and hands outstretched. But there is more to see, another side, a different dimension. For Jesus was not only the gracious giver. He was also a joyful and gracious receiver. He gave love, but how could he have done that had he not first received it – from Mary, from Joseph, from friends, from God. He had received Mary's loving care as a child. At the outset of his ministry he went to John to ask for and receive baptism. He was cared for by the Bethany sisters, and when he was tired and thirsty he was glad to receive a drink of water from a foreigner. The hands that gave so freely, so graciously, were also the hands of gracious receiving.

We, too, are called to be giving and receiving people – and to be gracious in both. We have every reason to believe that the Lord loves a cheerful giver. It is sometimes forgotten that there is also a graciousness in being a cheerful receiver. To accept from others is to admit dependence, to admit that we have needs, to admit that others are in a stronger position than we are. To receive is to honour the other person's wish to give. It is not because we have innate worth that we can offer ourselves to God; it is his receiving of our offering that gives us worth. We affirm one another, love one another, not only in our giving but also in our receiving. But the hands that gave and received remind us, too, that at a deeper level there is an even more telling mystery. Jesus was willing to be handed over. His openness in love, his graciousness in receiving, made him vulnerable to what no escape hatch. As he gave us his love he gave to us also the freedom *not* to love, gave us the freedom to treat him any way we liked. We are free to respond to his love or not, and that freedom is our awesome responsibility. We can do with him what we will.

And this is at the heart of his Passion. Jesus was willing, prepared to be handed over. It is what is meant when we say he was betrayed by Judas. He was handed over to the leaders, to Pilate, to the crowds, to the soldiers. They could do what they liked to him. In receiving him into their hands, their actions judged not Jesus but themselves.

They handed out a fiasco of a trial. Mockery and violence. He took it all and, as it were, held the evil, gripped it, let no part of it escape into resentment, into retaliation. The evil is held and the pain is all the greater. Hitting back when we are hurt seems to ease our pain. To hold on to it, to transform cruelty, misunderstanding, jealousy, stupidity, to melt it with forgiveness – that is more painful, that is love's aching agony. That is the fearful cost of receiving evil and forgiving it. The suffering on the cross is *not* some awful punishment that God inflicts on Jesus so that he can then love us. The cross's true suffering is love's agony at taking all the evil the world hands out and giving back forgiveness. This is the cost of the cross – the cost of receiving, giving and forgiving. It is the cost to Christ, the cost to God.

The head of Christ (Mark 15:33-39)

The Gospels tell us nothing about what Jesus looked like physically. That hasn't stopped countless artists giving us their impression of him. The TV series *Son of God* produced a clay bust of him, giving him the appearance of a typical Jew of the time. How unlike the usual portraits. Statues, crucifixes, stained glass and paintings all portray him. As often as not they tell us more about the artist or the culture of the period than they do about Jesus' actual looks. It matters little, for he is the universal man and portraying Jesus as black is no less true than portraying him as white, and no less wrong.

But as we look at him this Good Friday, it is the bowed head we now think about, not the colour or look of his eyes, or the shape of his mouth or nose.

The head is bowed and there is blood upon it where the thorns dug in. The soldiers twisted some thornbush twigs together and jammed it on his head. That it hurt was hardly the point. Thorns add little to physical suffering when you have had your back scourged raw with metal-tipped ropes. It was there as mockery, like the board above his head bearing the accusation 'The King of the Jews'.

But is it not possible that Jesus felt some sympathy with their mocking? Such a crown was also a self-mockery. Throughout his ministry, and no doubt for years before it, he had lived under the conviction of the truth of his faith in his loving Father and the destiny he had been called to. He had lived with it, lived it out, remained true to it, never compromised it even though he had prayed he might be spared its consequences. He had preached of the rule of the loving Father, his coming kingdom already dawning. But nailed against a crucifixion post, fighting for breath, humiliated and scorned, deserted by friends and followers, such faith stretches thin. A circlet of thorns is not much of a crowning achievement. Hardly the garland of the new age.

Of Christ's inner turmoil we know little, but Mark gives us one stark and terrifying glimpse. In a loud shout of anguish Jesus called out to question why the God he had served had deserted him. Defeat at the hands of men was also desolation at God's deserting. There is an austerity in the telling of this moment. Jesus the man of faith had no certainties, no guarantees, no divinely-given assurance that all would be well for him. He had only faith, and faith offered only an empty void at that moment. Mark gives us no reassuring outcome. Christ's final shout was for him no renewed moment of trusting. It is to Luke we have to go for that. For Luke the end comes in trust, not desolation. 'Father, into your hands I commend my spirit' (Luke 23:46).

The one does not cancel the other. They are both there; both are the cries of the man for whom there is no certainty beyond faith. The God who is felt as the forsaking God, the absent Father, is also the only one there is to trust. Faith has both experiences, and if Jesus did not know them then he is not much use to me or to you.

When Dame Julian of Norwich had her vision of Christ crucified she recounted that she saw a garland of thorns on his head. We would call it a crown. It catches the ambiguity and the mystery of the Passion. For it isn't just the mocking circlet placed on the head of a defeated pretender; it is also the crown that best expresses the victory of all that Jesus and God in Jesus achieved.

So often we speak as though it is the power of God that is most important. Too often we address him as Almighty. It is assumed that God can do everything, that there is no limit to what he can do. But it is not power that is the crowning characteristic of God. Like everything else about the cross, the crown of thorns reminds us that the victory is not the victory of power at all. It is the victory of love. You may call it love's power if you like, but it is not naked power, the power that dominates.

We have too often talked of God's omni competence as though he can do anything he likes, as though that were the very mark of God. Of a god it might be; of the God and Father of Jesus it is not. God our Father cannot do everything. All he does, and is, is love – and there are things that love cannot do. He could not win by power, for the victory had to be love's victory. Jesus experienced the force of the temptation to follow the way of power at the very start of his ministry. It would no doubt have assured him of quicker results, but he resisted power's lure, refusing to sell out to the demon of power. Love was the source and the way and the means and the end of all that he had to do, if he was to be obedient to God.

Love does not coerce, it does not manipulate, it does not enforce. It has to be open and offer invitations; it has to allow others freedom, even to be rejecting and mocking. Love's submission can appear like defeat, but in remaining true to itself love proves to be the victor.

The thorn-torn head of Jesus is crowned with glory – the two come together. It is not just that Easter will bring vindication, a reversal of the tragedy. This tragic end is itself glorious; this defeated king is himself victorious. The victim Jesus is also the conqueror. It is only faith that sees it so. It is only faith that risks the depth of desolation of God deserting us and also trusts to his loving purposes to hold us finally safe. Faith knows these things, but there are no guarantees. Jesus knew he could be wrong, and so could we.

Nina Simone, the black jazz singer, wrote a song after Martin Luther King's death. 'The king of love is dead', she sang. Wherever love lives true to itself the divine is present. And in living true to love we all share in the glory and the kingship of Christ. Few of us are called to risk so much, but it is as we look at the dying Lord, the Lord of all love, it is in his crowned head we see the glory of his kingship. It is a kingship not of certainty but of faith, not of power but of love. That love should have to suffer is the tragedy of our human failing. That love is victorious through the suffering is the source of all our hope.

So Jesus breathed his last and with a loud cry gave up the ghost. The King of Love is dead.

20. Resurrection
(Matthew 28:1-15; Mark 16:1-8; John 20:1-10)

The vast majority of people, though not all, have no difficulty in believing that Jesus actually existed, lived in Israel / Palestine about two thousand years ago, went about preaching and teaching and ended up executed by crucifixion. They may not believe that such a death was anything more than a tragic end to a good man, but they consider that the basic events of Jesus' life and death fit with what they believe could have actually happened. They are credible enough. It's the kind of thing that happens so long as you don't start adding extra bits to them about virgins, and miracles and so on. It does not challenge most people's world view.

When it comes to the Resurrection it is quite a different matter. The claim that Jesus, having been put to death and buried in a garden cave-tomb, was then raised and seen alive again by numerous friends, stretches credibility and threatens to break it. It's just not how the world works. You would need a great deal of practise to believe such an impossible thing, even after breakfast. Of course there are stories about people dying and then being resuscitated – but that is quite different. There are also accounts in the gospels of Jesus bringing people back from the dead – Jarius' daughter, the widow of Nain's son, Lazarus. But these can be explained as stories that were told to boost Jesus' reputation or may be simply ignored. They don't count as evidence that such a thing as the Resurrection ever actually happened.

And yet belief in the Resurrection appears to be central to the Christian faith and was pivotal in the emergence of the Christian Church from out of its Jewish origins. For many Christians it is such a part of their faith that it has never been doubted. It may puzzle. It may raise questions. But it has been accepted. For some it is so impossible to square with how they feel this world, this space and time universe, works that they look for other explanations. So it is suggested that the Resurrection was not a physical matter at all but a spiritual one. The body of Jesus did what all bodies do; decomposed and turned to dust. But his spirit, his influence, the sense of his presence was so powerful to his friends that it was a living reality in their lives. Jesus lives – in the heavenly places and in the hearts of his followers.

His 'Resurrection' assures us that we too will have life after death and join him in heaven. Stories of empty tombs and bodily appearances were simply the early Church's way of conveying the mystery and power of this living promise, assuring people that Jesus was alive.

For a person of faith this way of looking at the Resurrection is credible. It may be mysterious and awesome, but credible. In a world where God is a reality, a spiritual reality, there is nothing incredible about the Spirit of Jesus being brought back from the power of death. It's the kind of 'happy' ending we would look for after the tragedy of Jesus' death. Our own spiritual experience supports this, for we experience Jesus as being alive, a vital factor in our lives.

But we have to ask the question; does such a 'spiritual' explanation do justice to the faith of the early Church, the teaching of the New Testament and to the radical nature of what the Resurrection means? And if it doesn't, then are we simply left with trying to swallow what is incredible?

Ever since the Enlightenment we have been bombarded with the view that for something to be true it must be repeatable. It's the way scientists work – repeating experiments to check that the result is the same. But by its very nature the Resurrection of Jesus is a one-off event. It is part of what makes it so incredible. And post-Enlightenment scepticism encourages us all to question a unique event – especially when it comes to claims within a religious setting. Of course, if we want to explore what the Resurrection means and what led to the claims that Jesus had been raised, then we shall want to ask questions. But that is not the same as dismissing it as a historical event just because it was unique. It's the nature of significant historical events to be unique. They are one-offs. They cannot be repeated exactly, because the situation has moved on. The discipline of historical study knows this and has ways of distinguishing between accounts of unique events and accounts of fantasies and fabrications.

And the Resurrection was a unique, historical event. It took everyone by surprise. Those who went to the tomb that early morning did not know what to make of it. The stone had been removed – but by whom and why? The body was not there. Who had moved it? Where had they put it? Mary Magdalene could only assume someone had stolen the body, the gardener perhaps. Resurrection as something that involved only one person was not simply incredible, it just didn't occur to the disciples as a possibility. The only resurrection they could have understood was the resurrection of all faithful Jews at the last day. Others, the dazzling figures in white, would have to point them in the right direction.

In Mark's account the reaction of the women is one of terror. Was it fear of the unknown or something even more powerfully primitive than that? Even though they had been told to give a message to the disciples, fear prevented them. Women, of course, were not considered to be credible witnesses. They had no standing in establishing what events had occurred. They could not be sure they would be believed. The Gospel accounts do not hide the fact that whatever it was that had happened, it was not always immediately understood, did not automatically produce faith. There was fear and doubt, not only that first morning but later as well.

The authorities had their own concerns. They didn't understand what had happened but they were certainly not going to be blamed for it. The immediate problem was the lost body. While the women thought others had stolen it, the authorities put it round that it was the disciples who had come and taken it. They were trying to cover their tracks. Why the disciples would want to take the body is unclear. Was it a trick to convince themselves and others that because the tomb was empty Jesus was alive again? If so, it was a shaky foundation. That such a trick could have resulted in the development of the early Church with all that meant in terms of persecution and martyrdom, is truly incredible.

But the empty tomb is of course highly significant. If the tomb was not empty then the Resurrection as the disciples came to understand it could not have happened. For the Resurrection faith of the disciples was a belief that Jesus had risen bodily – not simply spiritually. If the body had still been there it just could not have been a 'resurrection of the body.' And yet this was what they came to believe. What was incredible came to be essential to their belief, their credo.

21. Emmaus (Luke 24:13-33)

Over the centuries there have been many attempts to identify exactly where Emmaus is. At one level it is part of the age-old tourist business. Every attempt is made to identify places mentioned in the story of Jesus so that pilgrims can visit them, revere them and spend money at them.

On the road from Jerusalem to Jericho, for example, there was even an inn of the Good Samaritan! At another level it is the search for the place of the holy which is part of every pilgrim's search – a focus for the things of God where we take time to reflect, and pray and be met by the Lord.

There are four places that have at various times been identified as the place the companions journeyed to that Sunday afternoon. I mention just two. As you leave Jerusalem by the road to the coast you travel about 5.5km to the first of the Emmauses at a place called Amatza. There is little to be seen and few stop. It is **the Emmaus of desolation**. The village that stood here had its significance in the defence of the road to Jerusalem. There was an Arab village there and it was destroyed in 1948 to secure the road. It is a dead place, there is hardly anything to indicate it ever existed. The other Emmaus is called Imwas. Eusebius (fourth century bishop of Nicomedia) and St Jerome (AD 342–420) were among those who recognised Imwas as the site of Emmaus – or to put it more cautiously, as the place where the Emmaus event was to be remembered.

Like Amatza it was a place of strategic significance controlling the major natural routes from the coast to Jerusalem. It was a place of many battles and many different groups have arranged their defensive positions there. At one time Imwas was a flourishing city and the Roman general, Vespasion, gave it the name of the City of Victory. You can still visit the ruin of the large Byzantine church that was put up in the fourth century and the smaller Crusader one erected in its ruins. Between them the city was wiped out, possibly by the plague, and the memory of Emmaus was all but lost. It has only recently been recovered. The Arab village of Imwas was totally destroyed by the Israelis in the 1967 war. There is a sad similarity between so much of this Emmaus and the Emmaus of desolation at Amatza. Yet although Imwas was ruined and has no place even on a map, it is not desolate, it does not speak finally of what is destroyed. It speaks rather of hope and promise, despite efforts to blot out the memory of there ever having been a village there. Imwas is the **Emmaus of reconciliation and of hope**. It is now part of a recreation area called Canada Park.

Imwas attracted two groups of people who, in a land torn so often by enmity and conflicting nationalistic aspirations, have sought to bring reconciliation. Above the ruined church is a Trappist community house and the monks, through their prayers and communal living, work for peace and reconciliation between Jews and Arabs. And under the guidance of a Dominican monk, Father Bruno, a small community called Neve Shalom (an oasis of peace) was established where Christian, Jewish and Moslem families live together as an example, a working model, of reconciled and reconciling people. In a country like Israel and a world like ours, hope hangs on such slender and fragile threads. They are pinpricks of light amidst much that is shadow and dark. The little thing that makes all the difference in the world. Today there are 50 families living at Neve Shalom. In the context of what is happening at this time in Israel-Palestine these two places where the Emmaus story has been remembered capture so much that is present in that story and which makes it so relevant for today. For the story is of a journey between desolation and hope and if that same journey is not made by Jews and Palestinians in companionship, in the presence of each other and in the fellowship of meals taken together, then there will be no future for either of them. Who, we might ask, will be their travelling companion today to help them see events in a fuller light, to be present with them as both guest and host?

The companions started their journey devastated by the events around the Crucifixion of Jesus. Their world had been destroyed, their hopes shattered. They set out in the afternoon and were travelling towards evening – into darkness. It is a common experience, these times when we feel ourselves to be heading into the darkness of anxiety, trouble, guilt or depression. Dark times surrounding us because of our own situation or the dark times of those we love or care about.

Why the companions could not recognise Jesus as the man who joined them we do not know – Luke hints that it was by supernatural forces. But it gave Jesus the opportunity to lead them in what amounts to a Bible study. They feared that his death was proof that he was not the Messiah they had hoped for. He showed them that the Scriptures actually say that suffering and death are the destiny of the Messiah. He brings to them the authority of the Word of God to help them see things in a new light. As they were later to explain, that warmed their hearts even as they travelled. It began to melt the icy despair that had gripped them.

What began with the Word was confirmed in the action at the meal. This account has its liturgical equivalent in the Word and Sacrament of Holy Communion. Invited to stay with the friends, the stranger seems to have taken charge – he acts as the host of the meal – taking the bread, saying the prayer of thanks over it and then breaking it to divide between those who were going to eat. In that very act recognition suddenly dawned – they knew it was Jesus and as they recognised him so he disappeared. His presence was now to be understood and experienced within the heart, not dependent upon sight and sound. In this way he could be present for all.

Their desolation had been turned to joyful hope. The journey on which they had set out into darkness and despair had been transformed into a journey to Resurrection light. This is a holy story that takes us way beyond fact to truth – to the mysterious, transforming truth of hope in the Resurrection.

22. The power of Resurrection life
(John 20:19-23; Luke 22:44-49; Acts 2:1-4)

The physicist describes power in terms of the equation $P=W/T$; power equals work over time. For the mechanical engineer work is the force acting on an object times its displacement. Philosophers speak of a person's ability to control the environment including the behaviour of others, and among psychologists, Adler made power the core element of the human psyche. Politicians exercise power in ways that can be seen as benevolent or malevolent. And Lord Acton, the historian and moralist, famously said, 'Power tends to corrupt and absolute power corrupts absolutely' (Letter to Bishop Mandell Creighton 1887). Religious power is not exempt from that tendency. Indeed, for people like Professor Dawkins it is seen as almost totally destructive.

It is therefore wise to be careful in approaching the question of the power that the Risen Lord gave or would give to his disciples, and by implication to the Church. Just as the word 'love' has distinctive meanings in the Christian context that can easily be missed under the assumption that Christians use the word much as the secular world does, the same might be true for the word 'power'.

In the context of the Resurrection events it is worth noting that power is mentioned in relation to Jesus' greeting of Peace. That word itself has a particular richness in the biblical vocabulary conveying as it does much more than simply the absence of aggression or anxiety. That would certainly have been relevant in the situation of the disciples hiding in the locked room for fear of the Jews. But the word's Hebrew origin of 'Shalom' went beyond this to speak of the desire for the harmonious well-being of the other person, of society and indeed of creation. In the Hebrew Scriptures this is one of the most frequently occurring concepts and one of the richest in meaning. In the Resurrection accounts it is the typical greeting of the Risen Lord and frequently appears in Paul's letters as he greets his readers. It has been taken up in the liturgy of the church with the Eucharistic sharing of the Peace. It is then in the context of his gift of harmonious well-being that Jesus speaks of power. When he endows power upon the disciples Jesus is not speaking of aggression, competition or self-seeking but of the exercise of influence, persuasion, authority for the sake of the other's well-being. The life that springs from the Resurrection, and is the gift of the Risen Lord, is in the strength of this kind of power and stands as a critique beside our more commonly understood and sought-after aspects of power.

From the accounts we have received we can detect that there are three main areas of power that Jesus has particularly in mind: the power to forgive, the power to understand revelation, and the power to speak out in witness. It is the power which is the gift of the Holy Spirit, breathed out upon the disciples and which from this time forward would abide with them and in them. Both John and Luke are quite clear about this association of power and Holy Spirit, although their accounts vary considerably in terms of both time and place. For John, we have it in the locked room in Jerusalem during the evening of the first Easter Day. For Luke, it is focused in the dramatic events of Pentecost some forty days later. But the underlying point is the same, although with different emphases.

For John, the gift of the Holy Spirit and the power to forgive is a gift to all the disciples and therefore to the Church. It is not only St Peter who has the power to bind and release (Matthew 16:19) but is given as part of the general apostolic authority. When Jesus had pronounced forgiveness to the paralysed man (Matthew 9:2-8) the scribes accused him of blasphemy, of abrogating to himself the authority of God's power to forgive. The effectiveness of his healing miracle was demonstration of the efficacy of his pronouncing forgiveness, not because this showed he was equivalent to God but because all forgiveness is God's and when it is offered appropriately it conveys the mercy and grace of God. The authoritative pronouncement of forgiveness is effective in releasing the guilty from their sin and from their guilt. This is the power the Risen Lord 'breathes' into his disciples.

It is more than just the formal announcement of forgiveness, it is the living power to bring about release and peace, that harmonious, spiritual well-being that affects the whole person. But for forgiveness to be the work of the Holy Spirit it requires more than simply sympathy for the guilty, more than a complacent 'that's alright, it doesn't matter.' Wrong does matter for it breaks down peace, breaks down harmony. And those who have the authority and the power to forgive, also need the discernment which is the Holy Spirit's gift to distinguish, to make judgements and to know when forgiveness is not the appropriate response – at least at that time, in the circumstances of the particular instance. Some people cannot be forgiven because they do not acknowledge they have anything to be forgiven for. Once they have come to a better self-awareness forgiveness is a possibility. Forgiveness, no more than love, can be forced upon someone. It is offered as a gracious possibility – and then waits for a response.

There is therefore the gift of discernment within the gift of power that the Risen Lord bestows upon his disciples, his Church. And this is picked up in the passage from Luke's Gospel. The Risen Lord opens the disciples' minds to the meaning of the Scriptures as they relate to him and the events surrounding Golgotha and the Easter Garden. What had been the experience of the two companions who had travelled down the road to Emmaus, was to be the experience of all the disciples. It was not simply that Jesus made plain things he had said to them in the months and years before his death. He also laid out before them the way in which the revelation contained in the Scriptures could be understood as relating to him.

This is much more than simply a question of taking various texts and interpreting them to show they predict events in Jesus' life and death. There is a danger in such attempts although it was one of the forms of scriptural interpretation that Paul, for example, often used. What was much more important was the awareness that the God who revealed himself and his purposes to the Hebrew people was the same God as the one Jesus proclaimed, revealed, obeyed and called Father. The disciples and the Church are heirs of that whole revelation which the Church was to draw together in the Scriptures known as the Old and New Testaments. The discernment which led to the creation of the canon of Scripture is the discernment sought by all who 'search the Scriptures' for the Word of God for them. It is the gift and the power of the Holy Spirit.

Such power was vital to the ongoing mission of the Church to the world in proclaiming the Gospel of repentance and forgiveness. What was happening in that room of frightened people to whom Jesus had spoken Peace, was to be repeated in the early Church and throughout Christian history as people opened themselves to the guidance of the Holy Spirit in the reading of Scripture. But it goes beyond a matter of personal enlightenment. It prompts and enables action. Out of their understanding the disciples were called to witness. It is the vocation of the whole Church, which means each individual member of the church as well. John had spoken of the power being breathed into the disciples. Luke speaks of the disciples being clothed in the power from on high. In the book of Acts, Luke was to use the symbols of wind and flame to convey the power of the coming of the Holy Spirit into the lives of the apostles. Its effect was to transform communication. Representatives from all over the world heard what was said and were able to understand. In biblical terms it was a reverse of the fragmentation of society that had been caused by the confusion of languages at the Tower of Babel. The power given to the disciples not only gives them courage and determination in telling the Good News, it makes it possible for all people to receive the Good News. Through the power given to the Church by the Risen Lord and present throughout creation, the whole world is able to 'hear' and receive that Peace of God that makes for its harmonious well-being. It is made possible by the gift of that power which pronounces restoration of broken relationships, with God and between peoples, which is able to discern the purposes of God and which bears witness to the work of God both by word and action.

It is power as soft as breath and as dramatic as a fiery storm. It is the power of Resurrection life.

23. Pride

Pride, we are taught, comes before a fall (Proverbs 11:2, 16:18). Some have described it as the devil's sin; others suggest it was what lay behind Adam's first act of disobedience. The image of the self-important person puffed up with pride is common in fiction and unpleasant in reality.

Religions generally are condemning of pride. As one of the seven deadly sins, it is often used synonymously with hubris, which is that inflated level of self-importance that is a failure to retain a proper humility and becomes an affront to the nature and status of God. This was Adam and Eve's failure – a self-regard that heightens the importance of the self beyond its proper value or beyond an esteem it has properly earned. As such, it is a sin against God and is considered pretentious by others.

In comparing pride with vanity, Jane Austen in *Pride and Prejudice* had this to say: 'Pride relates more to our opinion of ourselves, vanity to what we would have others think of us.'[1] Pride appears, in both religious and psychological aspects, to be a person's failure to have a proper evaluation of oneself. It is a failure of truth and of a proper self-knowledge. It can prevent the resolution of disputes and reconciliation even between friends. But, as Bob Dylan says, 'Swallow up your pride; you will not die, it's not poison.'[2]

We are taught that we should take pride in our work, and psychologists suggest that a lack of pride is damaging for our sense of self-worth and hence of a healthy self-image. Indeed, it may well be that a lack of such basic pride can in fact result in that defensive, bloated pride which is so widely disapproved of. A proper self-confidence keeps both failings and achievements in proportion without inflating either. Pride can then be an appropriate celebration of the gifts one has and the achievements made. The Christian view sees all people as having an intrinsic value and worth as a child of God. Such value and worth are recognised through faith and through the love and care of other people. We gain our self-worth, and hence a proper pride in ourselves, through good relationships with others. In turn, our love and care for them helps build their self-worth so that they, too, might have a proper, or virtuous, pride.

Pride, it seems, can be a bad thing, but so can too little pride.

---

1. Jane Austen (first published 1813), *Pride and Prejudice*.
2. Bob Dylan, 'Tombstone blues'.

We can have pride in others' achievements as well our own, and pride in one's country is socially valuable when it does not deteriorate into jingoism or racism.

The twin character of pride was noted by the eighteenth-century eccentric cleric and writer C. C. Colton: 'There is this paradox in pride – it makes some men ridiculous, but prevents others from being so.'[3]

24. Ambition

Ambition is often associated with aggressive competitiveness by which a person advances their own status, reputation or power at the expense of others. As such, it has rightly been viewed with suspicion by Christians. Such behaviour echoes what lies behind the disobedience of Adam and Eve in the Genesis story of creation where it was their desire to have the divine knowledge of good and evil that led to the Fall. Group ambition and aggrandisement is found in the story of the Tower of Babel. The people wanted 'to make a name for themselves' and this ambition led them to a massive building programme – a tower reaching to heaven. In each account God is said to have taken a dim view of what was happening and he punished the perpetrators – Adam and Eve were driven from the garden; the builders of the Tower had their language confused and were scattered all over the earth.

The ambitions of James and John (or perhaps more correctly their mother) were for them to have top places next to Jesus in his kingdom. This caused dissent with the other disciples and led Jesus to remind them that to be great they must first become a servant, after the example of the Son of Man (Matthew 20:20-28).

But ambition need not necessarily be seen as a bad thing. An honest acknowledgement of the gifts God has given a person may well lead to the desire, the ambition, to make use of those gifts as fully and effectively as possible. To do so may mean aiming high in one's profession or calling, seeking a position of influence where those gifts can best be used for the good of others. For all Christians, the ambition to exercise their gifts well is a good thing. Doing so at the expense of others is not.

---

3. C. C. Colton (first published 1886), *Lacon or Many things in a few words: addressed to those who think.*

25. Tolerance

The speaker at the conference shocked his audience of liberal-minded Christians by declaring, 'We are becoming too tolerant.' The majority of those present would have expected quite the opposite from him – as a society, they felt, we are becoming less tolerant. Jewish cemeteries and synagogues are desecrated, incidents of racial abuse are on the rise again, Islamophobia simmers in too many cities. The law may declare equal rights for women and for gay men and women but attitudes swing and appear to be hardening again. Fundamentalism in religion and politics seeks to sharpen the divide between those with 'correct' views and the rest. An increasingly vocal secular society no longer simply ignores Christianity as an irrelevance; it seeks to attack it.

There is no shortage of evidence that we have a long way to go before we treat everyone as being made in the image of God with an innate value and personal worth that should be honoured and respected, regardless of gender, race, religion or political allegiance.

Surely the ancient call that we should view each other in Christ as brothers and sisters undifferentiated as to whether we are 'Jew or Greek, freeman or slave' demands a spirit of positive tolerance. But that does not mean that all things should be tolerated. The very racism and homophobia that display a lack of tolerance are themselves attitudes that should not be tolerated. Those who worship a God of justice should not tolerate injustice. Those who worship a God who has consistently revealed a bias towards the poor should be intolerant of economic systems and government priorities that disadvantage the least well-off. Those who follow the one who declared himself to be the way, the truth and the life are challenged to exercise a righteous intolerance of falsehood and deceit in individuals and in institutions and an intolerance of all that diminishes the quality of life of God's children.

To be truly tolerant, the Christian has also to exercise a proper intolerance.

In their own words – biblical characters

1. Sarah – you must be joking!
(Genesis 18:1-15; 21:1-3)

You wouldn't think it to look at me now, but when I was younger I was considered something of a beauty. Abraham always said I was the best-looking woman in the whole family. He was really quite proud of me, the men all turning to look at me, the way they do. Mind you, that has its disadvantages and on a couple of occasions my looks made things difficult for us. Abraham was afraid the local rulers would kill him just so that they could get me, so we pretended we were brother and sister. They took me just the same. Not that anything happened, if you know what I mean. But it made things awkward.

But looks aren't everything, are they? I'd have been much happier even if I'd been plain and could have had children. Barren, they called me. It's such an empty, soul-destroying word. I can't begin to tell you what it made me feel. There was the shame of it – not just for me but for Abraham as well. He never said anything but I could see it in his eyes. It was as though I had let him down, let my family down. I had failed them all. I tried everything I could think of. The other women were always giving me advice, offering me potions and things. Made no difference. Every month I'd hope, and every month the same. I don't blame Abraham but he didn't help. Well, it wasn't so much him I suppose as those visions of his. He'd tell me about them. Just made matters worse. I mean to say, what would you think if your husband kept telling you he'd been promised by God that he would be the father of a great nation, descendants too many to count, and you not able to bear him any children. It was awful. I got really low about it. I got so desperate that I did something I really regretted later. But I didn't know what else to do at the time.

We'd been in Canaan for ten years or so and I had this servant, a nice little thing she was in her way. An Egyptian girl called Hagar. I just came out with it one day. 'What about Hagar?' I said to Abraham. 'What about her?' he asked. So I said he could have her, sleep with her, have a child by her. At least that would mean he would have an heir. If that was the only way he was going to be a father then so be it. It wasn't so strange really, not where we come from. So he did and that's when the trouble started. Once she got pregnant she just changed. All haughty she was, giving herself airs and graces, looking down her nose at me. Started telling me what to do even. How I regretted it all. It was even worse than before and I just couldn't stand it. I told Abraham so. But he just said I had to sort it. So I did, God forgive me. I made her life hell. She ran off into the wild places. I don't know what happened but she came back eventually – all submissive she was then and when she had a son Abraham called him Ishmael. So there he was, a dad at last. Well, to cut a long story short, things went on much the same for the next ten years or so. We moved around a bit and ended up at a place called the Oaks of Mamre, near Hebron. One day three strangers turned up. I heard my husband talking to them outside the tent and eventually he came in and told me to get them a meal.

I wasn't really paying much attention but I could hear them outside as they ate the meal. Then one of them said something that really took the biscuit. 'I'll come back this way in due course,' he said, 'and visit you again. And when I do your wife Sarah shall have a son.' Ha! I didn't know whether to laugh or cry. What a joke, at my age. They must have heard me laughing but I denied it of course. Frightened I was. They weren't like ordinary folk and they scared me a bit.

But it wasn't a joke. I got pregnant just as they had said. Couldn't believe it. Got me in a right state. One moment I was over the moon, the next I'd be worrying and all anxious. But how good it felt – my belly all rounded and as it should be. No more that empty void. I started smiling again, like I hadn't done for years. And the pain and the joy of his birth, it was marvellous. Here was the son I never thought I'd have. I cried and laughed and laughed and cried. And so did Abraham. This was no joke, this was a laughter that went right through me, filled my heart. We called him 'laughter', our son Isaac. He'd brought joy to my old age. No more a failure, no more shame. It was the Lord's doing. You don't know how good it felt.

2. Abraham – a terrible test (Genesis 22:1-14)

Ishmael was my firstborn. Ask any father how he feels about his first son and they'll all tell you, that one's special. I had thought I might never have a son, no matter what the Lord kept telling me. Sarah was a good woman but she failed to produce a son for me. In the end we came to an agreement and she gave me Hagar, her Egyptian maidservant. And that was how Ishmael came to be born. My first son. I thought I'd never get another. Sarah treated Hagar badly after that. I don't really know whose fault it was, six of one, half a dozen of the other. I told Sarah to sort it out. Hagar left for a while but then she appeared again and everything was OK for quite a number of years.

Then the miracle happened. Sarah fell pregnant, just as the Lord had promised. I should never have doubted of course, but it had gone on for so many years I suppose we'd got impatient. As special as Ishmael was it was nothing beside what I felt when Sarah gave birth. All the waiting, all the hopes, all the years of frustration – everything seemed to come together in that moment. There were tears, I don't mind admitting it. And lots of laughter as well. We called him laughter, it was Sarah's idea.

You'd think everything would be fine after that, but it wasn't long before the trouble started again. I don't know what gets into these women. Isaac was a toddler by then and he and Ishmael used to play quite happily together. Sarah didn't like it. I think she was afraid Ishmael would get the inheritance as well as her son. Jealousy's a terrible thing. I tried to explain but there was no reasoning with her. She wanted Hagar and Ishmael out of it. It really upset me, I can tell you. I didn't want to throw them out. Why should I? But she was adamant. Made my life a misery, she did. I talked with the Lord about it and he told me not to be so upset and I should do as Sarah wanted. Isaac was the son of promise and through him my descendants would be named after me. But Ishmael was my son too and because of that God promised he too would become a great nation. I trusted God so I sent Hagar and Ishmael away and the Lord did look after them. But for all that, he might just as well have been dead as far as I was concerned.

I've always trusted the Lord. Right from the beginning when he told me to leave my homeland and set out without even telling me where I would end up. You don't always see things his way at the time but eventually it works out. I just get a bit impatient. But what he asked me to do with Isaac was more than I could bear. How could he give me a son only to demand him back from me? To sacrifice my own son, my only son now that Ishmael was as good as dead. What would become of all the promises? Trust him, he said, but what a cost! We were used to offerings of calves and goats, even a bullock, and we gladly gave them to the Lord. But a son – who should be asked to make that sacrifice?

But ask he did and I didn't really have a choice. I didn't tell Sarah or the boy – just said that we were going off to a mountain where the Lord wanted me to worship with an offering. Going was bad enough. I just dreaded coming back without the lad. I took a couple of the men along and we had the donkey and the wood. There aren't always trees on those mountain places. We got near on the third day. I just knew it was the place.

I ordered the men to stay with the donkey while I took the lad with me. I put the wood on his shoulders. He had to carry the very means by which he would die. I felt terrible. Couldn't look at him. I went ahead with the fire and the knife. We made the altar just right and put the wood on it. It was then he asked me where the animal for the sacrifice offering was. What could I say? 'The Lord will provide,' I answered. And in a way of course he had, giving barren Sarah a son. Then I bound him. The agony of it. His pleading and his tears tore my heart in two. I took the knife and stared at the spot where I would plunge it. It glinted as I raised my arm.

'Abraham, Abraham!' rang through my head. A voice calling my name – urgent and insistent. I knew who it was. 'Here I am,' I said, like I always did, putting the knife down. I was to do no harm to the boy. It had all been a test, a terrible test. I had chosen right, put the Lord first, even before my son. But did he have to do it that way?

I saw a ram caught up in a thicket by its horns and we sacrificed that as a burnt offering. The Lord had indeed provided, so that's what I called the place: Jehovah Jireh – 'The Lord will provide'. No one should have to go through all that – to offer your own son as a sacrifice. No one.

3. Rebekah – you're my favourite
(Genesis 25:21-34; 27:1-41)

I don't know what it was about the women in our family but we all seemed to have trouble conceiving. I know that was true for Sarah, my husband's mother, and it was the same for me. Just too anxious to please, perhaps. Anyhow my husband, who's quite religious really, told me he prayed about it. I don't know if that made the difference but it wasn't long after that I got pregnant. I realise you don't want all the details but I can tell you it was no fun. First there was the sickness and then when the movements started you'd think all hell had let loose. I didn't realise at first of course that I was expecting twins. But they sure let me know about it. I felt like death. My husband suggested I asked the priest about it and he said that it was like the two were battling with each other. 'It'll be the younger one who comes out on top,' he said. How did he know that? But it was true. Over the years I've thought about that a lot.

It was twin boys, I had. But they could hardly have been more different. The firstborn was the strangest thing I'd seen – covered in hair all over, ginger I suppose you'd call it. We named him Esau. The other followed on straightaway, hanging on to his brother's heels. That's why we gave him the name Jacob. He was a lovely baby – all soft and smooth and so quiet and good. I know you should love both the same, but I have to admit he was always my favourite. Esau was his dad's favourite – a bit of a lad when he grew up, off hunting, and bringing his dad game he'd shot. Jacob was much quieter. He'd just get on with things, though you didn't always know what he was thinking. Some said he was a bit crafty. I suppose he was in a way. Got that from me, perhaps.

Like the time he put one over on Esau. Made me quite proud of him, the artful little beggar. But then Esau shouldn't have been so lax over his birthright. I know he was starving when he came in from the day's hunting but even so, to have promised Jacob he could have all the rights of a first-born just for the meal Jacob had prepared was plain stupid. But give him his due, Jacob saw his opportunity and took it. I bided my time but years later I clinched things for him.

Isaac was getting old by then, losing his faculties. He could hardly see, though his sense of smell was still pretty sharp and so long as it was well seasoned he could still enjoy a good meal. He knew he wasn't going to live much longer and one day he called Esau to him and asked him to go out hunting and make his favourite game stew with the kill. Then he would give him the blessing due to the eldest son. It was jolly lucky I heard this going on, I can tell you. Esau and those Hittite wives of his had been giving me a really rough time so I was in just the right mood to get my own back.

Anyhow, in no time at all I knew what to do. I told Jacob to kill a couple of young kids and I'd make them up into this really good stew, well seasoned just like Isaac enjoys. Then he could take them to his dad, pretending to be Esau, and get the blessing. 'It won't work,' he said. 'Dad's only got to touch me and he'll know immediately it's not Esau. I'm all smooth and Esau's rough and hairy.' But I'd worked that one out as well. I got hold of some of Esau's clothes. They were his best, but you could still smell his sweat on them. And then I cut up the kids' skins and made like gloves and a neckerchief of them for Jacob to wear. So when he went close to Isaac he would feel his hairy hands and if he embraced him, as I knew Isaac would, he would feel the hairs on the back of his neck. It worked like a dream. Even though he was a bit cautious, my husband was convinced by it and gave Jacob a wonderful blessing. We got out of the way quick, before Esau came home. He did all his dad had asked him to do but of course when he went in for the blessing Isaac realised what had happened: he'd been tricked. Esau was really upset, as you can imagine. He begged his father for a blessing. There wasn't much Isaac could do. All he could offer was the promise that he would serve his brother but eventually break free.

Esau was livid. He really hated Jacob then. The servants told me he'd threatened to kill him. So I made sure Jacob went away while Esau got over it. I got Isaac to agree that it wouldn't be right for Jacob to marry one of the local women like Esau had, and he saw the sense of that. So we sent him off to my brother Laban. It broke my heart to see him go – but I couldn't have him killed. He did all right for himself and to give him his due, Esau did get over it. I even hoped there would come the time when they would get together again and make things up. But Jacob would always be my favourite.

I heard he got religion in quite a big way. But you'd have to ask him about that.

4. Jacob – what a struggle (Genesis 32:22-32)

All my life I've been on the move and soon I will be making my last journey. I don't want to be buried here in Egypt. I want to go back with my ancestors. Joseph has sworn he will see to it. He's a good boy.

All in all, it's not been a bad life. God has blessed me. Mind you, I didn't have it easy. I had to stick up for myself. I've always been a fighter, battling against the odds, making sure of my place. At times that's only made things more difficult. I got the better of Esau my brother even though he was the older one. But it was only by being smarter than he was and I had to run for my life over that.

For twenty years I went and worked for Laban. Now there was a wily old bird. He tricked me over Rachel after I'd worked seven years for her. Palmed me off with Leah, he did, and got another seven years of work out of me. He was always changing the terms of my employment. Mind you, I got the better of him in the end. He'd done very well by me, no mistake. I'd built up his flocks. Good at it I was. And we agreed that for my wages I could have all the spotted and speckled sheep. Blow me if he didn't sneak them all off, leaving just the white ones that were his. But I knew a thing or two and bred speckled offspring from his best sheep. That got him, because they were then mine. He couldn't do anything about it.

In the end I chose my moment, packed the family up and just left. He didn't like that one little bit. Chased after me he did and in the end I had to make an agreement with him and we went our separate ways. God was good, you could say.

But to be honest that's been a struggle too, the faith thing. I've had to work at it. Or perhaps it was God working at me. Looking back I can pick out certain moments that seem to have made all the difference. There was that time on my way to Haran when I was getting away from Esau. I had this dream. It was as though there was a set of steps, or a ladder maybe, stretching right up into heaven with God's messengers going up and down. And blow me if the Lord didn't come and stand right near me. Really shook me it did, I can tell you. He promised to bless me and go with me. I woke up then. It was all so real it must have come from God. Awesome. I put up an altar there and called the place, the House of God, Bethel.

I suppose he did go with me – one way and another. He gave me a fine set of sons and he made sure Laban, the old cheat, never really hurt me. It was God who helped me over that matter of the speckled sheep and told me to leave Laban. Even Esau didn't pick a fight when we met up again. That was when I had a real struggle with the Lord. By the ford at Jabbock it was. I'd sent all the flocks and the household over the river and I was there on my own. Everything seemed to come to a head that night, about the Lord I mean. I knew I had to do things his way. But it was easy. There were things I wanted to do my way. Always had. And we battled it out all night. I was no push over. Well, you have to stand up for yourself. In the end it was only when he put my hip out that he won. I still have a limp. But I got a blessing out of him – and a new name. I'd struggled with God, face to face, you might say, so that's what he called me: Israel – he who strives with God. I did battle too – but, thinking about it, I'm glad he won. Taught me a lot that did.

Yes, looking back it's not been a bad life, not easy but OK – even for a crafty old devil like me. Better than I deserved!

5. Aaron – the pressure of leadership
(Exodus 32:1-35)

There are always people willing to criticise. Indeed there were times when he was downright unpopular. I might be biased because he's my brother, I have to say that without Moses we would never have made it. We didn't always see eye to eye, Moses and me, but overall he's a great leader, perhaps the greatest. He's not always been the easiest person to get on with, I'll grant you that. But he wouldn't be the person he is without a bit of edge to him, a bit of attitude. Actually, to be honest, it's more than that, he's got quite a temper. You wouldn't want to get the wrong side of him, and I should know.

He's always had it – that temper. Nice as you like most of the time, and then suddenly up it flares. He could be quite violent. In fairness there's usually good reason. Even in the early days while he was still a lad you could see it. Touch him on the raw, like in a matter of honesty or justice, and he'd go berserk. Killed a man once because he felt the man was being unfair to a Hebrew slave. He had to run for it.

I don't know where it came from, that temper. People have different ideas. I used to think it was because he sometimes found it difficult to get his words out. He knew what he wanted to say but the words would just get stuck. And then he could let fly. Perhaps it was frustration. I never had that problem. I always had the gift of the gab – didn't matter where I was or who I was with, I could always talk. You'd have thought he might have resented that, but he never did. Instead I became his sort of spokesman. We'd discuss what he wanted, like all those times we had to deal with Pharaoh, and I'd do the talking. He once said, 'I speak for God and you do the speaking for me.' Fair enough. It seemed to work, most of the time.

He even had a go at our sister Miriam on one occasion. But that was as nothing to the time he had a go at me. I've never seen him so angry. It wasn't my fault really. I didn't have a choice. He didn't know what the pressure was like when he went off up the mountain for his talks with God. All the responsibility fell on me and, as I said, there were always those who would have a go when Moses wasn't there. Good as a rebellion it was sometimes.

There was this time he'd been gone for ages. The people got restless, out there in the wilderness not knowing what was going to happen next. They talked about the old days in Egypt and you'd have thought from the things they said that it had all been a bed of roses. Ridiculous really. But they kept on at me and then it turned religious. They wanted something more tangible, more immediate than the God Moses was always on about. 'It's all right for him,' they said, 'we never really see this God – just clouds and things.' There had been amazing gods in Egypt. And the people round about, they had gods as well, gods you could see. Anyhow they kept on and on about it. How there was no one to lead them now and for all they knew Moses was dead.

I got so tired of it all I just told them to get me all their gold, their rings and bracelets and things and we'd put them in a furnace and see what happened. I made a mould of a calf like I'd seen somewhere, can't remember where. And there we were. We'd got ourselves a golden calf. 'That's our god,' the people said. 'Here's the one who brought us out of Egypt.' And because I was the priest they made me build an altar and I told them they could have a festival day. I thought it would be good for morale. I didn't think it could hurt. If it wasn't a real god then nothing could happen. If it was a god then it would help us through the wilderness. We made burnt offerings and sacrifices and the people had a great time. A bit too good really. It was beginning to get out of hand and then Moses appeared.

Was he angry? Dear Lord, he was beside himself. He told me later it had taken all his persuading to prevent the Lord from destroying all of us on the spot. But there he was. Magnificent and so angry. He'd got a couple of stone tablets in his hands. He'd been writing down God's rules for the people. He saw all the revelling and riotous behaviour going on and he raised the tablets over his head and sent them crashing down the mountain. It was terrible to see. He went for me something rotten. I told him the people had insisted and when we put the gold in the furnace this calf came out. In spite of all the excuses I realised, of course, I had made a terrible mistake – and so had the people. I knew there would be repercussions. The Lord wouldn't let it rest. How could he?

When Moses had calmed down he went back to the Lord to plead for us. For all his temper he always did his best for the people. He was a terrific leader. The Lord forgave us – but he didn't forget.

6. Naomi – a wonderful daughter-in-law
(The Book of Ruth)

You see that child over there, the one jumping up and down. That's my son, Obed. A fine boy. Well strictly he's my adopted son, my grandson actually. That's his mother standing by the table, she's called Ruth. Yes, I know what you're thinking: she's a Moabitess, not one of us. Well let me tell you that by her goodness and her love she has been blessed by the Lord and has entered the faith. So no more talk about foreigners.

Those whom the Lord blesses we should welcome and I couldn't have asked for a better daughter-in-law. I've never told you, have I?

It all began when my husband Elimelech and our two sons went to live in Moab. We didn't really want to go but what with the famine here in Bethlehem we had no choice. It was that or starve. My husband died not long after we arrived and I was left with the two boys. Then they married and for ten years we got on well. But when they too suddenly died I was devastated. It was as though the Lord had turned right against me. No husband, no children and no one to carry on the family name. I had no choice, I had to return here. I got very bitter and I don't know how I would have managed if it had not been for Ruth. Not that I expected her to come back here with me. I told both her and her sister-in-law Orpah that they should go to their own homes where they could get husbands to give them security. I wasn't going to have further sons for them to marry and even if I had they could never have waited. No, I told them straight and Orpah did go but Ruth insisted on staying with me. I'll never forget what she said.

'Where you go, I'll go,' she said. 'Your people will be my people, your God will be my God, where you die I will die.' She swore she'd never leave me. Well, what could I say? I never heard anything like it. She's an amazing young woman.

So we came back here to Bethlehem. Made quite a stir we did. But I told them I shouldn't be called Naomi, the sweet one, any more, rather they should call me Mara, Bitter. I had gone away full and returned empty. I felt very bitter about the way the Lord had dealt with me at that time. He had brought calamity on me. It's different now of course.

As I was saying, we came back here. It was harvest time. Ruth went out to the fields to pick up what she could behind the reapers. She ended up in the fields of Boaz, a rich kinsman of mine on my husband's side. You met him once, I think. She says it was chance that took her there but personally I think it was the Lord's doing. Boaz saw her and when he found out who she was, how she had left her own family and been so good to me, he treated her very well and called upon the Lord to reward her according to her goodness. He's a good man, Boaz. He told her to stay in his fields and to keep close to the other servants. I learned afterwards he even told the men to let her glean among the standing sheaves and not to molest her. You know what some of them can be like, especially with a foreigner. They think it gives them the right to do whatever they want. She did very well. That first day alone she came back with about a bushel of grain.

But I was worried for her in the long run. She needed security. So I told her to get dressed up and go down to the threshing floor and when Boaz dozed off after the evening meal, she should go to him and lie at his feet to show she would be prepared to marry him. You know how that goes, spreading her skirt out and uncovering his feet. It would mean the family name would not die out. I wasn't really sure how he would react but by all accounts it went well. He was a bit surprised to find her there when he woke but he took the hint and felt quite flattered that she should have chosen him rather than going off after the younger men.

There was just one fly in the ointment. There was a closer relative, one who had the responsibility for the family property and to look after the needy members of the family. Boaz had to sort it out with him first. So next morning he met up with him and in front of witnesses offered him the right to buy the bit of land Elimelech had had but told him that if he did, he would have to have Ruth as well. I think he laid it on a bit thick about her being a Moabitess and all that. Anyhow, be that as it may, the upshot was that the man found an excuse not to buy the land on those conditions. That left Boaz to take Ruth as his wife. It was a happy outcome all round. And the town elders approved as well, even giving them a wonderful blessing – comparing them to the mighty Judah and Tamar.

And then when the Lord gave Ruth a son it really was a blessing. To me I mean. I was no longer without a family. I nursed the little one. It was as though I had had another son of my own. Just watch him. Isn't he a lovely looking lad? The Lord has been good to us – so no more talk about her being a foreigner.

7. Samuel – not happy (1 Samuel 7-15)

This business about getting a king. I was never really happy with it.

In fact to begin with I was dead against it. But the people kept on insisting. It was partly because they feared the Philistines, partly because they knew other nations had kings and they wanted one for themselves. They thought it would solve all their problems. People can be very foolish at times!

They should have had more trust in the Lord. He was their King. He was their Ruler and Protector. I told them – this demand for a king merely showed their lack of trust in the Lord. It was all part of their disobedience, following the ways of other peoples, worshipping other gods. There was a time when they had made an effort. They had followed the Lord, begging me to ask him to protect them from the Philistines. I even got them to worship again in the proper way. And they could see it paid dividends. The Lord had protected them and had sent the Philistines packing. But the people are fickle. It did not take long for them to take up this call for a king.

They made an excuse, of course – said I was getting old and my sons were not up to the job. The fact is they were a big disappointment to me too. I had made them judges to follow me but they had no respect for the people or for God. They would take bribes and pervert justice. It reminded me of all the trouble old Eli had had with his sons. So I could see the people had a point. But I wasn't happy. Couldn't they be content with me? I went and spoke to the Lord about it. He made it plain it wasn't me the people were rejecting, it was him. He told me to go and talk with the people, tell them what it would mean to have a king.

So that's what I did. I laid it on thick, I can tell you. I told them a king would take their sons from them for his army and his chariots. He would take their daughters to gratify his whim and to serve in his palace. He would take their servants and their draught animals to work for him. He would tax them and enslave them and it would be no use crying out to the Lord then. He would not answer them.

I couldn't have made it plainer. But it was no use. They wouldn't listen to me. They still wanted a king. So I went back to the Lord and told him. I think he was as fed up with them as I was but he gave way and told me to set a king over them. He would show me who it should be. It happened this way.

I was at home in Ramah and the Lord revealed to me that on the following day a man from the land of Benjamin would visit me. I was to anoint him as a ruler over the people. And that's how it turned out. This young Benjamite man Saul came, along with his servant, enquiring of me where his lost donkeys were. In those days that's how many people saw me – as someone who could sort out their problems, see the future, interpret puzzles. We went up to the sanctuary together for the evening sacrifice and after we had a meal I invited Saul to stay the night. At dawn next day we went out into the town and, privately, I told him what God had in mind for him. I poured oil on his head and greeted him with a kiss and told him the Lord had anointed him as ruler over the people. I gave him three signs of what would happen to him on his journey, ending up at Gilbeah where the spirit of the Lord would come on him, driving him into a prophetic frenzy. And that's the way it turned out.

I summoned all the people to Mizpah, once more warned them of their folly in rejecting the Lord as their King, and then went about the task of electing Saul by lot. It was a popular choice. He was head and shoulders above the rest of them. A handsome young man with charm and courage. I told them the rights and duties of a king. It was sad how it turned out but I warned them all, Saul as well.

I longed for Saul to do what was right but twice I had to reprimand him. Twice I regretted having anointed him. The first time was at Gilgal. He couldn't wait for me to arrive to make the sacrifice before going into battle so, against all the rules, he made the sacrifice himself. On the second occasion he refused to destroy all the enemy, man and beast, as he had been commanded. He kept some of the herds and flocks for himself and then pretended that he had done so to provide a sacrifice to God. I was so angry. I told him: God wanted obedience more than sacrifices. His rejection of God meant God would reject him, would wrench the kingdom from him and his family and another would be anointed in his place. It tore my heart to have to tell him but the Lord was adamant. His commandment had been clear and Saul had thought he knew better, he'd disobeyed. Once someone gets all that power it goes to their head. I never saw Saul again after that.

So much should have come from it all, but right from the beginning I wasn't happy about them having a king. The only King is the Lord.

8. The Queen of Sheba – a matter of trade
(1 Kings 10:1-13)

I have never been a great lover of long journeys. They're much too tiring, no matter how well everything is organised. And camels are not my favourite animals – nasty-tempered creatures. They spit! But they make such travelling possible, so I suppose I should not grumble. I restricted the distance we did each day and it must have taken us a couple of months to get from Sheba to Jerusalem.

There had been long discussions about going at all. I was certainly intrigued by this Israelite king. His wisdom was legendary, outdoing the wise men of Egypt for his clever sayings and wise proverbs. Solomon, I was reliably informed, was a man of culture, an author and a songwriter. His reputation had spread throughout the whole region, down into Africa and across the north-east to the edges of Asia. Was he really such a paragon of virtue? How would he stand up to the kind of questions I could put to him, I wondered.

Politically the story is not that unusual but he made the best of his situation. He had inherited the territory from his father David and he had the skill to maintain its borders and strengthen its position. Under Solomon, the Hebrew people were no longer just a confederation of tribes held together by a charismatic leader. He centralised the government into administrative regions – which in the end of course is just a way of ensuring you can collect taxes, build up a sizeable standing army and guarantee a reliable labour force. But he was also strong and wily enough to keep peace and that made a big difference.

His real skill was the way he developed trade in the area. Much more than Saul, more even than David, he appreciated the significance of Palestine's position as a land-bridge between Egypt and Asia. He simply controlled the major trade routes and in the process amassed enormous wealth through taxes and commercial enterprises. He got a stranglehold on the supply of horses to the Hittites and Arameans and the same was true of chariots from Egypt. The sea routes were under his control as well, through an alliance he made with Hiram, King of Tyre. The Israelites don't make good sailors. Like many desert people they are ill at ease on the sea. So the boats were all built and manned by Phoenicians – but the trade was Solomon's, especially the smelted copper to Ophir from where the ships returned laden with jewels, and gold, and spices, and fabrics.

Solomon spelt danger to us in Sheba. Our own commercial trade was suffering and several of my people warned me of dangers from Israeli expansionism. It was those same advisers who pressured me to go and visit Solomon. So between my curiosity and national interest I had little choice. I was determined I was not going to be overawed by him and of course we could not appear less than a major trading country. So we travelled with an enormous baggage train of gifts. I don't suppose anyone had taken him such a quantity of spices before. It's how diplomacy is done.

We emphasised the personal side of the visit, for I did not want to show my hand too early and I knew the negotiations would not be easy. I was told that Solomon had an eye for the ladies and although I say it myself, I am renowned for my beauty, so I had certain advantages. But it did complicate matters and in the long run gave people all the wrong ideas. I've even heard stories that I slept with Solomon and since returning home have had a son by him. What nonsense! I would like to make it quite clear there is no truth in such stories, none at all. Not that I didn't find him attractive.

And clever, and wise, and of course very wealthy. Jerusalem was much more splendid than I had ever imagined. His court was magnificent. The palace was as fine as any I have seen – dazzling with gold everywhere and the chambers scented with the subtle smell of the Lebanese cedar panelling along with the spices in the perfumeries. The arrangements of his court, the officials with their clear hierarchy of duties and regalia, the sumptuous food set before us at every meal, and the abundance of the burnt offerings made at the temple were all beyond comparison. But the most telling was still the depth of his conversation, the astuteness of his judgements, the clarity of his analysis. It was breathtaking. Hard as I tried to ensure favourable terms for our trading arrangements I knew I was never going to get one over on him. I came away with less than I had hoped for but more than I had feared. I still have a collection of his proverbs but the book that really intrigues me is a poem he is supposed to have written after we had met – a love poem, no less. They say it is called the Song of Solomon although there is no certainty that he actually wrote it. I would like to think he did.

9. Jonah – where's the justice in that?
(The Book of Jonah)

So, my friend, you think it was just a matter of simple disobedience, those tales you've heard about me. You should not be so hasty to condemn. If I've learnt nothing else, I've learnt that. When dealing with God things are never that simple and justice is more than condemnation. You say you know the story. Well, be patient and let me tell you how I saw it. You might learn something. I did.

I was, still am, a prophet of the Lord. Prophets aren't comfortable people – they see things in the light of God's law, his holiness, his judgement. We see what is wrong in the lives of individuals and of nations and speak out in God's name about the retribution to come.

The Lord's word came to me to go and pronounce against Nineveh for all its wickedness. There was no worse place in all the world than Nineveh. Its violence and evil, its lack of justice and decency were legendary. Above all other cities it deserved the full wrath of God upon it. No second chances. I couldn't wait to pronounce their punishment. But I had this niggling fear that if I did as the Lord required they might take notice and repent. The sneaky lot would appeal to God's mercy and he would forgive them. Where's the justice in that? I decided to go west, to Tarshish, opposite end of the world to Nineveh. But my journey, you might say, was neither east nor west. It was down.

Down first to Joppa where I bought passage on a ship. Then down to a small cabin in the bowels of the boat. And later it was down to the deepest depths of the sea. But I get ahead of myself.

We set sail and I went for a rest after my journey. I was rudely woken by the captain telling me a great storm had blown up. The sailors, a mixed bunch, had done all they could, including praying to their various gods, and now he wanted me to pray to my God. In their superstitious way they threw dice to discover whose fault the storm was. It wasn't a total surprise when they pointed to me. They made me tell them all about myself. I told them I was a prophet of the Hebrew people and that I worshipped the Lord of heaven, sovereign creator of sea and land, and I was fleeing from him. They were terrified and asked me what they should do.

The only thing I could think of was for them to fling me off the ship into the sea. Give them their due, they were really reluctant to do that. They doubled their efforts with the oars but to no avail. So, asking God, and me, to forgive them, they did what I had asked and threw me into the raging sea. It did the trick. The storm ceased and I learnt later that they all came to believe in the Lord God. Ironic that. Conversion of those pagan sailors wasn't on my agenda at all. It was God who saved them.

He saved me too. A great fish brought me back up from the depths of death. Salvation, they say, is always a journey up – from darkness to light, from depths to height, from death to life. I praised God for all he had done for me.

But he hadn't finished with me or Nineveh. A second time he told me to go and proclaim against that den of wickedness. I had no great heart for it, I must say. Soon after I got there I went to a market square and made a brief declaration of doom on all their wickedness. I'd hoped no one would take any notice because then the judgement would come upon them as promised. It's what they deserved.

But the reaction was amazing. No sooner had I spoken than people began worshipping the Lord, bewailing their sins, calling for mercy. They stripped off their finery and put on rough sacking, bags used for flour and vegetables and such like. The king made a decree calling upon everyone to fast and to humble themselves before the Lord. 'Who knows,' he said, 'the Lord might relent of his anger and not destroy us.'

And that's exactly what he did. I knew it, I knew it! It made no difference how evil they'd been. A show of repentance, a call for mercy and God forgave them. I ask you, where's the justice in that? It made me really angry. I yelled at the Lord. I told him I knew this would happen. It was why I had run away the first time. It's so frustrating – I proclaim judgement and then he lets them off. I couldn't stand it. Or rather, I couldn't understand it, that was the real problem.

I went off into the desert to try and get my head round it. I was in a right mood. I stayed there all day. It was blistering hot but overnight a great plant sprang up to shade me from the sun and sirocco wind. It didn't last. By the next day it was all shrivelled up. It was so unfair. God had let the people of Nineveh off for their wickedness and yet he couldn't let me have more than a day's shade. I just wanted to die, to be shot of the whole thing: of being a prophet, of trying to work things out, of serving God.

I didn't die and I still have trouble sorting it all out. You're clever, you think everything is simple. What do you make of it? I've always thought a holy God must be a God of judgement, punishing disobedience and wickedness. Surely that's more important than being soft, with all that mercy and forgiveness stuff? And yet where would I be without forgiveness? Down in Davey Jones' locker, that's where. It makes my head hurt, all these questions.

10. Anne – just an ordinary child really
(Luke 1:26-38)

I was always proud of her, of course. You'd expect that of a mother, wouldn't you? But I wouldn't say she ever struck me as anything exceptional. Nothing out of the ordinary. Of course there were the times she would go off on her own a bit – in a sort of reverie. All tied up in her own little world she'd be and she'd sometimes say the funniest things. She'd come in from one of her little wanderings and I'd ask her what she'd been doing. 'Nothing much,' she'd say. 'I've been talking with the angels.' I just put it down to the way kids are. They all seem to have their little made-up friends when they are that age. Hannah, my neighbour's child, used to have someone called Joanna. You'd see her walking along the street chatting away as chirpy as anything and she'd get quite cross if you suggested there was no one there. 'Of course there is,' she'd say. 'It's Joanna. She's my friend.'

But for Mary it was always angels, though we never knew what they talked about. She'd just say that she was sending messages to God. In those days I never heard she ever had a message back. That was only later when she was in her teens. And it wasn't the kind of thing a mother wanted to hear. We had always brought the children up to behave properly, especially when it came to personal matters, you know, things like sex. Now of course it all seems so wonderful, quite extraordinary, but at the time it was a shock, I can tell you. Her father and I had talked about her future quite a lot. We wanted the best for her, the right kind of husband. Someone with a bit of standing in the community, who'd care for her. We'd picked on Joseph. He was quite a bit older than her but that's no bad thing I always said. He was established. Already shown he was a hard worker. Had built up his carpentry business and was well respected in the village. We were delighted when the arrangements met his approval and the betrothal was arranged. There was no hurry – things had to be done properly.

And then she told us! I remember like it was yesterday. I was making bread, with flour up to my elbows. She just walked into the kitchen, sat down as calm as you like and came straight out with it: 'I'm with child,' she said. You could have knocked me down with a feather. 'What do you mean?' I said, knowing full well what she meant. 'I'm with child,' she repeated. 'Going to have a baby, as special as it could possibly be.' I had to sit down. 'So what's so special about that?' I asked. 'It's nothing to be proud about, young lady. A disgrace more like. What could you have been thinking of?' I had expected more of you – and Joseph. 'Oh, it's not his,' she exclaimed, with a great grin on her face. I could have hit her, the little hussy. 'It's God's.' 'What on earth are you talking about, child?' I said. And then it all came out.

To start with I thought she was making it all up. More of her 'talks with the angels'. But she insisted and insisted that it was true. It seems Angel Gabriel had come with a message to say she was going to have a baby. Not an ordinary baby but one born of God's spirit. She was adamant. She swore on the Torah that she had not been with Joseph. I just didn't know what to make of it. Nor did her father. I kept thinking about what the neighbours would say. It's not the kind of thing you can keep quiet. Not in a small village like this. And you know how some like to gossip. But Mary had always been such a straight child. She'd never given us any real trouble. And I don't think I'd ever known her to lie, even when it would have kept her from getting into trouble. It was Joseph I was really worried about. What on earth would he make of it? If it was as she said and they hadn't slept together, then he'd have to think she'd been unfaithful to him, even before getting married. There was nothing for it. We had to go and see him and tell him all we knew. I wasn't looking forward to it, I can tell you. He was well within his rights if he demanded her to be thrown out or worse. We would all have to leave and go and live somewhere else. I was dreading it.

I should have had more faith in him. He was a good man. He didn't rant or turn nasty. He just sat there listening to Mary while I held my breath. You could tell it had shaken him. He just looked at Mary in a sort of quizzical way and then quite quietly kept asking her questions. He left us for a while and I think he went off to pray. We'd done a lot of praying too, I can tell you. When he came back he looked drawn and sort of sorrowful. 'We must do the right thing,' he said. 'I don't want any fuss. We'll just arrange for the betrothal to be set aside. We'll say as little as possible. Perhaps Mary could go to a relative until it's over.'

So that's what we did. Mary went to her cousin Elizabeth for a few months. I thought that would be the end of it as far as Joseph was concerned but he had second thoughts and he took her back – just as though nothing had happened. I put it down to these angels Mary kept talking about. The Lord's ways are very strange. Of course all that was several years back. It was amazing – and she was such an ordinary child in many ways.

11. Elizabeth – miracles run in the family
(Luke 1:5-66)

We have lived in amazing days – the like of which we will never see again. It has been the Lord's doing. I still find it hard to believe that I have been a part of it. Even with someone from my background it is to be wondered at. My mind keeps going back to the story of Hannah. It's a passage of the scriptures I often get my husband to read to me.

My name is Elizabeth and I come from a priestly family. We can trace our descendants all the way back to Aaron. My husband is Zechariah, a priest from a small country town where we have lived together for many, many years. Our only sadness was the fact that that we could not have children. You can't imagine what that meant to me. Twice a year Zach would go to Jerusalem to the temple to take his turn on duty with the rest of his division of priests. But that year, the one I want to tell you about, was like no other.

I was particularly proud of him because, as the custom among the priests is, he had been chosen by lot to enter the sanctuary and offer incense before the Lord. It was a great honour. But that wasn't the half of it. Lord, how we have talked about it, time and time again.

It was while he was in the sanctuary, doing whatever it is the priest has to do, that he had this amazing experience. The Lord sent his messenger, Gabriel and there he was standing by the right-hand side of the altar. It scared my old man, I can tell you. Well, it would do. You don't expect that sort of thing coming on you all of a sudden, even if you are a priest. He feared the worst and couldn't believe it when he was promised the fulfilment of all our hopes and dreams. Far from a message of doom, Gabriel spoke of joy and gladness, not just for us but for God's people. Our prayers would be answered and I would have a son, old as I was. His name was to be John. It's a Hebrew name meaning 'God has shown favour'. And as if that wasn't enough, he was to be specially dedicated to the Lord, and would be filled with the spirit of God to speak to the people with the power of an Elijah of old. He would prepare the people for the work the Lord was about to accomplish.

It was such a shock. My poor old boy couldn't really take it in. To be honest he didn't believe it was possible – seeing how old we both were. He told me later that he was dumbstruck. And that's precisely what happened. Couldn't speak – not a word. When he came out of the Sanctuary the people were waiting for him. All he could do was make signals. Couldn't say a thing. What with that and the way he was behaving they realised he had seen a vision, although to tell you the truth I don't think I would have worked it out. I think I would have thought he was just ill. Anyhow, the long and the short of it was that when his turn of duty ended he came back here to me. As best he could he explained things by writing down messages and so on. I'm not sure what I made of it all really. I prayed about it, I tried to make sense of it but it all seemed so unlikely – folks like us, I mean. And then I got pregnant! To start with I hardly dared believe it – just thought I was a bit late, like. But it soon became obvious and I knew that this was the Lord at work, just as he had promised. Half of me wanted to go and shout it out to all the world, I was that thrilled. But we decided to keep it quiet, not say anything to anyone.

And then my cousin, Mary, came to stay with me. She's a lot younger than I am but what a surprise when she told me her news. I knew something was up, well you could tell, but directly she came through the door the babe in my belly gave such a shove – like a great leap for joy. I swear he knew what was going on. A prophet even in the womb, he was! God was certainly doing something special and here we were in the midst of it: Mary with a child conceived through the Holy Spirit and me pregnant at my age. It seems miracles run in the family. Amazing days.

Mary stayed with me for nearly three months until my time was approaching. We had so much to talk about. Zach would just sit there listening, taking it all in, not saying a word. When John was born the whole neighbourhood went mad and we had quite a celebration. They didn't fully understand of course, were just glad for Zach and me to have a child at last. But the real celebration came a few days later at the circumcision. I had always known that the boy was to be called John but when I suggested it the neighbours were quite indignant. 'No,' they said, 'he must be called after his father.' Zach got really agitated. He waved his writing board at them, the one he used for messages. He wrote on it, 'His name is John.' That settled it of course and blow me if it didn't loosen his tongue as well and he was able to speak again. It was just as Gabriel had told him. Everyone was amazed and the story spread round all the villages in this area.

Me, I just gave thanks to God. I was that thrilled to have my son. I couldn't really understand what it would all lead to but I knew the hand of the Lord was with him. Amazing times. We'll not see the like of them again.

12. The lodging keeper – don't blame me
(Matthew 1:18 - 2:18; Luke 2:1-22)

It's no use blaming me. I did the best I could for them. But the place was throbbing. It was a nightmare. All week people had been arriving from all over the place, staying a night, getting registered and moving on. Oh, I know it was OK for business but frankly I could have done without it. Everyone was grumbling. There was even talk among some of the hot heads of rioting, as a protest against the census. They said it was against the Lord to number the people. A lot of notice the Romans took of that. It wasn't going to stop them. Orders from Rome. Anything to get more taxes out of us. Poll tax here, property tax there. The census made sure they milked us dry. A real pain.

Anyhow, back to this couple I was telling you about. Ordinarily I wouldn't have taken much notice of them, certainly wouldn't have gone out of my way for them, seeing they were northerners. But my missus took one look at the woman and that was that. We were overflowing in the house but there was the caravan lodge and the animal cave out the back and as I told them, that was the best I could do. The missus fussed over them and it must have been sometime the next afternoon the kid was born. Don't remember exactly when but I think the fellow had got back from registering by then. I had to let them stay – couldn't just throw them out.

It was after that that things got a bit strange. Never really did get to the bottom of it. Nothing like it had ever happened before – or since for that matter.

It was later that night. I'd got to bed around midnight – absolutely bushed I was – when there was this banging and calling. Well, to be honest it's never exactly quiet round here but this was out of order. I jumped out of bed, got my staff, just in case, and went out front. Just like I thought. A crowd of shepherds. They're always making trouble when they come into town. I told them to clear off. Well, they quietened down but just stood there. One of them said something but I couldn't make sense of it. 'A baby,' he shouted, 'is there a baby here?' 'No,' I said, 'my boys are all grown up.' 'A newborn,' he persisted. 'Born today.' 'What's that to you?' I asked. 'We want to see him,' another of them said. 'The way we've been told he should be all wrapped up in a manger of all places.'

So I took them out back and there it was just as they said. They just stood around like they were dumb founded. 'It was the angels,' one of them said to me. 'They told us about him. It was amazing. Lots of lights and things. He's going to be a great leader and save us from the Romans. Honest.' Well, that's a laugh for a start – an honest shepherd. I thought it was the drink. But they didn't cause any trouble and after a while they left. I don't know what the man and woman made of it. Just talked a bit and seemed to treat it as though it was normal. I went back to bed.

I don't suppose I would have thought anything more about it – stranger things do happen. And they did. That was what made it so weird. The crowds in town had thinned out a bit and after a couple of days we had a spare room. The missus insisted we let the couple have it – after all they weren't poor, they could afford it and you couldn't just leave them outside.

Anyhow they said they would be grateful if they could have it for a week before making their journey back home. 'No more shepherds,' I said, joking. 'No,' they said.

But then there were the travellers! We get a lot of them of course. Caravans from the east, stopping by for the night before going into Jerusalem with their goods. But these were different. They were from the east right enough, but not business people, not your usual traders. Strange they were – astrologers, magicians, something like that. Very classy. They'd been to the palace apparently, looking for a newborn prince but had been turned away, directed this way. They said something about stars, as far as I could make out. Didn't make any sense to me. I told them straight – we're not exactly the sort of place you'd find a prince in. But they just insisted.

And there it was – that couple from up north again and their new baby. Well, you should have seen the travellers. Down on their knees they went and showered him with gifts. I don't understand these foreigners. They've got some very strange ways. They stayed just the night and then left. It wasn't long after that the couple went – all in a bit of a hurry it was, very early one morning. And that was the last I saw of them.

We had one hell of a time just after that. Terrible it was. Soldiers came, raiding the houses, assaulting people, killing children. Terrible. No reason for it. No wonder we hate them. I sometimes get to thinking about that couple and their baby. All that fuss. What was so special about him? Couldn't see it myself. I wonder what became of him?

13. Melchior, the wise man – we thought we knew (Matthew 2:1-12)

Pray, forgive my keeping you waiting. I have been to the bazaar and was unusually delayed. I hope my servants have welcomed you and offered you some mint tea.

As I say, I was in the bazaar when out of nowhere I was confronted by a question of great profundity. An urchin ran from behind a carpet stall, stood right there in front of me and stared at me. 'Who are you?' he asked and without waiting for an answer ran off again. Not *What* but *Who* are you? I've been repeating that question to myself all the way home. I am Melchior I might have said – but my name is no more than a label on the market stall of humanity. A man? Yes. A son, a father, an uncle, a neighbour? Yes. Perhaps then I am the sum of my relationships. But I am also a Magus, a so-called wise man. An observer of events in nature and the world. A watcher and waiter who sees, but more than that, interprets what he sees. If you wish to have knowledge you must seek more than mere data. It is the meaning within and behind and between the facts that makes for wisdom. Interpretations and meanings are discovered after much searching. They reveal themselves to the true seeker. But even then I have no guarantees they are right. There are surprises in the search that can merely lead to more questions. Let me explain with a story – a true one.

Many years ago some friends and I were particularly interested in the message given to us in the stars. Their regularity tells much but it was the disjunction of that regularity that was of particular interest. We had noticed the way in which the path of the stars you would know as Venus and Saturn was being crossed by Jupiter, accompanied by the appearance of a different very bright, evanescent star. It presented us with a puzzle. All that we had learnt indicated that this was herald to a birth. Not just an ordinary birth but one of great significance, somewhere to the west. A king, we thought. I was intrigued and we decided to test our theory, for that is the way the quest for knowledge works.

We prepared for a long journey with both camels and donkeys and each of us, myself and my two companions, had a couple of servants for both our comfort and our protection. We set out with no precise knowledge of where we would end up. Our guides were the stars and we made careful observations each night so as to determine the direction for the following day. We went via Babylonia, followed the Euphrates and entered Palestine from the northeast. The general direction was clearly towards Jerusalem, and that of course made great sense since it was there that Herod had his palace. All the signs indicated that the birth we had seen heralded in the star formation was that of a new king of the Jews. So it was to Herod's palace that we made our way, convinced both of the accuracy of our observations and of their meaning.

We were given a polite, though not particularly warm welcome. As our custom dictates, we had gifts to present both to the king and to the newborn child. The latter we wished to present in person and so we asked if we could see the infant king. The response was guarded and we were kept waiting for a considerable time – way beyond the point of courtesy. We were also puzzled for there were no signs of celebration that we had expected at the birth of an heir. But we had had little contact previously with the Jews and we put it down to local custom. After what must have been several hours we were told that no birth had occurred at the palace but that we should go to a town to the south east, called Bethlehem. Apparently their own wise men in the past had predicted a king would be born there. These things are possible of course and we had, perhaps unwisely, made assumptions in directing our path to the palace.

We set off again and soon came to this rather unpromising little town. We found the caravan lodge and, having left the camels and donkeys along with the other camel trains, set off to the nearby resting house to enquire of news of the royal baby. It was there we found this young couple and their child.

There are times when despite the careful observations, the calculations and hypotheses, the weighing of the evidence and reference to the manuals, it's not your head that gets the answer but your heart. You just know that the answer you sought is there in front of you. Not at all as you expected. Not at all in the place you were looking for it. The answer finds you. In a tatty little lodging-house in downtown Bethlehem, amidst the traders and travellers was this ordinary family with an extraordinary son. It didn't make sense. It turned all we had expected upside down. We were certain yet unsure, all at the same time. Certain enough to pay him homage and present our gifts, but uncertain where it left our science. We had made our observations. We were sure of our interpretation, but what in fact we had come to, who in fact we had seen, we were never sure.

We never did return to the palace to give them the news. Caspar had a dream of warning and we left next morning by a different route.

14. The woman at the well – a life-changing meeting (John 4:5-30, 39-42)

I hear you want to know what changed my life. I've told the story many times and yet even in the telling I seem to understand it a little more. At one time I would have said it was just about my meeting with a stranger at the well, how we spoke about religious things and personal things. How he made me look at things in a new way. But the more I have thought about it, the more it has seemed it wasn't just about me. It was as though I stood for all our people, for all Samaritans.

I can only make sense of it if I tell you about us. We are descendants of Jacob just like the Jews. We believe the law is the Word of God for us and that Moses was the prophet who gave us the law. One day, Samaritans believe, a great prophet like him will come again. The great division with the Jews began when our land of Samaria was invaded by the Assyrians and many of us were captured and taken away. The Assyrians brought people from five provinces of their land to settle here. They brought their strange gods and although many of our people married the foreigners, most of us kept faithful to our religion. The Jews never gave us credit for that. They despised us for our mixed ancestry and they treated us badly, though I have to admit it wasn't all one-sided. There were fanatics from among us who went and desecrated the temple in Jerusalem one Passover because God had told us in the law that sacrifice should be on Mount Gerizim, not in the city. It only made things worse. I don't think most Jews really knew what to make of us. We aren't Jews and we're not Gentiles. We're sort of in-betweens. We worship the same God and even have the same laws of tithing but we are seen as heretics.

So it was a surprise when the Jewish stranger asked me for water. I had gone out to the well near Sychar, Jacob's well, to get water for the day. And there he was. It was midday and so hot. He looked exhausted and he had nothing to get water with. It was a surprise that he should even speak to me, a woman and a Samaritan, but to suggest we might share a drink from the same vessel – that was unheard of. I told him how surprised I was, him being a Jew and me a Samaritan. And that's where the conversation began to get strange. At first I really had no idea what he was on about. He said that if I really understood the law, the gift of God, and who he was, it would be me asking him for water, running water. Now that didn't make sense. He couldn't get water from the well, it's a hundred feet deep and he had no jar. Was he going to get water from somewhere else? Was he greater than our ancestor Jacob who dug this well for all to drink from? But he said that the running water he was offering wasn't like the well water. To drink the water he offered meant you would never be thirsty again. Now that, I thought, is just what I need. Never to be thirsty again. It would save me the job of having to go out to the well every day. Here was someone to be respected, no matter he was a Jew. 'Sir,' I said, 'I'd like some of that water.'

But he ignored that and simply told me to go and fetch my husband. I wasn't happy about the way he had suddenly changed the subject. It was getting personal and, as it happened, my relationship at that time was a bit irregular. Well, I had had more than enough marriages, five in fact. And that wasn't going to please him. Jews only allow three. But amazingly he seemed to know all about that. And the way he spoke seemed to go deeper.

Was he talking about me or about our people, people of the five provinces, the five gods? I've thought more and more about that. He was so much more than I had imagined. He intrigued me, looked into me and knew me. It felt to me that only a prophet would know such things. What would the prophet make of the fact we believed worship should be at different places?

But he didn't favour either Mount Gerizim or Jerusalem. For him worship was to be in neither place. The time was coming, he said, when real worship, true worship wouldn't be in a temple but in the power of the Spirit, because God is Spirit. They were words like I had never heard before – powerful words, words of insight, words that seemed to know the very mind of God. Surely only the one who would come, the Messiah, could speak like this. I told him so. He just said 'I am he.'

Was it true? Had I met the one we were all waiting for, there at the well of Jacob? His companions came back and I went off back to the town, leaving my water jar behind. It seemed irrelevant, for something more precious than water had been there. I went and told the people all that had happened, and lots of them went out to see the man. They got him to stay with us for a couple of days and as you might expect, what he told them had much more impact than anything I could say.

It changed my life, that meeting at the well. And the more I have thought about it, the more I have come to understand about that water he spoke of – living, flowing water that fills your life, flowing from him as it were into your whole being. We had nothing like that in our faith, and I don't think the Jews did either. Here was something new – cleansing and purifying, refreshing your whole being for ever and ever. That weary man gave us a gift neither Jew nor Samaritan could match. I really do believe he was the one we had been waiting for.

15. Zacchaeus – repentant rogue
(Luke 19:1-10)

It's no good you looking down your nose at me like that. All self-righteous just because of what I used to be. OK, I admit it, I'm no saint, never was, but I've changed, turned over a new leaf. It's not like the old days. I was a bit dodgy back then, well more than a bit, to be honest. But that's all different now. I gave up all that tax business long ago. Got myself a small farm. Just a few sheep and some olive trees but we get by.

I knew right from the start that I would never be popular but then I didn't go into the business to make friends. I just wanted to make money – lots of it. And I did. But it cost me – I lost my friends, my family even, was excommunicated from the synagogue, was jostled and generally shunned when I went out. My own people despised me, treated me as though I was unclean, just because I dealt so much with the Romans.

The way people talk you'd think all I had to do was sit around, fiddle the books and the money would roll in. It wasn't like that. I was a businessman, not a crook. OK, a crooked businessman but I wasn't a thief. People seem to forget, I had to invest my own money in the first place. There was a risk. I could have taken a big loss, so why not get a good return on the investment? That's just good business. Ask any of the traders round here. And the fact is I was good at it. You don't get to being the boss tax man if you don't know the business, especially in a town like Jericho where there are rich pickings to be had, especially from the balsam trade.

I'm not going to let you into all my little secrets even now, but the way it worked was like this. The Roman governor in a province set the taxes. The poll tax they would collect themselves but the other taxes, on goods and things, were farmed out to the highest bidder. I got started by bidding a stupid amount, beating off the opposition. And then I had to make that up somehow. That's where the fiddling came in. And if people wouldn't pay up, well you had to apply a bit of persuasion. You know what I mean? I had a couple of lads to help out on that. A bit handy they were.

It was easier with the traders passing through Jericho on their way to Jerusalem or up north. You could always add a bit, invent a new tax, charge them extra. Half of them didn't know the system that well anyhow and you'd only have to rough one or two of them up a bit and the message soon got round. Not that I did that sort of thing myself. By the end I had a whole number of tax collectors working for me. They were getting their whack and I made sure they gave me mine. The fact is the system couldn't have worked without us. Everyone knew it was going on and so long as you didn't get too greedy, the Romans just turned a blind eye.

But then Jesus came along. I wasn't a great one for Rabbis and such, they always had it in for us. But from what I'd heard he was different. I was just curious, so when we learnt he was passing through Jericho I went out to have a look. There were crowds everywhere. I couldn't get near. Couldn't see a thing, what with me being on the short side and people jostling me out of the way. There was this sycamore tree, well it's a mulberry really, dead easy to climb, even for a little 'un like me. So up I shinnied and got a really good view. As he came past he looked up. Someone must have told him who I was. And blow me if he didn't tell me to get down and go and make the house ready because he wanted to stay with me. I nearly fell off my perch. Him talking to me, him wanting to have a meal with me! That really set the cat among the pigeons. I could hear the muttering going on as I ran home. 'What's he doing,' they said, 'having a meal with a sinner like that?' I took no notice. The Rabbi thought I was worth something after all. He wasn't going to shun me. I couldn't believe it. I'd not felt that good for years and years.

I had a good meal prepared and when he came along I was that pleased to see him I put on a great show. It changed everything. I felt good again, about myself, wanted to make up for some of the things I'd done. So I told him right there and then that I'd give half of what I owned to the poor – and it was a tidy sum, I can tell you. And I promised to make it up to those I'd cheated. The missus said I was being too generous, offering four times the amount but fair's fair, that's what I'd have had to pay if I'd ever been caught defrauding people. So that's what I did. And you know what – I've never felt better. That sense of being at peace with yourself – it's better than all the money. Jesus made all the difference. I know what it means now: 'once I was lost and now I'm found.' So don't you go looking down your nose at me.

16. Mary – nothing is too precious
(Luke 10:38-42; John 11:20-44; John 12:1-8)

I always seemed to end up at his feet. I don't know why. It just happened that way. It got me into trouble but I don't care. It was good to be there and I miss him so much.

I remember the first time he came to our home. Since our parents died Martha has run the household. She's the eldest and although there is

Lazarus, our brother, she was always the one to make the decisions. She's very able in a practical kind of way. Lazarus is a bit of a dreamer. And I'm more of a thinker, if you know what I mean. I love ideas and learning new things. If I'd been a man I would have sought out a Rabbi to learn from, become a disciple. But it's not easy for a woman. It was why I was so pleased when Martha invited Jesus to come and have a meal with us. I know the neighbours looked a bit askance at that, standing at their doorways tutting and muttering. They didn't think it was seemly for a woman to do the inviting. But Lazarus was off somewhere and we weren't going to miss the chance.

We had heard so much about Jesus. I had sometimes joined the crowds to listen to his preaching. It was so profound and yet he knew how to put it across in a simple way. He'd say, this is God's way, or this is what the kingdom is like. And then he would just tell a story, about a farmer or a shepherd or some such, and as often as not just leave you to think about it. He was wonderful. So when he came I just sat at his feet listening, spellbound. I could have sat there for hours. It made Martha a bit cross. She was always telling me I didn't pull my weight with the chores. She had been bustling around with her usual efficiency but I suppose it had just got too much for her. She complained to Jesus. 'Don't you care, Lord,' she said, 'that I have been left to get everything ready by myself while she just sits there? We'll never eat if someone doesn't lend a hand.' It made me feel awful. But he just looked at her and gentle as gentle he told her not to get so anxious. It would be all right. Things would get done. And then he looked at me and it was as though he knew all that was going on inside me, the yearning to learn, the longing just to be close to him. 'Don't let's tell her off,' he said, 'what she is doing is fine and it cannot be taken from her.' Martha just shrugged, and smiled and went off and got on with things. She's never cross for long and she actually loves being busy. Always on the go. It was as though Jesus saw what she had to offer and loved her for it. And the same for me even though I'm so different.

When Lazarus got sick, there was no one we wanted more than Jesus. Of course we hoped he could come and make Lazarus better. He'd done it for others. We couldn't understand why he took such a long time coming. When he did arrive Lazarus was already dead. As usual it was Martha who dashed out to meet him. I was sitting at home, so upset. And you know it was she who first told Jesus that we believed he was the Messiah, the one we had been promised. She came back and told me that Jesus was asking for me. I dashed out, my hair all over the place, such a sight what with crying and everything. I just fell at his feet and told how we had been sure Lazarus would not have died if only he had come earlier. He was really upset, seeing our grief and he asked where we had laid Lazarus. I couldn't bear to go there and so I hung back and I'm not really sure what happened. I heard him shouting Lazarus' name and the next thing I knew there he was, walking out of the tomb.

Don't ask me how Jesus did it. I just have faith that he did. It was all very strange at the time but later, after those terrible days when they killed him and the wonderful days when we knew he was alive again, it did all seem to make sense. It was not just that Jesus could raise people, it was as though he was the life of resurrection we could all share. It's as he told Martha – he is the resurrection and he is the life.

I didn't understand at the time. If truth be told I still don't. The more I think about it, the more I listen to the scriptures to see what clues they can give, the more of a mystery it is. My head puzzles away at it. Sometimes I get it all clear and then the fog comes in again. Perhaps Martha's right – I should just listen to my heart a bit more. It works for her.

After Jesus left us that time, I got more and more worried. Some of the people had rejoiced with us to have Lazarus back, marvelling at what they had seen. But others went off to the authorities. It got more and more dangerous for Jesus. I was convinced bad things were going to happen to him. I would lose him – we all would. We had one last meal with him and some of his disciples. As he sat there at the end of the meal I fetched a jar of expensive perfume I had been saving up. It's the kind rich people use to anoint the dead body of a loved one. I just sat at his feet, pouring it over his feet, rubbing it gently with the braids of my hair. All I could think about was how he would be killed and how I would miss him. Someone protested that I had wasted the perfume. It should have been sold and the money given to the poor. They had no idea! But Jesus knew. For him I would have done anything. Nothing is too precious.

17. The donkey owner – you only have to ask
(Mark 11:1-11; Matthew 21:1-11; Luke 19:28-40; John 12:12-16)

I'd never met Jesus before that day. It was my cousin who knew him really. He took up with him a year back, gave up his job and travelled round the countryside with some of the other followers. He was never one of the inner group but he said there was something really special about Jesus. He reckoned big things were going to happen that could make all the difference for us Jews, and even for the Gentiles as well.

He visited us once and told us some of the stories that Jesus used when he was teaching the people. They were about all sorts of things – some were just about people like you or me, country stories about farming and fishing, and there were others about kings and important folk, even some about Samaritans. They explained what God's kingdom was like – coming unexpectedly, in small ways that would grow and grow, with an invitation to everyone, and an urgency you shouldn't ignore. Anyhow that's what I made of it, best as I could. And then there were the healings – the blind and the lame. He told me Jesus would even go up to lepers and touch them to make them better. Now that's not something you see everyday. It obviously made a big impression on my cousin, and he's nobody's fool.

I couldn't leave the farm or I would have gone and seen this Jesus for myself. But, as I told my cousin, if ever they were this way and there was anything they needed, all they had to do was ask. To be honest I didn't expect anything to come of it – but I meant it all the same. And when they did come it was quite a party, I can tell you.

The first I knew about it was this row going on outside in the street. I'd planned to take the donkeys up to the other fields and I'd just popped in the house to tell the missus, leaving the creatures tied up outside. When all of a sudden there was all this shouting. Such a carry on. I could hear Zechariah, my neighbour, having a right go at someone, so I dashed out. And there was my cousin and another bloke about to lead one of my young colts off. 'What do you think you're doing?' Zechariah was shouting. 'You northerners think you can do what you like at festival time. Clear off!'

'What's going on?' I asked. 'It's the Master,' my cousin said. 'He needs an animal to ride on and he told us to come and fetch an untried colt. He'll send it back later. You always said we could have anything we needed.' I said it was fine and Zechariah calmed down after that. Apparently Jesus and some of his followers were on their way to Jerusalem for the festival and Jesus had decided he wasn't going to be like the other pilgrims, go in on foot, but he would ride. It didn't really make sense to me so I asked my cousin what was going on.

'The way I see it,' my cousin told me, 'Jesus is making some kind of statement. I think he sees himself as the king that has been promised. He keeps telling us to read the scriptures and then we would understand. But I'm not too sure about it myself. I just hope people don't get the wrong message. He keeps saying he's coming to bring peace but I've also heard him say he's come with a sword, not that I've ever seen one, apart from the one Peter has. He's certainly acting like a king – he as good as told us to requisition this colt of yours. But you don't go to war on an ass, so I suppose he really does mean he wants a kingdom of peace. We'll just have to see, but I don't think the Romans will be too happy.'

To be honest, I'm not sure I understood what he was on about but it intrigued me. So I left the rest of the animals where they were and followed my cousin and his friend.

We found Jesus and the others just outside Bethany on the road into Jerusalem. There was quite a crowd. Some of the disciples had stripped off their coats and they put them on the colt's back for Jesus to climb on. It looked uncomfortable to me, the way they had piled them up, like a throne, someone said. Others were putting their coats on the road. It was as though they were putting themselves at the king's disposal. A sign of their obedience to him. There was a lot of cheering and people were getting very excited. They began chanting and shouting hallelujah. And they waved branches they'd stripped off the trees by the roadside. It's like what we do at the Feast of Tabernacles during the recitation of the Exodus Psalms. It all seemed to make good sense then and I joined in the shouting: 'Hosanna! Blessed is he, blessed is the king who comes in the name of the Lord.' We wanted a king and here he was, riding to his city, the city of David and we didn't care if the Romans were going to be upset. It felt good.

I followed all the way into Jerusalem and then things sort of fizzled out. Jesus and his disciples went off to the temple and I took the colt home. The Romans did get upset. They killed Jesus and that would have been the end of it but my cousin is convinced he's alive again and that he now knows that Jesus really is a king. I don't quite get it. But then I'm just an owner of donkeys.

18. Pilate – what is the truth?
(Luke 23:1-25; Matthew 27:11-26; Mark 15:1-11; John 18:28 - 19:16)

From Pontius Pilate, prefect of the province of Judaea, to his cousin Aurelius, greetings.

Forgive the rough nature of this letter. I have not seen fit to dictate it to a scribe but, having regard to the nature of its contents, have chosen rather to write in my own hand. You know of my loyalty to our emperor, Tiberius, as indeed I know he can count on yours, but I weigh our friendship and our family lineage even more dearly and hence seek to write of recent events that are of a somewhat sensitive nature. I wish that you should hear of them from me first, since I have no doubt there will be the usual lies and rumours that will speed the tongue and tickle the ears.

I always saw it as an honour that, even while belonging to the lower ranks, the emperor should have made me a provincial prefect. Judaea is not the place I would have chosen – its people are easily roused to riot and hold strange religious beliefs and customs. Even the most ordinary become fanatical, risking death rather than accept the most normal of our practices. I had hardly arrived when I found myself having to tackle a riot. It seemed that the new cohorts I had sent to Jerusalem from Caesarea had entered the city at the end of a long day's march and had set up their standards as usual in the fortress. They were unaware, as indeed was I, that the standards should not have borne the usual effigies of the emperor. The Jews allow no such effigies in their holy city or so near the temple. I had a deputation at my door in no time and while I sought to ascertain the exact nature of the incident a threatening crowd gathered. I called out the guard and had the mob surrounded and told them to disperse or risk death for insurrection. They simply lay down and bared their throats. Personally I'd have had the lot cut, but my advisers suggested I hear out their complaint and resist unnecessary trouble so early in my time. We had the effigies removed. Such a fuss, but Tiberius appeared pleased with the way I had handled it. Why he had to interfere later in the matter of the gilded shields, I have no idea.

I could tell you of countless incidents. You no doubt heard of the trouble over the aqueduct. It was for the good of the people – Jerusalem needed the extra water. I had every right to use the temple funds to pay for it but you would think I was robbing them. They paid dearly that time for their sedition.

You never know with them. I try to be sensitive to their beliefs, if only to keep the peace, but they take advantage and the only way is to show that I will not have my authority (by which of course I mean the emperor's authority) flouted. But I have only 3000 troops for the whole province and many of them are local auxiliaries. With Lucius Aelius, the Syrian governor, retained in Rome, I cannot even depend on reinforcements from that quarter. I am placed in a most difficult position.

Herod blows hot and cold and while I respect Caiaphas, the High Priest, I fully know that at the end of the day it's his own skin he thinks most about. He's a wily old bird and plays the system for his own ends. He thinks I am fool enough not to know. But I know what he's up to. Take recent events.

It'd been one of the Jewish festivals, Passover, and I always go to Jerusalem at festival time – just in case. I take extra soldiers to strengthen the garrison. There's nearly always trouble. They claim it's a religious festival but there are always political undertones – recalling their escape from slavery, overturning the foreign powers. Some hothead or other is always using it to make claims against Rome.

This time it was a chap from Galilee. He'd obviously got across Caiaphas and his cronies on the Sanhedrin. There'd been a bit of a fuss on the Sunday with a procession into the city but it dispersed quickly enough. Then it was reported that he had been stirring things up in the temple. Caiaphas had him arrested eventually and it was clear he was determined to put an end to him. They brought him to me, saying they had found him guilty and wanted me to ratify the death penalty.

From what I could see it was a blasphemy matter. It was up to them what they did with him. But they insisted this Jesus had been encouraging people not to pay taxes, and had claimed he was a king. Sedition they said. I interrogated him but he had little to say except that his kingdom was from elsewhere. I think the man was raving. When I found he was from Galilee I sent the prisoner to Herod, just to keep him sweet but I don't think he saw any political gain in it, so sent the man back to me. My advisers differed – some, my wife included, were for dismissing the whole thing but others could see the way the crowd were turning, stirred up by the council. It was even suggested I was no friend of the emperor if I didn't condemn him. I had had enough of their Jewish twisting and turning. I washed my hands of the whole thing and had him flogged and sent for crucifixion. Even then they complained about the charge against him: 'King of the Jews'. They'd said sedition, that's what the charge read. 'No,' they complained, 'it ought to read "He said he was King of the Jews." ' I left it how it was.

You are the only one I can say this to, but it troubles me still. I don't know why. Innocent or guilty, it doesn't usually matter, one less of them helps to keep the peace. I wonder if I'm growing weak or just tired. I even allowed his friends to bury him instead of leaving him to rot where he was, eaten by the dogs and the birds. What was the truth of the matter? I really have no idea. Fifty years from now I don't suppose it will matter one way or another.

I shall have to send an official report. I can't let the emperor think I am going soft. But I just wanted to let you know how I really felt.

My greetings to your wife and your household.

19. The soldier – you never forget the first time
(Matthew 27:27-54; Mark 15:16-39; Luke 23:26-49; John 19:1-37)

You ask me if I'm proud of what I do. I don't know I've ever thought about it like that. I've always known I was going to be a soldier – it's in the blood you might say and if all goes well I expect I shall do my 25 years and retire with a nice little bit of land. That's what my dad did. It's hard mind you, especially the training – twenty miles we have to do, fully loaded, in just five hours, and all that formation practise. I'm not sure I want to still be doing that when I'm 45. I'd rather be in a good fight myself. You've got your mates round you, we know what we're doing and there aren't many who can better the Roman army.

We don't get much fighting out here – not proper battles. We've had a couple of skirmishes but a lot of the time it's more like crowd control. They can get quite excited, the Jews, especially when anything to do with religion is concerned. And that seems to be most of the time. Right touchy lot they are. I was up at Caesarea at the main camp for the first three years. We had one incident up in the Northern area where there were some fanatics going about causing mayhem but we soon got that sorted. They've got no discipline, no organisation. I don't know why they try it on.

It's a bit livelier here in Jerusalem. I've been here a little over a year. Our cohort came to reinforce the garrison for the Festival last year and my century stayed on. It's been all right I suppose. I prefer it in Gaul myself – you get more fighting there. But at least it's not Britain – now there's a cold miserable dump. And have you ever tasted their wine – terrible.

I'd been with the same eight blokes in our platoon for two years. We got on pretty well. But I've just been shifted and I'm not sure how I'm going to like it. I know I volunteered – well that's what they call it, but you don't really have a choice. They say it's specialist work – executions. A step up. I'm not sure. They tell me I'll soon get used to it. I've only done one lot so far and I don't think you ever forget the first, do you?

Marcellus, he's the centurion, ordered us out just after cock crow. There were two robbers who had already been sentenced and he said there was a possible third. A prisoner had just been brought in by the Jewish leaders – someone they wanted to get rid of. They had been to the Prefect's palace and there was a whole lot of toing and froing from what I could gather. The fourth century got called out when a crowd gathered and started baying and chanting. They wanted Pilate to release a terrorist we'd got locked up, bloke called Barabbas, and to have this other bloke, Jesus, executed instead. Didn't make much sense to me but they had their way in the end. The lads brought him down for the usual scourging. It's painful that. I should know, I had it once for falling asleep on duty. It really cuts you up.

Anyhow, Gallus decided to have some fun. He really does have a wicked sense of humour. He'd heard that this bloke Jesus had claimed to be king of the Jews. Some chance! So we dressed him up, with a purple cloak and all, and Gallus got some thorn twigs and twisted them into a crown and plonked it on his head. It was a right laugh. Then we took him out to start the trudge up to the Skull – it's what they call the place where we do executions. It's a bit of a rocky out-crop really, in an old quarry. But it's a good name. I didn't like the look of the way this Jesus was walking. He could have pegged out on us which would have made me look a proper fool, this being my first time, so I collared some bloke in the crowd to carry the cross-piece for him. When we got him to the Skull I got the spikes out and we nailed him down. I thought there was going to be all screams and that. There was with the other two. But do you know all he said was 'Father forgive them, they don't know what they're up to.' What kind of thing was that to say? I knew perfectly well what I was doing.

Anyhow we got him hoisted up and offered him some sour wine, but he wouldn't take any. And then it was just a matter of waiting. Apparently there's no telling how long it will take. We got his clothes and divided them between us – a bit of a perk like. The tunic was spare so we threw for it. Didn't get it. I'm never lucky at dice. After about three hours it got really dark. I thought we were going to have a storm. One of the blokes said he felt the earth move but I think it was just a rumble of thunder. There was the usual crowd watching. Even some of the religious leaders came out to have a look and pass comments. They said some of his friends were there but I can't say I noticed. Anyhow, round about three in the afternoon orders came that out of respect for the Jewish sabbath we should finish them off. We whacked the legs of the two thieves with the iron pole and that put an end to them. But before we got to Jesus he let out this cry, 'It is finished', or something like that, and then he died. So Marcellus told us to give him a poke in the side with a spear just to make sure.

I don't understand Marcellus. He's a long-serving officer. Seen it all. He's been in charge of execution parties for some time. But he just stood there staring at the Jesus fellow. 'That bloke was innocent,' he said. Well what would he know? He could be the son of God for all I care. We'd done our job – got it over in reasonable time and that was that. Proud of it? No I wouldn't say that. But I don't suppose I shall ever forget it.

20. Mary of Magdala – seeing isn't everything
(Matthew 27:57 - 28:10; Mark 15:40 - 16:8; Luke 23:50 - 24:12; John 19:31 - 20:18)

I'm thinking of going away. I haven't decided yet but I may join John. He's planning to go to Ephesus now that Mary has died and he no longer has her to look after. Her death brought so many things back. Not that a day goes by that I don't think about him. But somehow it made me think again about what happened. After all, I was there and saw it all. But as I always say, seeing isn't everything. There's more to it than that. There's sight but more than that there's insight. It's a gift from God. At least that's how I see it. There are times when the Lord feels just as close as when we were with him in those early days in Galilee, even closer in some ways.

It all seems so distant now, those days before I knew him. It's another world. I lived in Magdala, on the coast. After the death of my husband I became ill. Everything seemed so dark and pointless. I was so angry that he should have been taken from me. The wealth he left me could never make up for that. I know my friends got anxious about me, the way I was behaving. I didn't really care. And then they took me to see Jesus. I don't remember what he said but I could feel his touch on my head, the way he held my hands. I still see the way he looked at me. And then it was as though all the evil demons churning around inside me were taken away. I never felt so free. I had nothing to keep me in Magdala so I joined his followers and paid for what I could to see they ate properly. I just wanted to be close to him. There were other women in the group as well and I think we were all a bit in love with him. I still am.

We followed him when he left Galilee and headed towards Jerusalem. I had these terrible feelings that something dreadful was going to happen. He used to tell us he would be crucified and then rise again. I didn't really understand how that could be but it made me so anxious. And of course that's exactly what did happen. When we arrived in Jerusalem I stayed at Bethany and it was there we heard the terrible news that he had been arrested and was to be crucified. We were beside ourselves and went to the killing place, the Skull. There were the usual gawping crowds. We just wanted to be with him, even if we could only watch from a distance. I don't know what happened to the men but John was the only one there with us and he said it was dangerous just to be seen there. What did we care? How could they be doing such things to our beloved Jesus? Mary, Jesus' mother, was there as well. It must have been just terrible for her.

It was late afternoon when he died. Joseph and Nicodemus had the courage to go to Pilate and ask if they could take his body down and bury him before night came and the Sabbath started. Joseph had a tomb nearby that would do as a temporary burial place. We wrapped Jesus' body in a linen shroud but everything had to be done in such a hurry that we didn't have time to anoint him. Mary, Martha's sister, said it was all right – she had done it earlier! We watched as they blocked the tomb entrance and made sure we knew just where it was. I know people still say strange things, like he wasn't really dead or we later visited the wrong tomb. What nonsense! I was there. There was no way we could make a mistake like that.

After the Sabbath was over, some of us decided that as soon as we could, we would go back to the tomb. We even took some spices for anointing, though I'm not quite sure what we thought we would actually do. The sun was rising as we reached the tomb. I had to check we were in the right place because it felt different somehow. And then I realised – there was no stone blocking the entrance. We had no idea what had happened to it and then when I looked in the tomb I saw it was empty. My heart sank. What could have happened to Jesus' body? I wondered if Peter and the others had already moved it to a more permanent place. I left the others and just rushed to John's house where Peter was staying. I told them what we had found and Peter and John ran, as puzzled as I was. I followed behind and they had already left by the time I got there. I felt so desperately sad. Everything I had treasured had come to an end. Wasn't killing him enough, that now he should be stolen away? I just stood there weeping for some time. Then I went back to the tomb and looked in. There was no body – just the shroud and head cloth. And what seemed like two shining figures at either end of where he had lain. They asked me why I was weeping, as though there was no need for it. And I just poured out my grief – that even his body had been taken away. I turned to leave and saw someone standing a little way off. I thought he was the garden manager and asked him to tell me where he had taken the body. And then he spoke – just my name. That familiar way he had of calling me. And I saw it was the Lord. I ran to him and fell at his feet, clasping him. I didn't know what had happened. I just knew it was him. All that he had said made sense. He wouldn't let me cling to him – how could he? We all had to let him go, see him in new ways. He would be with God, his Father and our Father. That's how we would know him That's how we do know him.

I was amazed and terrified and awestruck all at the same time. I rushed back to tell the others and just blurted out 'I have seen the Lord.' Seen and believed.

21. Peter – what a boaster (John 21:1-19)

I don't know what the future will hold, all I know is that I shall spend it following my Lord. There's nothing else I want to do, nothing else I could do. The last few weeks have been a very bumpy journey – like riding a three-legged camel, as the saying goes. There was so much that seemed possible that day we followed Jesus into Jerusalem – so much that indicated here was indeed the Messiah. I hoped it would be the start of the new age. And I suppose it was, only not in the way I expected. So much about these days had not been as I expected – me included.

From what seemed like a high point, things began to go downhill. Jesus talked more and more about what he saw as his own future, dark and terrible. It began to feel inevitable and though he tried to make us understand there would be more than death, we couldn't see the light at the end of the tunnel. I tried to tell him there could be another way, that it was unthinkable that he should die the way he said. I had done that before when it first clicked with me that he was indeed the Christ and he had spoken of the need for him to die. He had really rounded on me then and he was just as straight now. It was as though, as much as he trusted me in so many ways, looked on me as a sort of leader of the others, he knew what was really in me, knew I was just as frail as they were. And yet he still didn't give up on me.

I suppose that was what he was saying at the last meal when he insisted on washing my feet. I wasn't happy about that to start with – it was such a menial thing for him to do for us. It was as though we could only really be part of his followers if we allowed him to wash us, purify us. I see that even clearer now.

There was so much going on that night. There was the meal itself and the way he shared the bread and the wine. It wasn't so much what he did, he always had that particular way of dividing the bread and passing the cup to us. It was what he said about it being his body and his blood.

And then he talked about going, to a place where we would only follow later. I didn't know what he was on about. Why couldn't I follow him then? It was getting to me and I got quite agitated. I told him straight, I would follow him anywhere, even if it cost me my life. What did he think I was? How could he think I wouldn't risk everything for him? I made a right scene out of it, even showed him the sword I'd brought along. The more worried I got, the stronger I protested. And oh the look he gave me, such sadness and trouble and love all mixed up in those eyes of his. And there, right in front of everyone, he told me that before the night was out, before the morning cock crow, I would deny him three times. I couldn't believe he'd said that. Not me, the one he'd called Rocky! Not me, the one who'd always given a lead, been there at special moments. How could he possibly think that of me? Because he knew me, that's why. Knew me through and through, better than I knew myself.

And it happened. To my shame it happened just as he said. It was in the palace courtyard after he'd been arrested. At least I hadn't run off. Perhaps it would have been better if I had. John had some connections and made it possible for us to get in. The woman at the gate asked if I was one of Jesus' disciples and I just denied it. I didn't want her to shut me out. I was hanging around not really knowing what to do, trying to keep warm by the charcoal fire. One of the blokes asked me the same question. 'Not me, mate,' I said. Someone who'd been out in the olive grove said he recognised me as one of Jesus' followers. That got me worried and I really let rip, telling them I didn't know the man. And then the cock crowed. I just fled. I've never felt so awful in my life. How could I have done that? Me, the big, brave, boasting Peter. I didn't dare even go to the execution place in case he saw me. He'd know what I'd done. He did anyway.

It all came out after breakfast on the beach. After the end of the Festival I got some of the lads, old fishing pals, to go back up north again to see if we could pick up the threads of our lives on the lake. It's true we had seen Jesus alive again, the tomb had been empty, he had shown himself to us but it didn't seem to be leading anywhere. Life had to go on, so we went back to our old trade.

Perhaps we'd lost our touch. We fished all night and caught nothing, not even a tiddler. In the early light we saw this figure on the shore and he called to us to try putting our nets on the other side. It was amazing. In no time at all we had all the fish we could dream of. John said, 'It's the Lord.' Without thinking I jumped overboard and went to greet him.

He had a meal ready for us and when we had finished it he took me to one side. I didn't know what was coming. 'Simon', he said. He'd hadn't called me that for years. 'Do you love me more than these others?' Well I didn't know about that. 'Lord,' I said, 'you know I care for you.' And then he told me to feed his lambs. He asked me three times. Three times, the same question. Three times! All I could think of was the three times I had denied him. I was crying and hurting so much inside. He knew me better than myself, he knew how much I loved him, even though I had denied him. In spite of it all he still wanted me – to do his work, to care for the flock. But he told me the price of it, the cost there would be. No freedom like I had as a youngster, there would be a death like his. That was what it would mean to follow him and to follow him was what he asked of me. Me the boaster, the one who had denied him. If I could be a follower then there was hope for anyone. I don't know what the future will hold, but wherever he leads me, I know I will follow. And that's not a boast, that's a promise.

Services for Holy Week and Easter

1. Palm Sunday – procession

Processions form a significant part of the witness and worship of Palm Sunday. Local situations will determine how elaborate or simple they are. In some places the procession will involve a walk around the village or neighbourhood and include an actual donkey. Elsewhere this will not be practical but there will be a procession around the church itself, either outside or inside or both. The theme of procession, acclamation and humility might well be given a quite different kind of expression with the Christ figure riding a bike and followers waving scarves. The detailed arrangements are up to local decision.

The service offered here is an outline that could be adapted for any of such settings. It incorporates readings, movement, singing and prayers. It is intended to be a resource rather than a fixed blueprint. Different voices could be used to lead at each station.

Station 1 – Gathering

We gather in the name of the Lord, the Christ,
the King of Glory.
We gather as the followers of the Prince of Peace,
the Servant of all.
We gather not knowing what he will ask of us,
not always understanding what he will do in us.
We will follow the One who comes in the name of the Lord.

'While Jesus was going up to Jerusalem, he took the twelve disciples aside by themselves, and said to them on the way, "See, we are going up to Jerusalem, and the Son of Man will be handed over to the chief priests and scribes, and they will condemn him to death; then they will hand him over to the Gentiles to be mocked and flogged and crucified; and on the third day he will be raised."' *(Matthew 20:17-19)*
We will follow the One who comes in the name of the Lord.

'Jesus said: "If any want to become my followers, let them deny themselves and take up their cross and follow me. For those who want to save their life will lose it, and those who lose their life for my sake will find it."' *(Matthew 16:24, 25)*
We will follow the One who comes in the name of the Lord.

Hymn

Will you come and follow me?

During the singing of this hymn palm crosses are distributed.

Prayers

Lord Jesus, you set your face to go to Jerusalem and told your disciples what would happen there. Grant us a trust like theirs, that we may follow you whatever is asked of us and wherever you may lead. Grant us through your Spirit the knowledge of your presence with us, to sustain us and guide us, to encourage and to challenge us, that we may witness to your truth and your love in all we do and say and are. In your name we ask this. **Amen.**

We hold the palm of acclamation.
May we always be bold in our witness to you, our King.
We hold the cross of sacrifice.
May we always be courageous in following your way of service to others, whatever the cost. Amen.

Further prayers of praise and commitment may be offered.

Lord Jesus, you are the Way we would follow, the Truth we would know, the Life we would experience and the King we would serve. Enable us by your Spirit to fulfil our intentions, to be steadfast in our loyalty and courageous in our actions. **Amen.**

The procession moves to its next station.

Station 2 – Preparation

'Rejoice greatly, O daughter Zion!
Shout aloud, O daughter Jerusalem!
Lo, your king comes to you;
triumphant and victorious is he,
humble and riding on a donkey,
on a colt, the foal of a donkey.' *(Zechariah 9:9)*
We will follow the One who comes in the name of the Lord.

'When they had come near Jerusalem and had reached Bethphage, at the
Mount of Olives, Jesus sent two disciples, saying to them, "Go into the
village ahead of you, and immediately you will find a donkey tied, and a
colt with her; untie them and bring them to me. If anyone says anything
to you, just say this, 'The Lord needs them.' And he will send them
immediately."' *(Matthew 21:1-3)*
We will follow the One who comes in the name of the Lord.

Hymn

We have a king who rides a donkey *(verses 4 and 5 may be omitted)*

If a donkey is to be used it should be brought in during this hymn.

All creatures give praise to the Lord,
for he has wonderfully made you and all are in his care.
None is too humble for the King to use.
None is too lowly for the Lord to call to his service.
We will follow the One who comes in the name of the Lord.

Lord, you call us to your service.
May we be prompt in our response and willing in our obedience.
We will follow the One who comes in the name of the Lord.

Lord, you invite us to share in your work of love.
It is not a burden to serve you but a joy;
it is not a hardship but a privilege.
We will follow the One who comes in the name of the Lord.

Lord Jesus, King of all, you sought the help of others in your needs and met the needs of others. We pray for all who are in special need: the hungry and the lonely, the lost and the forsaken, the oppressed and all victims of violence and abuse. May we be generous in our giving, sensitive in our helping and loving in our supporting. **Amen.**

Further prayers of intercession for the needs of the world and of individuals may be offered.

The procession moves to its next station.

Station 3 – Enthronement

'The Lord is king; let the peoples tremble!
He sits enthroned upon the cherubim;
let the earth quake!
The Lord is great in Zion;
he is exalted over all the peoples.
Let them praise your great and awesome name.
Holy is he!
Mighty King, lover of justice,
you have established equity;
you have executed justice and righteousness in Jacob.' *(Psalm 99:1-4)*
Blessed is the king. Hosanna in the highest!

'The disciples went and did as Jesus had directed them; they brought the donkey and the colt, and put their cloaks on them, and he sat on them. A very large crowd spread their cloaks on the road, and others cut branches from the trees and spread them on the road.' *(Matthew 21:6-8)*
Blessed is the king. Hosanna in the highest!

Hymn

All glory laud and honour
or You are the king of glory

If practicable, coats and branches could be laid down in front of the procession.

Lord, you are king,
enthroned in majesty,
come and rule in our hearts.
Blessed is the king. Hosanna in the highest!

Lord, you are king,
the ruler of nations,
bring peace to our world.
Blessed is the king. Hosanna in the highest!

Lord, you are king,
worshipped by angels,
accept our praise.
Blessed is the king. Hosanna in the highest!

Lord of lords and King of kings, we pray for all who have the responsibility of leadership in the nations of the world. Grant them integrity in all their dealings and decisions, and a desire to serve that is stronger than a desire for personal power. In Jesus' name. **Amen.**

Further prayers for the leaders of the nations may be offered.
The procession arrives at the church door or, if it has been taking place inside the church, moves to the back. The procession is met by people waving palm branches.

Station 4 – Acclamation

Blessed is the one who comes in the name of the Lord!
We bless you from the house of the Lord.
The Lord is God and he has given us light.
Bind the festal procession with branches
up to the horns of the altar.
Blessed is the One who comes in the name of the Lord.

'The great crowd that had come to the festival heard that Jesus was coming to Jerusalem. So they took branches of palm trees and went out to meet him, shouting, "Hosanna! Blessed is the one who comes in the name of the Lord – the King of Israel!"' *(John 12:12, 13)*
Blessed is the One who comes in the name of the Lord.

'The crowds that went ahead of him and that followed were shouting, "Hosanna to the Son of David! Blessed is the one who comes in the name of the Lord! Hosanna in the highest heaven."' *(Matthew 21:9)*
Blessed is the One who comes in the name of the Lord.

'The whole multitude of the disciples began to praise God joyfully with a loud voice for all the deeds of power that they had seen, saying, "Blessed is the king who comes in the name of the Lord! Peace in heaven, and glory in the highest heaven!"' *(Luke 19:37, 38)*
Blessed is the One who comes in the name of the Lord.

The procession moves through the church to the front during the singing of the hymn.

Hymn

Ride on! Ride on in majesty!

The palm branches are held up and waved.

Glory and honour, praise and adoration,
we offer to Jesus our King.
With crowds adoring,
we greet his coming.
He is our Lord and our God.
Hosanna in the highest!

The palm crosses are held up.

Glory and honour, praise and adoration,
we offer to Jesus our Saviour.
The cross will bring true victory;
the sacrifice of God's lamb will bring our peace.
Hosanna in the highest!

Reflection or Address

Prayer

Heavenly Father,
we have joined in the acclamation of your Son,
echoing the words of the crowds.
Forgive us when our praise grows silent,
when our acclamations give way to apathy.
Forgive us the times we ask for the wrong things
and look only to our own wants.
Forgive us the times when we hide from your demands,
and want your power but not your love.
Go with us through this coming week,
that we may accompany you on your road to the cross
and so discover the joy and the wonder of your resurrection.
We ask this in the name of our King and our Saviour. **Amen.**

Hymn

Praise to the Holiest

Blessing

May the Lord of Glory bless you and keep you.
May the Son of David bless you and keep you.
May the humble King bless you and keep you on this day of acclamation,
through this week of trial and execution
and in the wonder of his resurrection. **Amen.**

2. An evening act of worship for Monday of Holy Week

Come, bless the Lord, all you servants of the Lord,
who stand by night in the house of the Lord!
Lift up your hands to the holy place, and bless the Lord.
May the Lord, maker of heaven and earth, bless you from Zion.

Hymn

Be still and know that I am God
or As we are gathered

Draw us, Lord, to yourself by the power of your Spirit. Quieten our hearts and our minds as we approach in worship. Hold us in the love of your Son as we follow him through this Holy Week.
Journey with us, Lord.

Cleanse us, Lord, from all that distorts your image in us,
in your mercy, forgive us.
For all that divides us from one another and from you,
in your mercy, forgive us.
For our satisfaction with less than the truth,
in your mercy, forgive us.
For any dishonesty in thought or action,
in your mercy, forgive us.
For worship that is unworthy of you,
in your mercy, forgive us.

May the Lord forgive us (you).
May he grant us (you) peace in our (your) hearts.
May he lead us (you) by his Spirit. **Amen.**

Psalm

(this may be said together or antiphonally)

It is good to give thanks to the Lord,
to sing praises to your name, O Most High;

to declare your steadfast love in the morning,
and your faithfulness by night,

to the music of the lute and the harp,
to the melody of the lyre.

For you, O Lord, have made me glad by your work;
at the works of your hands I sing for joy.

(Psalm 92:1-4)

A suitable piece of music may be played.

Reading

Matthew 21:12, 13 *or* Mark 11:15-19 *or* Luke 19:45, 46 *or* John 2:13-22

A time for reflection during which a piece of music may be played.

Reflection or Address

Prayers

Lord, you came to the Temple.
May we delight in worshipping you.

You drove out traders and upturned tables.
May we be passionate for the truth.

You wanted the Temple to be a place of prayer for all.
May we welcome all who seek you in our midst.

You faced opposition with courage.
May we be brave in standing up for you.

Lord, we pray for all who lead worship,
that they may be true to your word and sensitive to the needs of your people;
that all they do may be for your glory and the honour of your name. **Amen.**

Lord, we pray for all who worship,
that they may do so in spirit and in truth,
open to your forgiveness and drawn by your Spirit. **Amen.**

Lord, we pray for all with whom we disagree,
that we may treat them with respect even when feelings run high.
Help us to find a way through our quarrels,
through the grace and the guidance of your Spirit. **Amen.**

Further intercessions and thanksgivings may be offered.

Our Father . . .

Hymn

Before the ending of the day

Blessing

May the Lord hold you in his loving arms;
may he grant you restful sleep and peace in your hearts;
may he bless you and keep you safe, this night and for evermore.
Amen.

3. An evening act of worship for Tuesday of Holy Week

Come, bless the Lord, all you servants of the Lord,
who stand by night in the house of the Lord!
Lift up your hands to the holy place, and bless the Lord.
May the Lord, maker of heaven and earth, bless you from Zion.

Hymn

When all thy mercies *or* Be the centre of my life *or* Ubi caritas

Draw us, Lord, to yourself by the power of your Spirit.
Quieten our hearts and our minds as we approach in worship.
Hold us in the love of your Son as we follow him through this Holy Week.
Journey with us, Lord.

Lord, for the blindness which prevents us from seeing your glory,
in your mercy, forgive us.
Lord, for the meanness that restricts our thankfulness,
in your mercy, forgive us.
Lord, for our failure to honour you as king,
in your mercy, forgive us.
Lord, for the pride that prevents us admitting our faults,
in your mercy, forgive us.
Lord, for our lack of faith,
in your mercy, forgive us.

May the Lord forgive us (you).
May he grant us (you) peace in our (your) hearts.
May he lead us (you) by his Spirit. **Amen.**

Psalm

(this may be said together or antiphonally)

Bless the Lord, O my soul,
and all that is within me, bless his holy name.

Bless the Lord, O my soul,
and do not forget all his benefits –

who forgives all your iniquity,
who heals all your diseases,

who redeems your life from the Pit,
who crowns you with steadfast love and mercy,

who satisfies you with good as long as you live
so that your youth is renewed like the eagle's.
(Psalm 103:1-5)

A suitable piece of music may be played.

Reading

John 12:1-11 *or* Matthew 26:1-13 *or* Mark 14:1-9

A time for reflection during which a piece of music may be played.

Reflection or Address

Prayers

Lord, you come to be with us, our most honoured guest.
May we welcome you with joy.

Lord, you are our king, the anointed one.
May we serve you and obey you.

Lord, you forgive us and love us.
May we praise you and worship you.

Lord, you died and you rose for us.
Prepare us for your Passion and your resurrection.

Lord, we pray for those who are burdened with guilt,
that they may know your forgiveness
and live to give you thanks. **Amen.**

Lord, we pray for the poor and the homeless,
for the hungry and the unloved,
that we may be generous in our giving. **Amen.**

Lord, we pray for those who suffer and are in pain,
for the dying and those who care for them,
that they may know your presence and your comfort. **Amen.**

Lord, we pray for all leaders and those who bear great responsibility, for wisdom in their decision-making and integrity in their actions, that all people may be ruled with justice and honesty. **Amen.**

Further intercessions and thanksgivings may be offered.

Our Father . . .

Hymn

Before the ending of the day

Blessing

May the Lord hold you in his loving arms;
may he grant you restful sleep and peace in your hearts;
may he bless you and keep you safe, this night and for evermore.
Amen.

4. An evening act of worship for Wednesday of Holy Week

Come, bless the Lord, all you servants of the Lord,
who stand by night in the house of the Lord!
Lift up your hands to the holy place, and bless the Lord.
May the Lord, maker of heaven and earth, bless you from Zion.

Hymn

Jesus, humble was your birth
or Christ is the world's light

Draw us, Lord, to yourself by the power of your Spirit.
Quieten our hearts and our minds as we approach in worship.
Hold us in the love of your Son as we follow him through this Holy Week.
Journey with us, Lord.

Jesus, our Lord and our Master, forgive us the times we deny you,
in your mercy, forgive us.

Jesus, our Teacher and our Friend, forgive us the times we betray you,
in your mercy, forgive us.

For lost opportunities to speak of your love,
in your mercy, forgive us.

For love of possessions and desire for wealth,
in your mercy, forgive us.

For the guilt that leads us to despair,
in your mercy, forgive us.

May the Lord forgive us (you).
May he grant us (you) peace in our (your) hearts.
May he lead us (you) by his Spirit. **Amen.**

Psalm

(this may be said together or antiphonally)

Happy are those who consider the poor;
the Lord delivers them in the day of trouble.

The Lord protects them and keeps them alive;
they are called happy in the land.
You do not give them up to the will of their enemies.

As for me, I said, 'O Lord, be gracious to me;
heal me, for I have sinned against you.'

My enemies wonder in malice
when I will die, and my name perish.

And when they come to see me, they utter empty words,
while their hearts gather mischief;
when they go out, they tell it abroad.

All who hate me whisper together about me;
they imagine the worst for me.

They think that a deadly thing has fastened on me,
that I will not rise again from where I lie.

Even my bosom friend in whom I trusted,
who ate of my bread, has lifted the heel against me.

But you, O Lord, be gracious to me,
and raise me up, that I may repay them.

(Psalm 41:1, 2, 4-10)

A suitable piece of music may be played.

Reading

John 13:21-32, 18:1-6
or Matthew 26:3-5, 14-16, 20-25, 47-50

A time for reflection during which a piece of music may be played.

Reflection or Address

Prayers

Lord, you have called us to be your friends.
May we delight in your presence and follow you always.

Lord, you welcome us to eat at your table.
May we gather with joy in communion with you.

Lord, you know what is in our hearts.
May we be loyal in all we do and say.

Lord, you are our light and our life.
May we walk in your light and live in your love.

Lord, we pray for all who have been let down,
for all who have been betrayed,
for those who have been deserted by friends or by family.
Lord, in your mercy hear our prayer.

Lord, we pray for all who fear the dark
and who face the night in loneliness,
for all who sleep rough and live on the streets.
Lord, in your mercy hear our prayer.

Lord, we pray for the police and special constables,
for street pastors and neighbourhood watch,
for all who work to keep us safe.
Lord, in your mercy hear our prayer.

Further intercessions and thanksgivings may be offered.

Our Father . . .

Hymn

Jesus, humble was your birth
or One whose heart is hard as steel

Blessing

May the Lord hold you in his loving arms;
may he grant you restful sleep and peace in your hearts;
may he bless you and keep you safe, this night and for evermore.
Amen.

5. A service for Maundy Thursday – the Exodus meal

In this service the various elements in the accounts of the Last Supper are not only read but 'enacted'. If possible the altar/table to be used is set at one side, unadorned. The cloth, the vessels, the lights and the linen are ready to be brought on. As far as possible the area at the front of the church is bare, waiting for the preparations to be made.

A large pottery jug containing warm water, a bowl and a towel should be set to one side. Ideally there should be a washing of feet, but in some churches it may be felt only possible to enact this part of the evening by washing people's hands. Three to five people will be needed for this, depending on the numbers attending. As well as the president/celebrant someone will be needed to carry the bowl and the jug.

A loaf, not wafers, should be used – ideally it should be unleavened bread. Wine is still in its bottle ready to be 'poured out'. If possible a pottery plate and goblet should be used.

Different people may be used for the readings and the prayers of intercession. The president/celebrant may be the person who also gives the Reflections, or this may be a different person.

All who are to be particularly involved should be well briefed beforehand and given a full explanation of what they are expected to do. All liturgy is drama, but on this occasion the dramatic element is especially obvious and should therefore be properly directed so that it runs smoothly and does not detract from but rather enhances the act of worship.

The following 'Foreword' might be printed at the beginning of the order of service:

> **The Liturgy of Maundy Thursday brings us close to the events of the night before our Lord's death. It is the night of fellowship and betrayal, a night of humility and humbling, a night of agonising conflict and courageous obedience, a night of brave words and a traitorous kiss. It is a night of such contrasts and such richness that we can only glimpse its meaning, only approach the edges of its tragic darkness and radiant glory.**

This service recalls the night of the institution of the Last Supper, and in doing so it seeks more explicitly than is usual at a regular Eucharist to recall that night of Passover. We shall share in preparation and offering. The Christ will serve us and we shall receive his service. We shall join in the meal and in the hymn of departure. We shall spend a short while watching with him and we shall leave with him.

Welcome and opening prayer

Lord, you welcome us to share this meal of celebration with you.
We will come, Lord Jesus.

Lord, you call us to prepare this place and the place in our hearts.
We will obey, Lord Jesus.

Lord, you reveal to us the way of humble service.
We will serve, Lord Jesus.

Lord, you share with us the broken bread and the wine poured out.
We will eat and drink, Lord Jesus.

Lord, you are on your way to crucifixion.
We will follow, Lord Jesus.

Hymn

Let all mortal flesh keep silence

Preparation and Passover

Reading

Luke 22:7-16

Reflection 1 – the table is prepared (see page 187)

Psalm

(part of Psalm 103)

(all stand)

During the saying of this psalm the altar/table is brought on and prepared with cloth, lights, etc.

Bless the Lord, O my soul, and all that is within me, bless his holy name.
Bless the Lord, O my soul, and all that is within me, bless his holy name.

The Lord works vindication and justice for all who are oppressed.
He made known his ways to Moses, his acts to the people of Israel.
Bless the Lord, O my soul, and all that is within me, bless his holy name.

The Lord is merciful and gracious, slow to anger and abounding in
steadfast love.
He does not deal with us according to our sins,
nor repay us according to our iniquities.
Bless the Lord, O my soul, and all that is within me, bless his holy name.

Let us admit to God the sin which always confronts us.
Lord God, we have sinned against you;
we have done evil in your sight.
We are sorry and repent.
Have mercy on us according to your love.
Wash away our wrongdoing and cleanse us from our sin.
Renew a right spirit within us
and restore to us the joy of your salvation,
through Jesus Christ our Lord. Amen.

Almighty God, who forgives all who truly repent,
have mercy upon you.
Through the love of Christ and his life given for you,
may he pardon and renew you,
that strong as goodness you may walk the path of holiness, now and for
ever. **Amen.**

The meal begins

(all sit)

Reading

John 13:1-17

Reflection 2 – the washing (see page 189)

(see page 189)

During the washing Psalm 51:1-10 will be said together.

Have mercy on me, O God, according to your steadfast love;
according to your abundant mercy blot out my transgressions.

Wash me thoroughly from my iniquity,
and cleanse me from my sin.

For I know my transgressions,
and my sin is ever before me.

Against you, you alone, have I sinned,
and done what is evil in your sight,
so that you are justified in your sentence
and blameless when you pass judgement.

Indeed, I was born guilty,
a sinner when my mother conceived me.

You desire truth in the inward being;
therefore teach me wisdom in my secret heart.

Purge me with hyssop, and I shall be clean;
wash me, and I shall be whiter than snow.
Let me hear joy and gladness;
let the bones that you have crushed rejoice.

Hide your face from my sins,
and blot out all my iniquities.

Create in me a clean heart, O God,
and put a new and right spirit within me.

Glory to the Father, and to the Son, and to the Holy Spirit,
as it was in the beginning, is now, and ever shall be,
world without end. Amen.

If necessary music may be played until the washing is completed.

Hymn

Brother, sister, let me serve you

The bread and wine are brought to the table.

Reading

1 Corinthians 11:23, 24

Reflection 3 – The bread (see page 190)

Prayers of thanksgiving

Father, we give you thanks for this night of fellowship, for the presence of our Lord amongst us and with us. He is the host, the head at our table and he invites us to join him. Let us bless the Lord.
Thanks be to God.

Father, we give you thanks for our world, for all its resources and for its beauty. We thank you for bread – for all that sustains us. We thank you for wine – for all that delights us. We remember with sadness the hungry and the unhappy. Let us bless the Lord.
Thanks be to God.

Father, we give you thanks for all who serve you in the church and in the community. For those who do the lowly jobs no one else wants to do. For those who are busy when we are at rest. Let us bless the Lord.
Thanks be to God.

Father, we give you thanks for freedom, for peace, for good health, and we remember all prisoners, all who suffer because of violence, all who are sick, at home and in hospital. Let us bless the Lord.
Thanks be to God.

Hymn

Broken for me
or My God, and is thy table spread

Reading

1 Corinthians 11:25, 26

Reflection 4 – The wine (see page 191)

Prayers of intercession

Father, on this night of meeting with his disciples Jesus was betrayed. We pray for all whose loyalty is being tested and who will tonight be tempted to betray friends, loved ones or themselves. Grant them your strength, and grant us grace when we are tempted to deny you.
Lord, in your mercy, **hear our prayer.**

Father, on this night Jesus prayed that his disciples might be one. We pray for your Church throughout the world and we pray for its unity. We pray for all church leaders, that they may be guided by your Spirit, be true to your teaching and serve your people with wisdom and humility.
Lord, in your mercy, **hear our prayer.**

Father, on this night your Son commanded his disciples to love but suffered rejection himself. We pray for all who feel themselves rejected and unloved and for those who feel that their lives are useless and who are in despair. We pray for those we know who are unwell and who grieve at this time. May we be bearers of love and hope to those around us who look to us for care and support.
Lord, in your mercy, **hear our prayer.**

Father, on this night they came with soldiers bearing arms to arrest your Son. We pray for all victims of injustice, persecution and war. We pray for members of the armed forces who fight on our behalf to maintain peace and justice. We pray for the injured and the maimed, for the terrified and the grieving, for all who work for reconciliation and peace.
Lord, in your mercy, **hear our prayer.**

Lord Jesus, on this night before your crucifixion, we pray for all who will die this night. For those whose lives will end in violence or accident, and for those who will slip peacefully into their final sleep. We pray for those who watch and wait and grieve.

Lord, in your mercy, **hear our prayer.**

Merciful Father, accept these prayers for the sake of your Son, our Saviour, Jesus Christ. Amen.

Collect

God our Father, you have invited us to share in the supper which your Son gave to his Church to proclaim his death until he comes again; may he nourish us by his presence and unite us in his love. For his sake we ask this. **Amen.**

The Peace

(all stand)

On the night he was betrayed and arrested Jesus said to his friends:
Peace I leave with you; my peace I give to you.
The peace of the Lord be always with you.
And also with you.

Hymn

Lord Jesus Christ
or A new commandment

A prayer of blessing for the gifts of bread and wine may be said.

Blessed art thou, O Lord of all creation; you bring forth wheat from the earth.
Blessed art thou, O Lord of all creation; you bring forth vines from the earth.
Blessed art thou, O Lord of all creation, for the bread and the wine we share together.

The Eucharistic Prayer

The Lord is here.
He is present among us.

He calls us to his table.
We come in his name.

Holy God, Father of us all,
you gave us your Son
and sent him to live among us.

He came in humility,
born of the Virgin.
He taught of your kingdom
and healed the sick.
He lived with integrity
and in obedience died on the cross,
revealing your forgiving love.
We praise his holy name.

On the night before he died
he had supper with his friends.
He took the towel of the servant
and washed their feet.
During the meal he took the bread,
he gave thanks and broke it.
He gave it to the disciples, saying:
Take, eat, this is my body which is given for you;
do this in remembrance of me.
We remember him:
he is the true bread,
the bread of life.

At the end of the meal
he took the cup of wine.
He gave thanks and shared it with his disciples, saying:
Drink this, all of you;
this is my blood of the new covenant,
which is shed for you for the forgiveness of sins;
do this in remembrance of me.
We remember him:
he is the true vine,
the wine of salvation.

We proclaim his death
and we celebrate his rising.
In the power of the Holy Spirit
may this bread and this wine
be for us his body and his blood.
Fill us with your grace,
empower us by the Spirit
and draw us into the glory of your kingdom.
Praise to our God,
the Holy One,
for all that he has done
through the Son
in the power of the Spirit.

Our Father . . .

Jesus is the Lamb of God
who takes away the sins of the world.
Blessed are those who are called to his supper.
Lord, I am not worthy to receive you,
but only say the word and I shall be healed.

All gather round the table/altar to receive the bread and wine or a blessing. After receiving, the people remain standing close to the table/altar.

Prayer

Lord, you are with us in the sacred meal;
you share fellowship with us and call us to follow you.
Nourish us through the gifts of your body and your blood;
they speak of your self-giving love and your death for us.
Grant us the courage and the faith that we may follow you in the way,
taking up our cross and looking for the coming of your kingdom.
In your name we ask this. **Amen.**

The table is cleared. As the hymn is sung the people move back to their seats.

Hymn

Thy way not mine, O Lord
or Go to dark Gethsemane

When they had sung the hymn, they went out to the Mount of Olives.

If there is no vigil the people leave quietly at this point.

A vigil may follow. Its length will depend on local wishes. The vigil that is set out here is quite brief but may be extended as appropriate.

The lights are dimmed. The scene changes from the Upper Room to the Garden of Gethsemane.

The vigil

Reading

Mark 14:32-40

Watch and pray.
The Lord is in distress of soul, torn between his own desires and the will of the Father; torn between escape and the demands of his own integrity.
We watch and pray.

Silent prayer and reflection.

Reading

Mark 14:41-50

Watch and pray.

The Lord is betrayed with a kiss. With swords and with cudgels they make the arrest. He has not hidden from them and he does not resist. He is to fulfil his destiny and the work of God's saving plan foretold in Scripture. **We watch and are afraid.**

Silent prayer and reflection.

All of them deserted him and fled.

In silence everyone leaves.

6. Good Friday – execution

Three sections are provided, corresponding to the traditional three hours. Each section could be used on its own where only one hour is required.

During times of quiet and reflection suitable music may be played – e.g. tracks from the CD *A Celtic Holy Week and Easter.* (Kevin Mayhew 1490191).

a. A dramatic reading of the Passion:

Matthew 26:57 – 27:66

The reading has been set out in dramatic form. It begins just after the arrest of Jesus. It assumes that the events of Gethsemane, including the betrayal and the moment of arrest, have been used in reflections on Maundy Thursday. If they have not it would be possible to start the reading, following the format used here, from the end of the Last Supper. The accounts in one of the other Gospels could be used rather than Matthew if so desired.

As far as possible, different voices should be used for each of the persons involved. For groups such as soldiers and chief priests a number of those voices could be used together. The whole congregation takes the part of the Crowd.

Opening sentence

Surely he has borne our infirmities and carried our diseases;
yet we accounted him stricken, struck down by God, and afflicted.
But he was wounded for our transgressions, crushed for our iniquities;
upon him was the punishment that made us whole,
and by his bruises we are healed. *(Isaiah 53:4, 5)*

Hymn

One whose heart is hard as steel
or My song is love unknown

Prayer

Look mercifully upon us, Lord,
as we come to this time of your Passion.
Reveal again to us the meaning of your suffering and your death,
that as we hear the story of your self-giving love
we may know the cost of our forgiveness
and the depth of your compassion.
In your dear name we ask it. **Amen.**

1. Denial

Narrator   Those who had arrested Jesus took him to Caiaphas the high priest, in whose house the scribes and the elders had gathered. But Peter was following him at a distance, as far as the courtyard of the high priest; and going inside, he sat with the guards to see how this would end. Now the chief priests and the whole council were looking for false testimony against Jesus so that they might put him to death, but they found none, though many false witnesses came forward. At last two came forward.

Witnesses	This fellow said, 'I am able to destroy the temple of God and to build it in three days.'
Narrator	The high priest stood up.
High priest	Have you no answer? What is it that they testify against you?
Narrator	But Jesus was silent.
High priest	I put you under oath before the living God, tell us if you are the Messiah, the Son of God.
Jesus	You have said so. But I tell you, from now on you will see the Son of Man seated at the right hand of Power and coming on the clouds of heaven.
Narrator	Then the high priest tore his clothes.
High priest	He has blasphemed! Why do we still need witnesses? You have now heard his blasphemy. What is your verdict?
Crowd	He deserves death.
Narrator	Then they spat in his face and struck him; and some slapped him.
Crowd	Prophesy to us, you Messiah. Who is it that struck you?
Narrator	Now Peter was sitting outside in the courtyard. A servant-girl came to him.
Servant girl	You also were with Jesus the Galilean.
Narrator	But he denied it before all of them.
Peter	I do not know what you are talking about.

Narrator   When he went out to the porch, another servant-girl saw him, and she said to the bystanders,

Servant girl This man was with Jesus of Nazareth.

Narrator   Again he denied it with an oath,

Peter   I do not know the man.

Narrator   After a little while the bystanders came up to Peter.

Crowd   Certainly you are also one of them, for your accent betrays you.

Narrator   Then he began to curse, and he swore an oath,

Peter   I do not know the man!

Narrator   At that moment the cock crowed. Then Peter remembered what Jesus had said:

Jesus   Before the cock crows, you will deny me three times.

Narrator   And he went out and wept bitterly.

A time of silent reflection.

Prayer

Forgive us, Lord, for all the times we have denied you, through fear of embarrassment or fear of ridicule, through the weakness of our love for you and the care we have for the opinion of others. Forgive us, Lord, and look on us in mercy. **Amen.**

Hymn

Ah holy Jesus
or I give you love

2. Trial

Narrator	When morning came, all the chief priests and the elders of the people conferred together against Jesus in order to bring about his death. They bound him, led him away, and handed him over to Pilate, the governor. When Judas, his betrayer, saw that Jesus was condemned, he repented and brought back the thirty pieces of silver to the chief priests and the elders.
Judas	I have sinned by betraying innocent blood.
Chief priests	What is that to us? See to it yourself.
Narrator	Throwing down the pieces of silver in the temple, he departed; and he went and hanged himself. But the chief priests, taking the pieces of silver, said,
Chief priests	It is not lawful to put them into the treasury, since they are blood money.
Narrator	After conferring together, they used them to buy the potter's field as a place to bury foreigners. For this reason that field has been called the Field of Blood to this day. Then was fulfilled what had been spoken through the prophet Jeremiah, 'And they took the thirty pieces of silver, the price of the one on whom a price had been set, on whom some of the people of Israel had set a price, and they gave it for the potter's field, as the Lord commanded me.' Now Jesus stood before the governor.
Pilate	Are you the King of the Jews?
Jesus	You say so.
Narrator	But when he was accused by the chief priests and elders, he did not answer.

Pilate	Do you not hear how many accusations they make against you?
Narrator	But he gave him no answer, not even to a single charge, so that the governor was greatly amazed. Now at the festival the governor was accustomed to release a prisoner for the crowd, anyone whom they wanted. At that time they had a notorious prisoner, called Jesus Barabbas. So after they had gathered, Pilate said to them,
Pilate	Whom do you want me to release for you, Jesus Barabbas or Jesus who is called the Messiah?
Narrator	For he realised that it was out of jealousy that they had handed him over. While he was sitting on the judgement seat, his wife sent word to him.
Pilate's wife	Have nothing to do with that innocent man, for today I have suffered a great deal because of a dream about him.
Narrator	Now the chief priests and the elders persuaded the crowds to ask for Barabbas and to have Jesus killed.
Pilate	Which of the two do you want me to release for you?
Crowd	Barabbas.
Pilate	Then what should I do with Jesus who is called the Messiah?
Crowd	Let him be crucified!
Pilate	Why, what evil has he done?
Crowd	Let him be crucified!

Narrator	So when Pilate saw that he could do nothing, but rather that a riot was beginning, he took some water and washed his hands before the crowd.
Pilate	I am innocent of this man's blood, see to it yourselves.
Crowd	His blood be on us and on our children!
Narrator	So he released Barabbas for them; and after flogging Jesus, he handed him over to be crucified. Then the soldiers of the governor took Jesus into the governor's headquarters, and they gathered the whole cohort around him. They stripped him and put a scarlet robe on him, and after twisting some thorns into a crown, they put it on his head. They put a reed in his right hand and knelt before him and mocked him.
Soldiers	Hail, King of the Jews!
Narrator	They spat on him, and took the reed and struck him on the head. After mocking him, they stripped him of the robe and put his own clothes on him. Then they led him away to crucify him.

A time of silent reflection.

Prayer

Your silence spoke of innocence
and the mockery revealed your majesty.
Give us eyes to see your glory
in the humility of your self-giving.
Give us grace
to respond to your love revealed in suffering;
our salvation declared upon your cross. **Amen.**

Hymn

My God I love thee
or When I survey the wondrous cross

3. Crucifixion

Narrator   As they went out, they came upon a man from Cyrene named Simon; they compelled this man to carry his cross. And when they came to a place called Golgotha (which means Place of a Skull), they offered him wine to drink, mixed with gall; but when he tasted it, he would not drink it. And when they had crucified him, they divided his clothes among themselves by casting lots; then they sat down there and kept watch over him. Over his head they put the charge against him, which read, 'This is Jesus, the King of the Jews.' Then two bandits were crucified with him, one on his right and one on his left. Those who passed by derided him, shaking their heads.

Crowds   You who would destroy the temple and build it in three days, save yourself! If you are the Son of God, come down from the cross.

Narrator   In the same way the chief priests also, along with the scribes and elders, were mocking him.

Chief priests   He saved others; he cannot save himself. He is the King of Israel; let him come down from the cross now, and we will believe in him. He trusts in God; let God deliver him now, if he wants to; for he said, 'I am God's Son.'

Narrator   The bandits who were crucified with him also taunted him in the same way. From noon on, darkness came over the whole land until three in the afternoon. And about three o'clock Jesus cried with a loud voice,

Jesus   Eli, Eli, lema sabachthani?

Narrator	That is, 'My God, my God, why have you forsaken me?' When some of the bystanders heard it, they said,
Crowd	This man is calling for Elijah.
Narrator	At once one of them ran and got a sponge, filled it with sour wine, put it on a stick, and gave it to him to drink. But the others said,
Crowd	Wait, let us see whether Elijah will come to save him.
Narrator	Then Jesus cried again with a loud voice and breathed his last. At that moment the curtain of the Temple was torn in two, from top to bottom. The earth shook, and the rocks were split. The tombs also were opened, and many bodies of the saints who had fallen asleep were raised. After his resurrection they came out of the tombs and entered the holy city and appeared to many. Now when the centurion and those with him, who were keeping watch over Jesus, saw the earthquake and what took place, they were terrified.
Soldier	Truly this man was God's Son!

A time of silent reflection.

Prayer

Son of God, victim and victor,
your work is finished,
and the cost of our salvation is revealed in full.
We bring you our repentance and our thanks,
the love of our hearts and the commitment of our lives.
To you be praise and honour, now and always. **Amen.**

Hymn

O sacred head, surrounded

4. Entombment

Narrator Many women were also there, looking on from a distance; they had followed Jesus from Galilee and had provided for him. Among them were Mary Magdalene, and Mary the mother of James and Joseph, and the mother of the sons of Zebedee. When it was evening, there came a rich man from Arimathea, named Joseph, who was also a disciple of Jesus. He went to Pilate and asked for the body of Jesus; then Pilate ordered it to be given to him. So Joseph took the body and wrapped it in a clean linen cloth and laid it in his own new tomb, which he had hewn in the rock. He then rolled a great stone to the door of the tomb and went away. Mary Magdalene and the other Mary were there, sitting opposite the tomb. The next day, that is, after the day of Preparation, the chief priests and the Pharisees gathered before Pilate.

Chief priests Sir, we remember what that impostor said while he was still alive, 'After three days I will rise again.' Therefore command that the tomb be made secure until the third day; otherwise his disciples may go and steal him away, and tell the people, 'He has been raised from the dead', and the last deception would be worse than the first.

Pilate You have a guard of soldiers; go, make it as secure as you can.

Narrator So they went with the guard and made the tomb secure by sealing the stone.

A time of silent reflection.

Prayer

Go with us, Lord, from this place of your Passion,
that in hope and expectation
we may look beyond the tomb
and meet again to celebrate your resurrection,
for through your death we come to new life. **Amen.**

Hymn

It is finished

or We sing the praise of him who died

b. Christ crucified – meditations on the Passion

Opening sentence

'He himself bore our sins in his body on the cross, so that, free from sins, we might live for righteousness; by his wounds you have been healed.' *(1 Peter 2:24)*

Hymn

There is a green hill

or It is a thing most wonderful

Reading 1 – Mark 15:1-24

As soon as it was morning, the chief priests held a consultation with the elders and scribes and the whole council. They bound Jesus, led him away, and handed him over to Pilate. Pilate asked him, 'Are you the King of the Jews?' He answered him, 'You say so.' Then the chief priests accused him of many things. Pilate asked him again, 'Have you no answer? See how many charges they bring against you.' But Jesus made no further reply, so that Pilate was amazed.

Now at the festival he used to release a prisoner for them, anyone for whom they asked. Now a man called Barabbas was in prison with the rebels who had committed murder during the insurrection. So the crowd came and began to ask Pilate to do for them according to his custom. Then he answered them, 'Do you want me to release for you the King of the Jews?' For he realized that it was out of jealousy that the chief priests had handed him over. But the chief priests stirred up the crowd to have him release Barabbas for them instead. Pilate spoke to them again, 'Then what do you wish me to do with the man you call the King of the Jews?' They shouted back, 'Crucify him!' Pilate asked them, 'Why, what evil has he done?' But they shouted all the more, 'Crucify him!' So Pilate, wishing to satisfy the crowd, released Barabbas for them; and after flogging Jesus, he handed him over to be crucified.

Then the soldiers led him into the courtyard of the palace (that is, the governor's headquarters); and they called together the whole cohort. And they clothed him in a purple cloak; and after twisting some thorns into a crown, they put it on him. And they began saluting him, 'Hail, King of the Jews!' They struck his head with a reed, spat upon him, and knelt down in homage to him. After mocking him, they stripped him of the purple cloak and put his own clothes on him. Then they led him out to crucify him.

They compelled a passer-by, who was coming in from the country, to carry his cross; it was Simon of Cyrene, the father of Alexander and Rufus. Then they brought Jesus to the place called Golgotha (which means the place of a skull). And they offered him wine mixed with myrrh; but he did not take it. And they crucified him, and divided his clothes among them, casting lots to decide what each should take.

Meditation 1 – the feet of Christ (see page 191)

A time of silent reflection.

Prayer

Lord Jesus Christ, your way of love became the way of the cross. As you walk in obedience to the Father, give us the faith and the courage to follow you who are the Way, walking always in the path of your truth and under the guidance of your holy and life-giving Spirit. **Amen.**

Hymn

My song is love unknown *(verses 1, 2, 3, 5, 7)*

Reading 2 – Mark 15:25-32

It was nine o'clock in the morning when they crucified him. The inscription of the charge against him read, 'The King of the Jews.' And with him they crucified two bandits, one on his right and one on his left. Those who passed by derided him, shaking their heads and saying, 'Aha! You who would destroy the temple and build it in three days, save yourself, and come down from the cross!' In the same way the chief priests, along with the scribes, were also mocking him among themselves and saying, 'He saved others; he cannot save himself. Let the Messiah, the King of Israel, come down from the cross now, so that we may see and believe.' Those who were crucified with him also taunted him.

Meditation 2 – the hands of Christ (see page 194)

A time of quiet reflection.

Prayer

Lord Jesus Christ, your outstretched arms offer us love and life.
Give us grace to accept your love and to offer ourselves in your service.
Forgive what is false in us and by your love nurture us in holiness.
For your dear name's sake. **Amen.**

Hymn

When I survey the wondrous cross

Reading 3 – Mark 15:33-39

When it was noon, darkness came over the whole land until three in the afternoon. At three o'clock Jesus cried out with a loud voice, 'Eloi, Eloi, lema sabachthani?' which means, 'My God, my God, why have you forsaken me?' When some of the bystanders heard it, they said, 'Listen, he is calling for Elijah.' And someone ran, filled a sponge with sour wine, put it on a stick, and gave it to him to drink, saying, 'Wait, let us see whether Elijah will come to take him down.' Then Jesus gave a loud cry and breathed his last. And the curtain of the temple was torn in two, from top to bottom. Now when the centurion, who stood facing him, saw that in this way he breathed his last, he said, 'Truly this man was God's Son!'

Meditation 3 – the head of Christ (see page 196)

A time of quiet reflection

Prayer

Jesus Christ, crucified Lord and King of all, show us the mystery of your suffering and death, that the defeat of the cross may become the throne of victory, that its humiliation may become the place of glory, and that love may rule both in heaven and in our hearts. We ask it in your dear name. **Amen.**

Hymn

O sacred head, surrounded
or O dearest Lord, thy sacred head

Prayers

Our Father . . .

Most merciful God, who by the death and resurrection of your Son Jesus Christ delivered and saved the world, grant that by faith in him who suffered on the cross we may triumph in the power of his victory, through Jesus Christ our Lord. **Amen.**

Go in the peace and the love of Christ. **Amen.**

c. The Crucifixion – the witness of the Scriptures

Different voices should be used for the readings.

Introduction

Let us come to the foot of the cross and watch a while.
Lord, be with us in this time of your agony.
Let us hear the words of Scripture and reflect on their meaning.
Lord, be with us in this time of your glory.

Let us open our hearts to all that Christ achieved in this costly act of self-giving.
Lord, be with us in this time of your victory.

Hymn

When I survey the wondrous cross
or Glory be to Jesus

Reading

Isaiah 52:13 – 53:12

See, my servant shall prosper;
he shall be exalted and lifted up,
and shall be very high.
Just as there were many who were astonished at him
– so marred was his appearance, beyond human semblance,
and his form beyond that of mortals –
so he shall startle many nations;
kings shall shut their mouths because of him;
for that which had not been told them they shall see,
and that which they had not heard they shall contemplate.
Who has believed what we have heard?
And to whom has the arm of the Lord been revealed?
For he grew up before him like a young plant,
and like a root out of dry ground;
he had no form or majesty that we should look at him,
nothing in his appearance that we should desire him.
He was despised and rejected by others;
a man of suffering and acquainted with infirmity;
and as one from whom others hide their faces
he was despised, and we held him of no account.

Surely he has borne our infirmities
and carried our diseases;
yet we accounted him stricken,
struck down by God, and afflicted.

But he was wounded for our transgressions,
crushed for our iniquities;
upon him was the punishment that made us whole,
and by his bruises we are healed.
All we like sheep have gone astray;
we have all turned to our own way,
and the Lord has laid on him the iniquity of us all.

He was oppressed, and he was afflicted,
yet he did not open his mouth;
like a lamb that is led to the slaughter,
and like a sheep that before its shearers is silent,
so he did not open his mouth.
By a perversion of justice he was taken away.
Who could have imagined his future?
For he was cut off from the land of the living,
stricken for the transgression of my people.
They made his grave with the wicked
and his tomb with the rich,
although he had done no violence,
and there was no deceit in his mouth.

Yet it was the will of the Lord to crush him with pain.
When you make his life an offering for sin,
he shall see his offspring, and shall prolong his days;
through him the will of the Lord shall prosper.
Out of his anguish he shall see light;
he shall find satisfaction through his knowledge.
The righteous one, my servant, shall make many righteous,
and he shall bear their iniquities.
Therefore I will allot him a portion with the great,
and he shall divide the spoil with the strong;
because he poured out himself to death,
and was numbered with the transgressors;
yet he bore the sin of many,
and made intercession for the transgressors.

A time of quiet reflection during which a suitable piece of music may be played.

Hymn

At the Lamb's high feast we sing *(verses 1-3)*

Reading

Exodus 12:21-27; John 19:14, 16b-22; Revelation 5:12, 13

Then Moses called all the elders of Israel and said to them, 'Go, select lambs for your families, and slaughter the passover lamb. Take a bunch of hyssop, dip it in the blood that is in the basin, and touch the lintel and the two doorposts with the blood in the basin. None of you shall go outside the door of your house until morning. For the Lord will pass through to strike down the Egyptians; when he sees the blood on the lintel and on the two doorposts, the Lord will pass over that door and will not allow the destroyer to enter your houses to strike you down. You shall observe this rite as a perpetual ordinance for you and your children. When you come to the land that the Lord will give you, as he has promised, you shall keep this observance. And when your children ask you, "What do you mean by this observance?" you shall say, "It is the passover sacrifice to the Lord, for he passed over the houses of the Israelites in Egypt, when he struck down the Egyptians but spared our houses."' And the people bowed down and worshipped.

It was the day of the preparation for the Passover; and it was about noon.

So they took Jesus; and carrying the cross by himself, he went out to what is called The Place of the Skull, which in Hebrew is called Golgotha. There they crucified him, and with him two others, one on either side, with Jesus between them. Pilate also had an inscription written and put on the cross. It read, 'Jesus of Nazareth, the King of the Jews.' Many of the Jews read this inscription, because the place where Jesus was crucified was near the city; and it was written in Hebrew, in Latin, and in Greek. Then the chief priests of the Jews said to Pilate, 'Do not write, "The King of the Jews", but, "This man said, I am King of the Jews."' Pilate answered, 'What I have written I have written.'

'Worthy is the Lamb that was slaughtered
to receive power and wealth and wisdom and might
and honour and glory and blessing!'
Then I heard every creature in heaven and on earth
and under the earth and in the sea, and all that is in them, singing,
'To the one seated on the throne and to the Lamb
be blessing and honour and glory and might
for ever and ever!'

Agnus Dei
Lamb of God, you take away the sin of the world,
have mercy on us.
Lamb of God, you take away the sin of the world,
have mercy on us.
Lamb of God, you take away the sin of the world,
grant us peace.

Hymn

There is a green hill far away
or On the holy cross I see

Reading

Psalm 69:1-4, 6-8, 13-20; Luke 23:32-43

Save me, O God,
for the waters have come up to my neck.
I sink in deep mire,
where there is no foothold;
I have come into deep waters,
and the flood sweeps over me.
I am weary with my crying;
my throat is parched.
My eyes grow dim
with waiting for my God.

More in number than the hairs of my head
are those who hate me without cause;
many are those who would destroy me,
my enemies who accuse me falsely.

Do not let those who hope in you be put to shame because of me,
O Lord God of hosts;
do not let those who seek you be dishonoured because of me,
O God of Israel.
It is for your sake that I have borne reproach,
that shame has covered my face.
I have become a stranger to my kindred,
an alien to my mother's children.

But as for me, my prayer is to you, O Lord.
At an acceptable time, O God,
in the abundance of your steadfast love, answer me.
With your faithful help rescue me
from sinking in the mire;
let me be delivered from my enemies
and from the deep waters.
Do not let the flood sweep over me,
or the deep swallow me up,
or the Pit close its mouth over me.

Answer me, O Lord, for your steadfast love is good;
according to your abundant mercy, turn to me.
Do not hide your face from your servant,
for I am in distress – make haste to answer me.

Draw near to me, redeem me,
set me free because of my enemies.
You know the insults I receive,
and my shame and dishonour;
my foes are all known to you.

Insults have broken my heart,
so that I am in despair.
I looked for pity, but there was none;
and for comforters, but I found none.

Two others also, who were criminals, were led away to be put to death with him. When they came to the place that is called The Skull, they crucified Jesus there with the criminals, one on his right and one on his left. Then Jesus said, 'Father, forgive them; for they do not know what they are doing.' And they cast lots to divide his clothing. And the people stood by, watching; but the leaders scoffed at him, saying, 'He saved others; let him save himself if he is the Messiah of God, his chosen one!' The soldiers also mocked him, coming up and offering him sour wine, and saying, 'If you are the King of the Jews, save yourself!' There was also an inscription over him, 'This is the King of the Jews.'

One of the criminals who were hanged there kept deriding him and saying, 'Are you not the Messiah? Save yourself and us!' But the other rebuked him, saying, 'Do you not fear God, since you are under the same sentence of condemnation? And we indeed have been condemned justly, for we are getting what we deserve for our deeds, but this man has done nothing wrong.' Then he said, 'Jesus, remember me when you come into your kingdom.' He replied, 'Truly I tell you, today you will be with me in Paradise.'

A time of quiet reflection during which a suitable piece of music may be played.

Crucified Lord, you were insulted and scorned, reviled and derided,
yet you remained silent.
They pierced you with nails and fixed you to the cross,
yet you forgave them.
As you hung between criminals, one asked you to remember him.
You promised him a place in Paradise.

Hymn

Bless the Lord, O my soul
or Father of heaven, whose love profound

Reading

Psalm 22:1-11, 14-20; Mark 15:33-36

My God, my God, why have you forsaken me?
Why are you so far from helping me, from the words of my groaning?
O my God, I cry by day, but you do not answer;
and by night, but find no rest.
Yet you are holy,
enthroned on the praises of Israel.
In you our ancestors trusted;
they trusted, and you delivered them.
To you they cried, and were saved;
in you they trusted, and were not put to shame.
But I am a worm, and not human;
scorned by others, and despised by the people.
All who see me mock at me;
they make mouths at me, they shake their heads;
'Commit your cause to the Lord; let him deliver –
let him rescue the one in whom he delights!'

Yet it was you who took me from the womb;
you kept me safe on my mother's breast.
On you I was cast from my birth,
and since my mother bore me you have been my God.
Do not be far from me,
for trouble is near
and there is no one to help.

I am poured out like water,
and all my bones are out of joint;
my heart is like wax;
it is melted within my breast;
my mouth is dried up like a potsherd,
and my tongue sticks to my jaws;
you lay me in the dust of death.

For dogs are all around me;
a company of evildoers encircles me.
My hands and feet have shrivelled;
I can count all my bones.
They stare and gloat over me;
they divide my clothes among themselves,
and for my clothing they cast lots.

But you, O Lord, do not be far away!
O my help, come quickly to my aid!
Deliver my soul from the sword,
my life from the power of the dog!

When it was noon, darkness came over the whole land until three in the afternoon. At three o'clock Jesus cried out with a loud voice, 'Eloi, Eloi, lema sabachthani?' which means, 'My God, my God, why have you forsaken me?' When some of the bystanders heard it, they said, 'Listen, he is calling for Elijah.' And someone ran, filled a sponge with sour wine, put it on a stick, and gave it to him to drink, saying, 'Wait, let us see whether Elijah will come to take him down.'

A time of quiet reflection during which a suitable piece of music may be played.

Lord, in our times of doubt,
strengthen the faith within us.
Lord, in times when we feel abandoned,
grant us knowledge of your presence.
Lord, when all seems lost,
search for us and bring us home.

Hymn

We sing the praise of him who died
or Come, wounded healer

Reading

Psalm 22:22-31; Luke 23:44-57

I will tell of your name to my brothers and sisters;
in the midst of the congregation I will praise you:
You who fear the Lord, praise him!
All you offspring of Jacob, glorify him;
stand in awe of him, all you offspring of Israel!
For he did not despise or abhor
the affliction of the afflicted;
he did not hide his face from me,
but heard when I cried to him.

From you comes my praise in the great congregation;
my vows I will pay before those who fear him.
The poor shall eat and be satisfied;
those who seek him shall praise the Lord.
May your hearts live for ever!

All the ends of the earth shall remember
and turn to the Lord;
and all the families of the nations
shall worship before him.
For dominion belongs to the Lord,
and he rules over the nations.

To him, indeed, shall all who sleep in the earth bow down;
before him shall bow all who go down to the dust,
and I shall live for him.
Posterity will serve him;
future generations will be told about the Lord,
and proclaim his deliverance to a people yet unborn,
saying that he has done it.

It was now about noon, and darkness came over the whole land until three in the afternoon, while the sun's light failed; and the curtain of the temple was torn in two. Then Jesus, crying with a loud voice, said, 'Father, into your hands I commend my spirit.' Having said this, he breathed his last. When the centurion saw what had taken place, he praised God and said, 'Certainly this man was innocent.' And when all the crowds who had gathered there for this spectacle saw what had taken place, they returned home, beating their breasts. But all his acquaintances, including the women who had followed him from Galilee, stood at a distance, watching these things.

Now there was a good and righteous man named Joseph, who, though a member of the council, had not agreed to their plan and action. He came from the Jewish town of Arimathea, and he was waiting expectantly for the kingdom of God. This man went to Pilate and asked for the body of Jesus. Then he took it down, wrapped it in a linen cloth, and laid it in a rock-hewn tomb where no one had ever been laid. It was the day of Preparation, and the sabbath was beginning. The women who had come with him from Galilee followed, and they saw the tomb and how his body was laid. Then they returned, and prepared spices and ointments.

On the sabbath they rested according to the commandment.

A time of quiet reflection during which a suitable piece of music may be played.

Father, in the darkness we look to you for light,
we place ourselves in your hands.
Father, amidst pain and suffering,
we place ourselves in your hands.
Father, at our end and our departing,
we place ourselves in your hands.

Crucified Christ, go with us,
forgiving Christ, go with us,
forsaken and trusting Christ, go with us,
into the waiting time, Christ go with us.
All leave in silence.

7. Holy Saturday – the in-between time

A vigil

If possible there should be a gradual increase in the lighting level as the vigil progresses, reflecting the movement of the subject matter from the sinful condition of humankind to the possibility of new life through Christ's death and resurrection, from the darkness of night to the light of the coming glorious Easter Day. Hymns are suggested but may be omitted if not felt to be appropriate at a vigil. This is not intended to be a Service of Light – provision for that is made in the Easter Liturgy.

Opening reflection

This vigil is by its very nature a dark time. It takes place when the world around is dark. It is night-time. But more than that, this Holy Saturday vigil reflects a dark time in the story of Holy Week – not the darkness of the hours on Skull Hill but the darkness of entombment. It is the darkness of a time 'between' when we are not sure whether our worst fears will be realised or our highest hopes will come true.

For the disciples it was a time of waiting – a dark time of in-between while the shock of the crucifixion was still raw within them, shock and the darkness of grief and of guilt, for they had done nothing to prevent his death. Some had run away, some had just stood by and watched. They were caught between reflecting on all that had happened and reflecting on what might happen next. They remembered all that Jesus had said as he had sought to prepare them for the worst. They pondered on their last meal with him and the evening in the olive grove as they tried to piece together the clues, weighing all that he had said and done. They clung on to the fragments of promise he had spoken and which they had neither understood nor really believed – the hints that this would not be the end, that there would be something after his death that would return him to them. They were fearful that as followers of the one executed as 'King of the Jews' they would be arrested as insurgents. They stayed indoors behind locked doors, afraid of the authorities. It was still the sabbath so perhaps for the time being they were safe. But the women had already determined to go to the tomb to do what the coming of the sabbath had prevented them from doing – anointing his body. It wasn't their fault, his death coming so late in the day, but they felt guilty for failing to do even this before they laid him in the tomb.

This is a time of reflection for us and we, too, are caught in the in-between – between the knowledge of why the events of these past days were necessary and the hope that through them new possibilities will open up. For here is a pivotal point in the human condition between the fact of our sinfulness and the promise of forgiveness and transformed lives. It is a time when we are reminded of the dark side of our humanity and when we look for the coming of the light of God's gift of new life, of resurrection life. In the darkness there is nothing we can do but wait, watch and trust.

Hymn

Put thou thy trust in God
or All my hope on God is founded

Prayer

Be present with us, good Lord,
in the darkness of this night
as we await the coming of the dawn
and the light of your new life.
Hold us as we acknowledge the darkness of our common sin
and hear the story of your saving acts.
Grant us the faith to know the truth of your promises
and discover the glory of your victory.
Be present, good Lord. Amen.

Reading

Genesis 1:1-5, 26-31

In the beginning when God created the heavens and the earth, the earth was a formless void and darkness covered the face of the deep, while a wind from God swept over the face of the waters. Then God said, 'Let there be light'; and there was light. And God saw that the light was good; and God separated the light from the darkness. God called the light Day, and the darkness he called Night. And there was evening and there was morning, the first day.

Then God said, 'Let us make humankind in our image, according to our likeness; and let them have dominion over the fish of the sea, and over the birds of the air, and over the cattle, and over all the wild animals of the earth, and over every creeping thing that creeps upon the earth.'

So God created humankind in his image,
in the image of God he created them;
male and female he created them.

God blessed them, and God said to them, 'Be fruitful and multiply, and fill the earth and subdue it; and have dominion over the fish of the sea and over the birds of the air and over every living thing that moves upon the earth.' God said, 'See, I have given you every plant yielding seed that is upon the face of all the earth, and every tree with seed in its fruit; you shall have them for food. And to every beast of the earth, and to every bird of the air, and to everything that creeps on the earth, everything that has the breath of life, I have given every green plant for food.' And it was so. God saw everything that he had made, and indeed, it was very good. And there was evening and there was morning, the sixth day.

A time of quiet reflection.

Psalm

Psalm 33:6-9, 13-15

By the word of the Lord the heavens were made,
and all their host by the breath of his mouth.
He gathered the waters of the sea as in a bottle;
he put the deeps in storehouses.

**Let your steadfast love, O Lord, be upon us,
even as we hope in you.**

Let all the earth fear the Lord;
let all the inhabitants of the world stand in awe of him.
For he spoke, and it came to be;
he commanded, and it stood firm.

**Let your steadfast love, O Lord, be upon us,
even as we hope in you.**

The Lord looks down from heaven;
he sees all humankind.
From where he sits enthroned he watches
all the inhabitants of the earth –
he who fashions the hearts of them all,
and observes all their deeds.

**Let your steadfast love, O Lord, be upon us,
even as we hope in you.**

Prayer

Almighty God, we praise you for the wonder of your creation.
By your love you formed us in your image
and made us stewards of the earth.
We have spoilt your image
and exploited your world.
Renew our sense of responsibility,
that the good things of the earth may be shared by all
and our lives renewed through the Passion of your Son. **Amen.**

Reading

Genesis 3:8-13, 22-24

They heard the sound of the Lord God walking in the garden at the time
of the evening breeze, and the man and his wife hid themselves from the
presence of the Lord God among the trees of the garden. But the Lord God
called to the man, and said to him, 'Where are you?' He said, 'I heard the

sound of you in the garden, and I was afraid, because I was naked; and I hid myself.' He said, 'Who told you that you were naked? Have you eaten from the tree of which I commanded you not to eat?' The man said, 'The woman whom you gave to be with me, she gave me fruit from the tree, and I ate.' Then the Lord God said to the woman, 'What is this that you have done?' The woman said, 'The serpent tricked me, and I ate.'

Then the Lord God said, 'See, the man has become like one of us, knowing good and evil; and now, he might reach out his hand and take also from the tree of life, and eat, and live for ever' – therefore the Lord God sent him forth from the garden of Eden, to till the ground from which he was taken. He drove out the man; and at the east of the garden of Eden he placed the cherubim, and a sword flaming and turning to guard the way to the tree of life.

A time of quiet reflection.

Psalm

Psalm 51:1-4, 6, 7, 10-12

Have mercy on me, O God,
according to your steadfast love;
according to your abundant mercy
blot out my transgressions.
Wash me thoroughly from my iniquity,
and cleanse me from my sin.

A broken and a contrite heart, O God, you will not despise.

For I know my transgressions,
and my sin is ever before me.
Against you, you alone, have I sinned,
and done what is evil in your sight,
so that you are justified in your sentence
and blameless when you pass judgement.

A broken and a contrite heart, O God, you will not despise.

You desire truth in the inward being;
therefore teach me wisdom in my secret heart.
Purge me with hyssop, and I shall be clean;
wash me, and I shall be whiter than snow.

A broken and a contrite heart, O God, you will not despise.

Create in me a clean heart, O God,
and put a new and right spirit within me.
Do not cast me away from your presence,
and do not take your holy spirit from me.
Restore to me the joy of your salvation,
and sustain in me a willing spirit.

A broken and a contrite heart, O God, you will not despise.

Hymn

Lord Jesus, think on me

Reading

Isaiah 55:1-11

Ho, everyone who thirsts,
come to the waters;
and you that have no money,
come, buy and eat!
Come, buy wine and milk
without money and without price.
Why do you spend your money for that which is not bread,
and your labour for that which does not satisfy?
Listen carefully to me, and eat what is good,
and delight yourselves in rich food.
Incline your ear, and come to me;
listen, so that you may live.
I will make with you an everlasting covenant,
my steadfast, sure love for David.

See, I made him a witness to the peoples,
a leader and commander for the peoples.
See, you shall call nations that you do not know,
and nations that do not know you shall run to you,
because of the Lord your God, the Holy One of Israel,
for he has glorified you.

Seek the Lord while he may be found,
call upon him while he is near;
let the wicked forsake their way,
and the unrighteous their thoughts;
let them return to the Lord, that he may have mercy on them,
and to our God, for he will abundantly pardon.
For my thoughts are not your thoughts,
nor are your ways my ways, says the Lord.
For as the heavens are higher than the earth,
so are my ways higher than your ways
and my thoughts than your thoughts.

For as the rain and the snow come down from heaven,
and do not return there until they have watered the earth,
making it bring forth and sprout,
giving seed to the sower and bread to the eater,
so shall my word be that goes out from my mouth;
it shall not return to me empty,
but it shall accomplish that which I purpose,
and succeed in the thing for which I sent it.

Psalm

Psalm 42:1-3, 6-8; 43:3-5

As a deer longs for flowing streams,
so my soul longs for you, O God.
My soul thirsts for God,
for the living God.
When shall I come and behold
the face of God?

**O send out your light and your truth;
let them lead me.**

My tears have been my food
day and night,
while people say to me continually,
'Where is your God?'
My soul is cast down within me;
therefore I remember you
from the land of Jordan and of Hermon,
from Mount Mizar.

**O send out your light and your truth;
let them lead me.**

Deep calls to deep
at the thunder of your cataracts;
all your waves and your billows
have gone over me.
By day the Lord commands his steadfast love,
and at night his song is with me,
a prayer to the God of my life.

**O send out your light and your truth;
let them lead me.**

O send out your light and your truth;
let them lead me;
let them bring me to your holy hill
and to your dwelling.
Then I will go to the altar of God,
to God my exceeding joy;
and I will praise you with the harp,
O God, my God.

Why are you cast down, O my soul,
and why are you disquieted within me?
Hope in God; for I shall again praise him,
my help and my God.

**O send out your light and your truth;
let them lead me.**

Prayer

God of hope and inspiration,
send out your light and your truth
that we may walk in the way of your Son;
bearing our cross in service and obedience,
and living in the power of your resurrection. **Amen.**

Reading

Romans 6:3-11

Do you not know that all of us who have been baptized into Christ Jesus were baptized into his death? Therefore we have been buried with him by baptism into death, so that, just as Christ was raised from the dead by the glory of the Father, so we too might walk in newness of life.

For if we have been united with him in a death like his, we will certainly be united with him in a resurrection like his. We know that our old self was crucified with him so that the body of sin might be destroyed, and we might no longer be enslaved to sin. For whoever has died is freed from sin. But if we have died with Christ, we believe that we will also live with him. We know that Christ, being raised from the dead, will never die again; death no longer has dominion over him. The death he died, he died to sin, once for all; but the life he lives, he lives to God. So you also must consider yourselves dead to sin and alive to God in Christ Jesus.

Hymn

Jesus lives

Reading

Luke 24:1-12

But on the first day of the week, at early dawn, they came to the tomb, taking the spices that they had prepared. They found the stone rolled away from the tomb, but when they went in, they did not find the body. While they were perplexed about this, suddenly two men in dazzling clothes stood beside them. The women were terrified and bowed their faces to the ground, but the men said to them, 'Why do you look for the living among the dead? He is not here, but has risen. Remember how he told you, while he was still in Galilee, that the Son of Man must be handed over to sinners, and be crucified, and on the third day rise again.' Then they remembered his words, and returning from the tomb, they told all this to the eleven and to all the rest. Now it was Mary Magdalene, Joanna, Mary the mother of James, and the other women with them who told this to the apostles. But these words seemed to them an idle tale, and they did not believe them. But Peter got up and ran to the tomb; stooping and looking in, he saw the linen cloths by themselves; then he went home, amazed at what had happened.

A time of quiet reflection.

Prayer

Lord, you lead us from the darkness of your death
into the glorious light of your resurrection.
May we leave the path of sin and death
and follow you in the way of eternal life.
**May we leave the darkness of the night
and rejoice once more in the coming of the new day. Amen.**

Jesus lives.
He lives indeed. Hallelujah.

7. EASTER DAY

a. The Easter Light

This short service could form the opening section of an Easter morning service of Holy Communion or Family Worship. As far as possible, the service should begin in the dark with the lights out or the curtains drawn as the Light of Christ is processed through the church. It is the custom in some churches to light the candle from a small brazier, in which case due precautions should be taken.

The night is over and the light of God's new dawn approaches.
Come, Christ our Light.

The darkness of sin is dispelled in forgiveness.
Come, Christ our Light.

The shadow of death gives way to the light of life.
Come, Christ our Light.

You, O Christ, are the Light of the world.
Come, Christ our Light.

This is the light no darkness can quench.
Come, Christ our Light.

Be not afraid but be filled with the joy of resurrection.
Christ is our Light, our joy and our life. Hallelujah.

Lord Jesus Christ, you endured the cross for us,
revealing the costly love with which you forgive us.
Lead us from the place of sin and death
to the glory of your resurrection,
that we may rejoice in your light
and walk in your way. **Amen.**

The candle is lit

Away with all that is dark,
for Christ has risen and his light shines throughout the earth.
Christ is our Light, our joy and our life. Hallelujah.

The candle is processed to the front of the church in three stages.
At each stage the following is said:

This is the light of Christ.
Christ is our Light, our joy and our life. Hallelujah.

The candle is placed on a stand in a prominent place at the front of the church.
Lights are switched on and candles around the church may be lit from the
main candle.

Hymn

Light's glittering morn *(first verse and doxology)*
or Jesus Christ is risen today

Jesus Christ is risen.
He is risen indeed. Hallelujah.

If there is an Easter garden, this might be a suitable time for it to be blessed.
Children might be invited to gather round the garden and place flowers in it.

b. The Easter Garden

Come to the place where the women came.
We come to the garden of resurrection.

Come to the place where the stone was rolled away.
We come to the empty tomb.

Come to the place where the angels sat.
We come to hear the news of Christ's rising.

Come to the place where new life was proclaimed.
We come to meet with the Risen Lord.

God in whom we live, you raised your Son to new life.
May this Easter garden be a blessing to all who visit it.
May it be a witness to the power of your love to overcome death,
and may we be filled with resurrection joy. **Amen.**

Hymn

All in an Easter garden

c. Easter service – a celebration of resurrection

This service could follow on from the Easter Light and / or Easter garden or stand alone.

In planning this service visual material should be drawn on, but how this is done will depend on the resources available to the church. Where there are facilities for projection, suitable images could be projected at key points during the service – e.g. a picture of a bright dawn at the beginning of the service, a picture of the garden with the stone rolled away. Pictures are available on various websites but they need to be chosen with care. It may also be appropriate to involve children in activities on the various themes to engage them as well as adults.

This is the day of the resurrection of our Lord.
Hallelujah! We will rejoice and be glad.

This is the day when new life burst from the tomb.
Hallelujah! We will rejoice and be glad.

This is the day the risen Lord was present again with his followers.
Hallelujah! We will rejoice and be glad.

Hymn

The day of resurrection

Prayer

Great and all-loving God,
we praise you for this day
when you raised your Son to new life.
Grant us the ears to hear the message of resurrection,
grant us the eyes to see his risen presence,
grant us the voices to tell the good news to all,
grant us the feet to follow in the way of our risen, living Lord. **Amen.**

In the garden

If the Easter garden has not already been used, this would be a suitable place for it.

Reading

Matthew 28:1-10

Narrator   After the sabbath, as the first day of the week was dawning, Mary Magdalene and the other Mary went to see the tomb. And suddenly there was a great earthquake; for an angel of the Lord, descending from heaven, came and rolled back the stone and sat on it. His appearance was like lightning, and his clothing white as snow. For fear of him the guards shook and became like dead men. But the angel said to the women,

Angel   Do not be afraid; I know that you are looking for Jesus who was crucified. He is not here; for he has been raised, as he said. Come, see the place where he lay. Then go quickly and tell his disciples, 'He has been raised from the dead, and indeed he is going ahead of you to Galilee; there you will see him.' This is my message for you.

Narrator   So they left the tomb quickly with fear and great joy, and ran to tell his disciples. Suddenly Jesus met them and said,

Jesus   Greetings!

Narrator	And they came to him, took hold of his feet, and worshipped him.

Jesus	Do not be afraid; go and tell my brothers to go to Galilee; there they will see me.

Reflection

A brief talk/presentation may be given on the theme of 'Do not be afraid' because Jesus is alive again. People may be asked what things make them afraid and what helps them when they are afraid. These will be picked up in the prayer after the hymn.

Hymn

Be bold, be strong

Prayer

Jesus, there are many times when we are afraid:
afraid to be hurt,
afraid to be lost,
afraid to be . . .
We thank you for all who help us when we are afraid:
our mums and dads,
our friends . . .
Lord, be with us in our fear,
and fill us with your love and your life. **Amen.**

In the room

Reading

John 20:19-29

Narrator	When it was evening on that day, the first day of the week, and the doors of the house where the disciples had met were locked for fear of the Jews, Jesus came and stood among them.

Jesus	Peace be with you.
Narrator	After he said this, he showed them his hands and his side. Then the disciples rejoiced when they saw the Lord.
Jesus	Peace be with you. As the Father has sent me, so I send you.
Narrator	When he had said this, he breathed on them.
Jesus	Receive the Holy Spirit. If you forgive the sins of any, they are forgiven them; if you retain the sins of any, they are retained.
Narrator	But Thomas (who was called the Twin), one of the twelve, was not with them when Jesus came. So the other disciples told him,
Disciples	We have seen the Lord.
Narrator	But he said to them,
Thomas	Unless I see the mark of the nails in his hands, and put my finger in the mark of the nails and my hand in his side, I will not believe.
Narrator	A week later his disciples were again in the house, and Thomas was with them. Although the doors were shut, Jesus came and stood among them.
Jesus	Peace be with you. Put your finger here and see my hands. Reach out your hand and put it in my side. Do not doubt but believe.
Thomas	My Lord and my God!
Jesus	Have you believed because you have seen me? Blessed are those who have not seen and yet have come to believe.

Reflection

A brief talk/presentation may given on the theme of 'faith and doubt' and the way we trust in people and things we do not see.

Hymn

As we are gathered
or Hail the day that sees him rise

Prayer

In you we trust, O Lord.
Forgive our lack of faith.

Your love surrounds our every moment.
Forgive our lack of love.

You call us to your service.
Forgive our disobedience.

You go before us in all we do.
Forgive us when we do not follow.

In his love and his mercy,
God promises us forgiveness,
sets us on our feet again
and walks beside us in the way.
As forgiven people,
we offer him thanks and praise.

On the beach

Reading

John 21:1-19

Narrator	After these things Jesus showed himself again to the disciples by the Sea of Tiberias; and he showed himself in this way. Gathered there together were Simon Peter, Thomas called the Twin, Nathanael of Cana in Galilee, the sons of Zebedee, and two others of his disciples. Simon Peter said to them,
Peter	I am going fishing.
Disciples	We will go with you.
Narrator	They went out and got into the boat, but that night they caught nothing. Just after daybreak, Jesus stood on the beach; but the disciples did not know that it was Jesus.
Jesus	Children, you have no fish, have you?
Peter *James* *and* *John*	No.
Jesus	Cast the net to the right side of the boat, and you will find some.
Narrator	So they cast it, and now they were not able to haul it in because there were so many fish. That disciple whom Jesus loved said to Peter,
John	It is the Lord!
Narrator	When Simon Peter heard that it was the Lord, he put on some clothes, for he was naked, and jumped into the lake. But the other disciples came in the boat, dragging the net full of fish, for they were not far from the land, only about a hundred yards off. When they had gone ashore, they saw a charcoal fire there, with fish on it, and bread.

Jesus	Bring some of the fish that you have just caught.
Narrator	So Simon Peter went aboard and hauled the net ashore, full of large fish, a hundred and fifty-three of them; and though there were so many, the net was not torn.
Jesus	Come and have breakfast.
Narrator	Now none of the disciples dared to ask him, 'Who are you?' because they knew it was the Lord. Jesus came and took the bread and gave it to them, and did the same with the fish. This was now the third time that Jesus appeared to the disciples after he was raised from the dead. When they had finished breakfast, Jesus said to Simon Peter,
Jesus	Simon son of John, do you love me more than these?
Peter	Yes, Lord; you know that I love you.
Jesus	Feed my lambs. Simon son of John, do you love me?
Peter	Yes, Lord; you know that I love you.
Jesus	Tend my sheep. Simon son of John, do you love me?
Peter	Lord, you know everything; you know that I love you.
Jesus	Feed my sheep. Very truly, I tell you, when you were younger, you used to fasten your own belt and to go wherever you wished. But when you grow old, you will stretch out your hands, and someone else will fasten a belt around you and take you where you do not wish to go. Follow me.

As everyone leaves they may sing 'We are marching'. Alternatively, 'Resurrection Song' from the CD A Celtic Holy Week and Easter (Kevin Mayhew 1490191) *would be suitable to dance out to.*